Weatherby

Other books by the authors

by Grits Gresham
Fishes and Fishing in Louisiana
Fishing and Boating in Louisiana
The Complete Book of Bass Fishing
The Sportsman and His Family Outdoors
The Complete Wildfowler
Grits on Guns

by Tom Gresham
Close Calls
The Steel Magnolias Scrapbook

Weatherby

The Man. The Gun. The Legend.

By
Grits Gresham and
Tom Gresham

CANE RIVER
PUBLISHING
P.O. Box 666
Natchitoches, LA 71458

Published by Cane River Publishing
P.O. Box 666
Natchitoches, LA 71458

Library of Congress Cataloging-in-Publication Data
Gresham, Grits, 1922-
    Weatherby: The man, the gun, the legend / Grits
    Gresham and Tom Gresham
            p.   cm.
    Includes Index
    ISBN 0-944438-02-4 : $24.95
    1. Weatherby, Roy E. 2. Industrialists—United
States—Biography. 3. Firearms industry and trade—
United States—History. 4. Hunting rifles—United States—
History. I. Gresham, Tom. II. Title.
HD9744.F552W434 1992
338.7'62344'092—dc20
[B]   90–84174
                                        CIP

Library of Congress Catalog Card Number: 91-77172

Printed and bound in the United States of America

ISBN 0-944438-02-4

First printing January 1992
Second printing March 1992

Contents

Preface by Ed Weatherby   ix

Introduction   xi

1 How it Began   1

How did the son of a tenant farmer in Kansas become the world's best known advocate of high velocity cartridges? Why did he quit a good job to jump into the risky venture of customizing rifles to fire magnum cartridges of his own design. Roy tells of his beginnings in the gun business, including the many times bankruptcy seemed imminent.

2 The Rough Years   9

Heavy debts, little or no profit, a serious auto accident, and litterally selling the farm to raise money . . . that's what Weatherby faced the first few years. From fighting the I.R.S. to battling his suppliers, the setbacks were many and the successes few in those early years. He took on partners. While their money was critical to the continued survival of the company, all did not go well. Partners came and went, but Weatherby stayed.

3 Weatherby: The Man   57

Roy and celebrities just clicked. Hollywood figures, professional athletes and politicians all made the trip to South Gate to visit Roy and to get those famous rifles. Roy's promotional genius may have the been the biggest reason for the ultimate success of Weatherby, Inc. Many people who worked and hunted with Roy describe their personal relationships with him in a section titled: "I Knew Roy."

4   The Weatherby Big Game Trophy Award   107

It started as a way to recognize the hunters who had made the greatest accomplishments in the hunting world. The recipients include some of the best hunters in the world, and the celebrity presenters are among the best-known actors, athletes, politicians and military heros.

5   Weatherby's Hunting Trips   115

Developing new magnum cartridges required that Roy test them under hunting condition, and he did just that all over the world. His personal diary from his first African hunt details the wonders of a full scale safari as seen through the eyes of a meticulous observer.

6   Weatherby Magnum Cartridges   181

Compared to the other cartridges available at the time of their introduction, the Weatherby Magnum calibers were revolutionary. Many magnums from other gun companies were developed to answer the Weatherby cartridges—yet another tribute to Roy.

7   Building the Rifle   187

From England to Europe to Japan, Weatherby searched for someone to make his rifles. In the Mark V action, he finally had what has been called the strongest rifle action in the world.

8   Rimfires and Shotguns   215

Weatherby Mark XXII rimfire rifles and shotguns filled out the line to make the company a full-line gun manufacturer. Getting those guns produced at a reasonable price (and on time) took all the skill Roy had, and at times even that wasn't enough.

9 Weatherby Collectors Association   227

Formed only recently, the Weatherby Collectors Association has become an important source of information on all Weatherby guns.

10 Ed Weatherby: The New Era   229

Not content to just keep the company going, Ed Weatherby has been the innovative president who created the Lasermark, the Fibermark (the first factory-made rifle with a synthetic stock) and the .416 Weatherby Magnum cartridge. And he isn't through, yet.

11 37 Years With Weatherby   237

Betty Noonan was Roy Weatherby's personal secretary for many years. She held several positions, including Vice President of Sales, and she knows as much about Roy Weatherby and the company he created as does anyone. Betty talks about the early days, as well as the present.

12 Weatherby Firearms   249

Through the company's history it has made a number of special guns commemorating the Bicentennial, the Olympics, Ducks Unlimited, and other events. There was even a Weatherby pistol. Also included in this chapter is the only list of models, dates of manufacture, and serial numbers ever compiled by Weatherby. Rifles, shotguns, and rimfires are included.

Index   285

Preface

It seems as though it were yesterday that I listened to my father tell one of his hunting stories, as only he could tell. Yet in a way it seems a lifetime since we've laughed and shared and worried together. He must just be on one of his hunting trips, testing one of his magnums. Surely he'll be home soon.

In the meantime, I trust you will enjoy reliving his hunting adventures, along with the trials, tribulations and successes of the life he devoted to his business.

I am deeply devoted to Betty Noonan, whose unyielding effort has made this book a reality. And to Grits and Tom Gresham for spending hundreds of hours putting it all together.

Today is a special day...not only to have this book complete, but because it marks the anniversary of when it all began...eighty-one years ago, the birth of Roy E. Weatherby.

Roy Edward Weatherby, Jr.
September 4, 1991

Introduction

"It's a Weatherby"

The legend lives on, and one of the most interesting aspects of the saga of Weatherby is that this American success story didn't begin with a grandiose plan. The young man from Kansas had no idea, in the beginning, that he would eventually, forever, alter the world of sporting rifles.

Roy E. Weatherby simply wanted a hunting rifle that would do the job better than anything then available. There were many twists and turns in the trail he trod from that point, true, but in the final analysis he accomplished his goal in the time-honored tradition of this nation's frontier heritage: he did it himself.

This book is the story of that trail. It is an account of the enormous difficulties Roy faced time and again, of the huge odds he overcame. It is a testament to unfettered enthusiasm, to continued perseverance where conditions warranted despair, to a consuming belief that Roy E. Weatherby had a better idea.

And this book is about and by some of the people who trod that trail with Roy, for all or part of the way, or who crossed it now and then. This flamboyant, dedicated, kind, inventive man left his imprint on all who encountered him.

From his simple need for a better hunting tool came a revolution in big game rifles. The Weatherby look and the Weatherby philosophy for such rifles did not find universal favor with hunters, but many shooters and hunters found that both the look and the philosophy fit them like a glove. They still do.

One measure of the incredible marketing success of this rifle is the fact that, although total sales rank far behind Remington, Winchester and others, the Weatherby is undoubtedly one of the best known rifles in the world. Gun people in remote regions of the globe know *Weatherby*, even when they've never seen one. Everybody in the U.S. who shoots or hunts is familiar with a *Weatherby*, love it or not.

Another measure, of course, is the "Weatherby" influence that permeates the firearms industry today. Imitation is indeed one of the sincerest forms of flattery, and rifle makers have certainly lavished upon Weatherby a goodly portion of that commodity. "Magnums" is virtually synonymous with "Weatherby," and Roy's dedication to the big, blown-out cases caused industry across the board to recognize them, and in many instances to follow his lead. The "Weatherby look," the flash and the shine and the lines of the stocks, is readily identifiable in countless other brand models around the world today.

Weatherby: The Man. The Gun. The Legend. is about that Weatherby rifle, and about Roy E. Weatherby, the man who made it happen.

Weatherby

The Man. The Gun. The Legend.

1

How It Began

"On my first deer hunt in Utah, in 1942, I wounded a buck with the 30-06, and after following the blood trail until dark I finally had to give up. I had a sad feeling for that animal because I knew he was going to die a lingering death. I also knew that I would be trying to take another buck, and I didn't think that was good conservation. That's when I started thinking about getting a bullet to travel fast enough so it would disintegrate inside the animal's body, and the shock would cause instant death even though the animal was not hit in a particularly vital area. Then, too, the animals would not suffer and the hunter would get the first animal he shot and wouldn't be wounding one and taking another."—Roy Weatherby

In 1945 Roy Weatherby read an article in the January issue of *Sports Afield,* written by Major Charles Askins, entitled "Mania for Speed." He sat down and wrote a rebuttal of sorts to Major Askins, telling about his experiences with high velocity. Weatherby's letter was published in the March issue of *Sports Afield* under the heading, "This Speedster Doesn't Guess," and he immediately started receiving many letters from people who agreed with his theory and who wanted a rifle with that kind of velocity.

Roy answered every letter, enlisting the services of a secretary at the local bank to work with him in the evening at his home. Before long, he started receiving actual orders from individuals requesting that he rechamber their existing rifles for his larger capacity cartridges.

New rifles of any kind just weren't available in those years, because all of the arms companies had been producing for the military during World War II. There wasn't much on the market in the way of firearms for a long time following the war.

In his garage Roy had a small lathe, a drill press and a few other pieces of light equipment, including a bluing tank. There, he started to fill those orders, to build rifles for customers from all over the country. He wasn't a riflesmith nor machinist nor stockmaker, didn't claim to be, but he learned much about each of these trades, the hard way. He farmed out the work that he couldn't do himself.

Ammunition was a problem. His friend, George Fuller, who had made the chambering reamers for him, also made a few sets of loading dies and sold them to customers who were interested in doing their own handloading. If they weren't, he would fireform cases after rechambering each rifle and provide reloaded ammunition with the rifle.

The orders kept coming in. The workload got so heavy that Roy finally hired a friend to work with him in his garage in the evenings and on weekends, for he was still maintaining his job with the Auto Club, selling insurance.

This tremendous response to his "letter to the editor" helped convince Roy that he should get into the business on a full-time basis. It was a difficult decision.

Although Roy was making about $600 a month at the Auto Club, a pretty good salary in those days, he had little savings, and he had already started to build a new home in Downey, California. In fact, it was the first G.I. financed home built in that particular area after World War II, with a 4.5 percent loan! He realized he would be taking a terrific gamble to go into this kind of business, but he was convinced there was a great demand for a practical, serviceable rifle with very high velocity. Roy was confident the public would accept his ideas on gun designs, rifles that would not only shoot better but be attractive.

Starting His Business

Howard Merrill, a friend and co-worker at the Auto Club, provided the impetus that pushed Roy over the edge into the gun making profession. He owned a building on the corner of Long Beach Blvd. and Firestone Blvd. in South Gate, and was renting one of the four stores in it to a barber. On being notified that the rent was increasing from $50 to $100 a month, the barber moved out. Howard had often heard Roy talk about going into business, so offered him the 25 by 70 foot space at his new rent rate of $100 a month. Roy took the plunge.

But Roy hedged his bet. Feeling that the income from building his rifles just for specific customers wouldn't be enough, he decided to utilize the front 30 feet of the building for a retail sporting goods store, and the "back 40" space for a workshop and a small office.

Roy had many friends and now called on them. One, a cabinet maker, offered to build cabinets and showcases for the retail store, allowing Roy to pay him off by the month. Another, Ed Seidel, loaned him $2,500 (which it took him six years to repay) in order to buy inventory to put in those cases and on those shelves.

Roy opened the store on September 1, 1945. His total investment in everything—inventory, fixtures and the equipment in the shop, was less than $5000.

During the eight years he was with the Auto Club, Roy was consistently the highest producer of any of the salesmen. He was also astute enough not to burn any of his bridges and on August 21, 1945, he wrote the following letter of resignation to his boss, Jim Magee:

Dear Mr. Magee:

For many years I have studied ballistics. I have been keenly interested in guns and ammunition. Almost a lifetime desire of mine has been to own a first-class sporting goods store, dealing with guns and ammunition, and catering to those people who have so much in common with me. At long last, this opportunity has presented itself and with mixed emotions of regret and happiness, I find myself at those crossroads, wondering just which way to turn.

This letter is to serve as a letter of resignation; however, I want you to know how very much I have enjoyed working for you and the Automobile Club for the past eight years. Of the positions I have held in my lifetime, this one has definitely been the outstanding one. I have never felt more secure or enjoyed my work more thoroughly than I have since I have been with you and your company.

Even though this letter is to serve as my resignation, I want you to know that I will remain your employee until such time as you find someone suitable to take my place - whether the time be two weeks, 30 days, or whatever period of time you deem necessary. During this time,

I will continue to do my job to the best of my ability, keeping the interest of you and the Automobile Club in mind.

Again, I want to thank you, Mr. Magee, for hiring me back in 1937. You have been the finest boss I have ever had and the Automobile Club has been the finest organization I have ever worked for.

Very truly yours,

Roy E. Weatherby

On September 4, 1945, he received this reply:

My Dear Weatherby,

While it is never pleasant to lose a long-time employee, I have yet to have a real feeling of regret when I realize that the individual is "going on his own" on some business venture which promises him more of an opportunity in life than he could hope to gain by working on a salary for anyone.

My best wishes to you in your new undertaking.

With kind personal regards, I am,

Cordially yours,

J.L. Magee

And so began the legend of the Weatherby.

The Real Beginning According to Roy

(In 1980 Roy reminisced at length, following his custom of putting down on paper his thoughts about subjects important to him. Here are some of those thoughts.)

Most of my life has been one of poverty, which is probably why money and financial security are so important to me today. Why I watch expenditures like a miser. I'll probably never be able to act like a wealthy man.

When one grows up living far below the level government calls "poverty" today, with no money for even a pair of shoes, most of the time not enough food, it's very difficult to change.

I was born September 4, 1910 on a farm near White City in central Kansas. My parents were George and Martha Weatherby, and Dad was a tenant farmer. All 10 of us, parents, six sisters and a brother, kept moving from farm to farm.

Early on we didn't know we were poor. Everything was relative. It seems to me that I was happy in those days because none of us knew anything different. We didn't miss electricity or inside plumbing because none of us had ever experienced them, or anything like them.

But by the time I was six I began to wonder why we drove a horse and buggy when other farmers had automobiles, and some of them had electricity. Why Mom washed laundry in a tub with a washboard while others used washing machines.

We lived off the land: gardens in the summer and canning things for winter; butchering our meat and canning it, too; making our soap, hominy and sauerkraut; Mom making our clothes on a Singer sewing machine.

Things ceased to be relative when I was plowing a wheat field with one 12-inch shear pulled by three horses, after milking nine cows each morning and night, when the farmer next door was pulling five plows three times faster with a Fordson tractor. I was envious.

I had fun setting traps along the creek for possum, muskrats and raccoons. Now and then I'd catch one, skin and stretch it and take it to town. I'd sometimes get 50 or 60 cents for a skunk or a good raccoon, about 30 cents for a possum. In the summer I trapped gophers, crows and jackrabbits—ten cents bounty each from the county.

Mine was a typical depression-era boyhood, during which I developed a real inferiority complex. The kids at school made fun of me because my name was Weatherby. They called me "bee," or "bug." Or they'd ask when my old man was gonna pay their old man the money he owed. Kids can be cruel.

When I was 13 we began a series of moves. First to Salina, Kansas and our first indoor plumbing, primitive as it was. Dad opened a one-pump filling station—I still remember the hand-lettered sign, "Weatherby and Son"—where I worked some mighty long hours. I was always embarrassed of where and how we had to live, like squatters in the poorest part of town, while all my friends had nicer homes, nicer cars and better clothes.

Next came Wichita, where we lived in a vacant grocery store building in a residential area: one big room. Then, in 1924, we migrated to Florida, nine of us in a four-passenger Dodge that belonged to my brother-in-law, along with everything we owned. We had a tent and camped each night, quite a resemblance to *Grapes of Wrath*.

The Florida land boom was on and jobs were plentiful, and it seemed that everybody was prospering except us. Dad worked as a brick mason and other odd construction jobs, but wasn't a very good provider.

As the years passed I hauled mortar for brick layers, delivered papers, worked in a "dime" store, spent a summer in Chicago as an ice cream good humor man, was desk clerk in a hotel, clerked in a music store and in another that sold washing machines and refrigerators, drove a bakery truck, and .... realized more and more that I needed more education. I was back in Wichita at the time, and began to take afternoon and night courses at the University of Wichita. Night after night I worked like the devil, studying and cramming.

It was there in Wichita, in Sunday School where I'd gone for the sole purpose of finding a girlfriend, that 23-year old Roy E. Weatherby met one Camilla Jackman. A junior at the University, she would become my wife two years later, in 1936.

I worked for the Southwestern Bell Telephone Company in Wichita and Topeka, but we decided to leave the company and head west. With no work in Denver, we continued to San Diego. After working for San Diego Gas & Electric as a salesman for a short time, I got my first "good" job with the Automobile Club of Southern California, making $200 a month.

In one year I was the top producer for the Club, and soon brought my mother and sisters out from Kansas. Even though times were tough, I was no longer living in the poverty I had known all my life.

During all this time I liked to hunt, and was beginning to experiment with guns and ammunition and to study ballistics. I became a real gun nut. And I became convinced that if I could get a bullet going fast enough it would kill an animal humanely and quickly. It was the beginning.—*Roy Weatherby*

A year later, in February of 1981, Roy added other thoughts to his story.

In the beginning it would have been difficult for me to comprehend that this company would ever be where it is today. It would have been even more difficult for me to have realized, when I borrowed my first $5,000 from the Bank of America in 1946 by pledging everything I owned, that in later years I would have a five million dollar line of credit. Or to have imagined that my gross sales in 1946 of less than $50,000 would ever reach a million dollars a year.

My great dream was to have gross sales of a million. That was passed many years ago, and now I'm striving for the $20,000,000 mark. The increase came so slowly and was so difficult. For many years, although sales increased, there was no profit, for so much was being spent on research and development, promotion and advertising. I always felt that if I could just hold everything together, somehow keep from going bankrupt, the research and development of new products would eventually pay off, and it has.

For the first 15 or 20 years my anxiety and fears of going broke were overwhelming. I was on the brink of bankruptcy so many times. Although my business is now strong and prosperous, that fear still plagues me today. The thought of reverses that could bring the business to an end. This anxiety has kept me always alert, attempting to operate the business very conservatively. It has also caused me to become a bit pessimistic.

But, most of all, it has taught me to be a realist. I will still be pushing forward to bring out new and better products, for increased sales and profit, but I know I'll never take the gambles I took back in the early years.

My formal education is somewhat inadequate for the profession I chose. Although I took some courses in business administration, and thought I knew how to run a business, I found that actually operating a business doesn't always work out like the books teach you.

I received my greatest education since 1945, in the most difficult and expensive school anyone could ever attend. The long, hard days, months and years of study, and the learning experiences gained through costly trial and errors. This type of education can never be obtained in any university. It's also one from which you never graduate, nor receive a degree or diploma.

The sad part is that the term never ends. The school just keeps going on and on with the same gambles, risks and unsure decisions one has to make. The common sense judgment one gains through trial and error surely creates a true realist. And, after scores of years it has left me not with a satisfaction of success, or the ability to relax and begin to take life easier, but with a continued anxiety of what could happen to my life's work.

2

The Rough Years

Growth in the Late 1940's

Roy's first few months in business were tough days, but things got better. He had a tremendous amount of ambition. He was convinced that his high velocity concept was the answer to humane, clean kills, and that with proper promotion his business would prosper. He needed such confidence, for in those early days he was the janitor, the retail clerk, the shipping clerk, the polishing and bluing man, as well as the receptionist and correspondence secretary. Eventually, he was able to hire a very inexpensive secretary and then another man to work in the shop on guns. Little by little people were finding out where his business was located and, fortunately, he was also getting a little bit of editorial coverage in some of the magazines about high velocity.

Friends were invaluable. Wilbur Martin, who used to help him in his garage, would come over and work in the retail store just for fun. Bill Wittman, his attorney friend, would work in the retail store on Saturdays because he liked fishing tackle and enjoyed talking about fishing with the customers. Roy himself put in long hours, from 7:30 in the morning until about 10 every night at least six days a week, and sometimes on Sunday.

His national advertising at that time consisted of a small ad every few months. It was only three inches of one column, and it showed the different shape of one of his cartridges in comparison to a standard one, with a little squibb below telling the advantage of high velocity. As a result of each of these ads, he would receive a few more inquiries and build a few more rifles.

By the time he started in business, Roy had developed the .220 Rocket (based on the .220 Swift cartridge, with a changed taper and shoulder), the .257, .270, and .300 Weatherby Magnums. He would build new rifles on any kind of action that he could obtain, as well as rechambering customers' rifles. If they had a .300 H&H Model 70, he would rechamber it to the .300 Weatherby. If they had a .270 WCF caliber, he would rechamber it to take the .270 Weatherby Magnum, altering the bolt face and the magazine. The same applied to any .25 caliber. Weatherby's idea was to give the shooting public a service such as they had never had before; to answer promptly all correspondence and to give the customer exactly what he wanted.

After the first year in business, he had about six employees.

From the beginning, Roy displayed a talent for attracting people of prominence and fame as customers. Very shortly after he went into business, while he was still waiting on customers in the retail store, a tall lanky guy pulled up in front of the store in a Lagonda sports car. When he walked into the store Roy immediately recognized Gary Cooper. He told Roy he'd been reading about these high velocity guns he was building and he would like to have one.

Before he left the store, their conversation turned to automobiles, another avid interest of Roy's. Cooper quickly offered to take Roy for a ride in his new sports car, which he had just purchased the day before. That first meeting with Gary Cooper led to many more, and a long friendship developed. He used to come out to the store two or three times a month, and he and Roy would go to the rifle range together, where Weatherby would test new guns and calibers and check velocities on his homemade chronograph. Gary often helped him sight-in rifles that were ready to be returned to his customers.

Another early customer was Sheldon Coleman, of the Coleman Company in Wichita, Kansas. Sheldon did not realize, at first, that Weatherby was actually in the business of producing high velocity rifles and ammunition. He had read an article of Roy's, "Overgunned and Undergunned," which was published in the January 1946 issue of *Hunting and Fishing* magazine, and agreed with many of the things Weatherby had to say concerning super velocities. So he wrote a letter to Roy Weatherby, mailing it to *Hunting and Fishing* magazine in

Boston, Massachusetts, who forwarded it on to Roy Weatherby. When Roy replied, Coleman learned he was actually in business.

Coleman was planning an Alaskan trip for Brown Bear and sent Weatherby a .270 caliber Model 70 Winchester rifle to be not only rechambered to .270 Weatherby Magnum caliber, but also to be restocked to his personal measurements. At the same time, he sent along a .300 H&H Magnum rifle, not to be rechambered to Weatherby caliber, but to be restocked with the Weatherby style stock.

And so it began, with a determined, serious Roy Weatherby at his first office in 1945. The antique dictating machine, state of the art at the time, was a precursor of the Roy Weatherby mindset: he documented everything with copious notes, memos and photographs.

Struggles of the Early Years

Weatherby made a little profit in 1946, so it was a pretty good year for the embryonic firearms firm. This was due mainly to the fact that there was very little expense in maintaining a business, only a small store and shop. Overhead was low. Weatherby was taking only $400 in salary, far less than he had earned as an insurance salesman.

In addition to his mail order rifle building business continually increasing, the Weatherby retail store drew shooters because it was also the only one in the entire southern Los Angeles area that had a gunsmith. Weatherby had also received quite a bit of editorial coverage in the national outdoor magazines in the past 18 months. That caused more and more customers from all over the nation to single out his retail store when they were in the area. He realized that in order to make the business grow, he would need to expand, giving more room for inventory in the retail store and space for additional equipment in the shop.

All of the profit made in 1946 was put back into the business, and the retail store inventory increased from around $7,500 in March to over $20,000 by the end of that year. Roy also was able to pay Bill Wittman, his attorney friend and first partner, $4,000 profit on his initial $10,000 investment.

Just before Christmas in 1946 Roy had an auto accident, severely injuring his right knee. He spent almost a month in the hospital, another three months on crutches, and for the next six months had to use a cane to walk. None of that slowed him down.

In less than two years, Weatherby had succeeded in establishing a worldwide reputation with his "flashy" high velocity rifles. Customers from every state in the union, plus Canada, Alaska, Hawaii and Africa, were using his rifles. The December 1946 issue of the *American Rifleman* featured a Weatherby rifle on the cover. Weatherby had already displayed an inherent ability to meet important people and cultivate their friendship, and he frequently exploited these friendships in order to obtain additional publicity.

When building his home in Downey, Roy included a darkroom in his oversized garage for his photography hobby. In purchasing his photographic equipment from the Winters Company, a supply house in Los Angeles, he became well acquainted with the manager. Roy convinced him that it would be mutually beneficial if Weatherby were

Roy's office in the new quarters reflected the growing success of his rifle-making dreams.

to put a display of his guns in their Los Angeles showroom. He did just that, and got excellent free publicity.

Selling the Farm for Additional Capital

Camilla, Roy's wife, had inherited a 160 acre wheat farm in Kansas. It was worked by a tenant farmer and Camilla received a small income from the profits, up or down depending on the crop. But Weatherby knew that he needed additional capital to expand his business. He also wanted to buy back Bill Wittman's share of the company, despite the fact that Wittman was an ideal "silent partner," never interfering with the actual operation of the business. Camilla's farm was the answer, and early in 1947 she and Roy sold it, netting $21,000. Roy bought out Wittman's interest and had money left over.

About this time he became very well acquainted, through correspondence, with Philip B. Sharpe, who was considered an expert in the field of guns and ballistics. His book, "The Complete Guide to Handloading," was the handloading bible for many years.

Sharpe bought a .270 Weatherby Magnum custom rifle with a stock of Oregon myrtlewood. In ordering this rifle he wrote, "The 1947 season for chucks will soon be with us. I would like to try my .270 Weatherby this season so my observations can be included in Hand-loading 1948 revision. I will keep a shot-by-shot log of everything fired through the barrel, and after each session in the range and in the fields, diary notes will be kept on the wear, using a fine Berlin-made boroscope I picked up overseas. This is a fine precision optical instrument, with built-in 'grain-o-wheat' lamps, which permit minute examination of every spot in the bore, including the chamber. What this unit reveals is amazing. Using it, we will get the real picture of what life the barrel will give."

True to his word, the 1948 revised edition of Sharpe's "Complete Guide to Handloading" contained complete loading data and ballistics, as well as his personal comments, on each of the following Weatherby calibers: .220 Weatherby Rocket, .228 Weatherby Magnum (one of the original Weatherby calibers, it was the first one to be discontinued by Roy after only a few rifles were chambered for it), .257 Weatherby Magnum, .270 Weatherby Magnum, 7mm Weatherby Magnum, .300 Weatherby Magnum and .375 Weatherby Magnum. Although Sharpe's comments left no doubt with the reader that the .270 Weatherby Magnum was his favorite, he had this to say about the .375 Weatherby Magnum: "Weatherby's blown out version of the original .375 H&H Magnum has been stepped up to the point where the game almost dies before you pull the trigger."

Selling Stock to Incorporate

Weatherby had now grown out of the original small quarters, and was able to enlarge the retail store, his private office and the shop by taking over two additional store fronts. He now had about a 75 foot frontage, and occupied three-fourths of Howard Merrill's building. His business was growing, but so were his expenses.

Once again he was in dire need of new capital, so he approached Bill Wittman and told him he wanted to incorporate the company and sell stock. Accordingly, Weatherby's, Inc. (this was later changed to Weatherby, Inc.) was formed in May of 1949, with permission granted for the sale of $70,000 in stock. Officers of the company were Roy E. Weatherby, President; Herbert W. Klein, of Dallas, Texas, Vice-President; Philip B. Sharpe, of Fairfield, Pennsylvania, Vice-President; Isabel Field Peterson, of South Gate, California, Secretary-Treasurer.

14

Roy destroyed many Los Angeles telephone directories, soaked with water, testing his beliefs in high velocity. In addition, he exploded drums of water and even demonstrated that his cartridges would penetrate "bulletproof" glass, as shown here.

Early in 1946 Herb Klein, a wealthy oil man from Dallas, had ordered a .270 Weatherby Magnum custom rifle. It was the first of many custom Weatherbys that he would acquire. He and Roy Weatherby had become quite good friends, and when he learned of Roy's plans to incorporate and sell stock, he became one of the original shareholders by purchasing $10,000 worth of common stock.

Roy also sold shares to other individuals in amounts ranging from $1,000 to $15,000, most to friends who had faith in the abilities of Roy Weatherby. Later, Klein bought the remaining $40,000 worth of stock when he learned that Roy was having trouble finding additional investors. It made his total investment $50,000 and gave him half interest in the business.

Eastern Trip, Establishing Valuable Contacts

In 1949 Weatherby and his attorney friend, Bill Wittman, made a three week trip to the East Coast where he made many valuable contacts. One was Firearms International Corporation, where he met the president of the firm, Booker McClay, and Jan Winter, the sales manager. FIC was then the sole importer of the F.N. Mauser action, manufactured by Fabrique Nationale d'Armes de Guerre in Liege, Belgium. Weatherby had with him one of these Mauser actions on which he had made certain modifications, i.e., altering the feeding ramp and lengthening the magazine in order to better accommodate the larger Weatherby cartridge, and he asked FIC if they could build Weatherby rifles on the action. He also wanted the name "Weatherby, South Gate, California" stamped on the side of the F.N. receiver. Firearms International agreed to send this modified action to F.N. for a quotation.

Later, after receiving their quotation for an action with his specifications, Weatherby placed an order for 100 of them at a cost of $33.50. He wanted to begin standardizing and identifying his Weatherby Deluxe rifle as a true Weatherby.

Weatherby was also determined to find a company to manufacture his ammunition commercially, thus taking his calibers out of the wildcat class. So, along with the modified action, Firearms International also sent samples of Weatherby's cartridge cases to F.N. asking them to quote a price for making Weatherby cartridge cases and/or loaded ammunition.

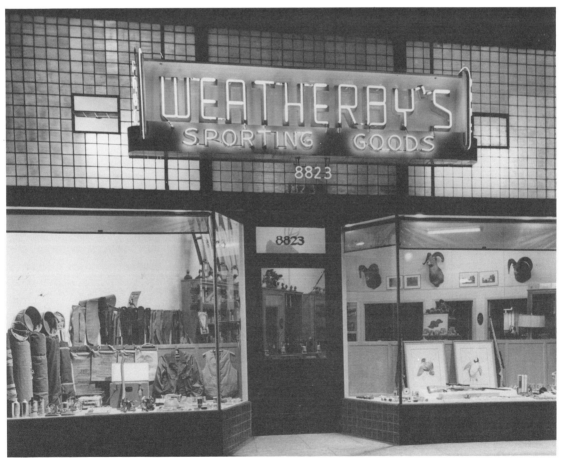

(Above) Weatherby Firearms began here, in a skinny 25x70 foot space on the corner of Long Beach and Firestone boulevards in South Gate, California. (Top) The new, enlarged "Weatherby's," built in 1951 on Firestone Boulevard just around the corner from the old one, became a showplace that attracted groups of visitors from throughout the area. The offices, shops, and 100-yard underground firing range were in the rear.

One evening during his stay on the East Coast Weatherby was on the NBC television station in Washington, D.C., an appearance arranged by Ray Stann of the National Rifle Association. Roy showed some of his rifles, explained the principle of the Weatherby cartridge, and also talked about his 1948 African safari.

While in Washington Weatherby met with General Julian Hatcher, who was with the National Rifle Association and author of "Hatcher's Notebook." Hatcher set up an appointment for Weatherby with a Captain Jervey, who was recognized as one of the top authorities in Army ordnance.

Jervey told Weatherby that Federal Cartridge Company in Minneapolis, Minnesota had bought surplus cartridge case machinery from the Army after the war, and now was ready to operate. He suggested that Weatherby contact Charles Horn, president of Federal about making Weatherby cartridge cases and ammunition. He also recommended that Roy contact a George Dawson at Winchester, as Western was only working three days a week at that time and might be interested in additional work for Weatherby. He was also able to provide Weatherby with the names of the proper people to contact at Remington Arms in this regard, Roy Swan or a Mr. Coleman.

Another great Washington contact Roy made was with Colonel Townsend Whelen, vice president of Parker-Whelen in Washington, D.C., as well as being arms editor for *Sports Afield* magazine. Whelen had just finished writing a book on custom rifles, devoting an entire chapter to Weatherby rifles, the only custom gun that was illustrated in his book. Weatherby never overlooked the importance of establishing and cultivating friendships such as this.

From Washington Weatherby went to Philadelphia and visited Paul Jaeger in Jenkintown, who had a small sporting goods store and gun shop with about 10 employees. Jaeger told Weatherby he was very impressed with his barrel blanks and ordered 27 of them. He also told Roy he would send his own stock pattern out to Weatherby for them to inlet and shape stocks on his pantograph machine, which Weatherby agreed to do at a price of $6.00 each. Weatherby's notes indicate that he felt this was a very good and profitable contact.

The next day he went to the Frankford Arsenal and met with Colonel George Miller, who had handled the sale of surplus loading equipment to Federal Cartridge Company. Miller tried to convince Weatherby that he should do the same thing, and start training men to manufacture cartridge cases on the West Coast. If Weatherby had a pilot line of his own cartridge cases being manufactured, he added, the government would give him enough contracts to keep the machinery in constant operation, making it pay for itself. He gave Weatherby all necessary information relative to every cartridge case machine and loading machine available, and also took him on a tour through the arsenal and gave him a demonstration of their new electric annealing machine. At that time there was no other machine like it in existence.

Weatherby went to New York the next day and had lunch with Warren Page, who had just been appointed the arms editor for *Field & Stream*. It was his first meeting with Page, although he had corresponded with him. It was another valuable initial contact, and was the beginning of a lifelong friendship with Warren.

That afternoon Weatherby visited Griffin & Howe, one of the largest gun stores in New York at the time, and met with Seymour Griffin and Mr. Johnstone. They gave him an order for ten of his rifle barrels, all in .416 caliber.

In Bridgeport, Connecticut, a day later, Roy met with Roy Swan at Remington Arms Company. Swan seemed interested in the possibility of Remington manufacturing Weatherby ammunition, and told Weatherby he would discuss it with company executives very shortly and let him know. Weatherby expressed reluctance to order ammunition from a foreign firm, there being two splendid ammunition companies here in the United States, and that seemed to appeal to Swan. Weatherby did tell him that if either Remington or Winchester would not furnish him with ammunition, and if he did not buy his own equipment to make it himself, then he would be ordering it from a foreign company.

While in Bridgeport, Weatherby also visited the Waterbury Farrel Company, a company that manufactured automatic loading equipment. It had built loading machines for the government during the war, but machines from current production would cost Roy twice as much. They suggested that the War Assets Administration might have surplus Waterbury Farrel loading machines available.

In Hartford, Connecticut Roy talked to Pratt & Whitney about barrel machinery. He was already using a Pratt & Whitney rifling machine in South Gate, but was experiencing some minor problems. Weatherby's next stop was to visit Winchester in New Haven. They advised him to

Three mounted heads—elk, moose and sheep—plus a lion rug on the counter, were the sparse decoration in the first Weatherby retail store.

stop using carbide bits, and also to change his barrel material so that the rifling process could be speeded up.

Not missing any bases, Weatherby also met with Winchester in New Haven. Again, they were receptive to the idea of producing Weatherby ammunition, but added that they would require an order for one million rounds before it would pay them to set up the necessary equipment.

At Winchester Roy met Mel Johnson, the inventor of the Johnson automatic rifle used by the Army, who was working for Winchester. Johnson seemed pleased to meet Weatherby, saying he had heard a lot about Roy's rifles and had seen many of them. He showed Weatherby extreme slow-motion movies, made by Winchester, that showed the function of automatic weapons and the behavior of shotgun charges

20

In his new retail store, Roy exhibited many of the trophies from his 1948 African safari.

and projectiles as they leave the barrel. In their experimental laboratories Roy saw the new Winchester Model 70 on the drawing board, soon to be brought out in competition to the Remington 721. It was an impressive and informative visit.

That was the first of many trips Weatherby was to make that combined public relations with seeking out ways and means of improving the production of his rifles.

On the way home, typically enough, he and Wittman stopped in Salina, Kansas to show his African pictures to a group of sportsmen.

The Need for Additional Space and Capital

When Roy incorporated in February of 1949 the Weatherby Company had a total indebtedness of $41,000, and he succeeded in selling

$63,000 of the $70,000 worth of stock the State had permitted him to sell. After paying off the debt Weatherby was left with about $22,000 for an expansion program. Although the orders were continuing to come in at a steady pace, he was operating under the hardships of too little space, too little time-saving equipment, too little money for the national advertising he felt would be required, and still no source for the manufacturing of his own ammunition.

Later in 1949 Roy signed a note for $25,000 loaned to the company by Herb Klein. By the end of June 1950, Weatherby was buying about 1400 pounds of rifle barrel steel each month to build 150 barrels. Sale of barrel blanks had continued to increase, mostly in response to some small black and white ads Roy ran in trade publications for gunsmiths. He was selling his standard blanks for $25.00, and the heavier #2 or #3 contour barrels for $30.00, less a discount to the trade of 25 percent.

He was also buying wood for stocks, 200 blanks at a time, paying $2.28 each for plain walnut and $4.18 for fancy walnut. By that time he was making full use of his 18-spindle stock carving machine, selling both unfinished and finished stocks inletted for F.N. or Model 98 Mauser, Springfield, Enfield, Winchester Model 70, Remington Models 721 and 722 and the JAP 6.5 and 31. Unfinished stocks sold for $20.00 for the standard grade walnut and $30.00 for the fancy grade. Finished stocks of the Weatherby design, completely finished inside and out and equipped with a rubber butt plate, were $42.50 without checkering and $57.50 with it. In addition, both gunsmiths and customers were sending Weatherby their stock blanks to be machine carved and semi-inletted at a price of $8.00 each.

By now he was also receiving shipments of 100 rifle actions every other month from F.N. with the name Weatherby on them, and serial numbered with a special series of four digit numbers. These were being used at the rate of 45 to 50 per month for the production of Deluxe and Custom rifles.

Despite the infusion of capital from the sale of stock, and the $25,000 loan from Herb Klein, by the end of June 1950 the Company was showing a net operating loss of nearly $18,000. Once again, Weatherby, with his proven abilities as a super salesman and promoter, approached Herb Klein and was able to convince him that an additional loan of $35,000 would help put the company in the black.

Moving To A New Building On Firestone Blvd.

By the end of 1950 Weatherby had expanded as far as he could go in the building at 8823 Long Beach Blvd., and he was still running out of room. There was a piece of land with a 240-foot frontage that was ideally located right around the corner on Firestone Blvd., but neither Roy himself nor the Company had the wherewithal to purchase it. Once again he contacted his friend and stockholder, Herb Klein, who by this time could be likened to the "angel" that playwrights seek out to finance their plays. Herb provided the money for the land and the building, and on April 1951, Weatherby moved into what was then very spacious headquarters of some 20,000 square feet.

The retail store, with its 100 foot all-glass front, was considered in those days to be a most modern showplace. Roy Weatherby personally designed the store, from the placement of counters and showcases to the attractive display of the numerous game animals he had collected over the years on his hunts in the U.S., the Yukon Territory, Canada and on his 1948 safari into Africa.

At one end of the store, mounted next to a fireplace, Roy positioned the full head, shoulders and forelegs of a giraffe. A few years later added an imposing mount of an elephant head over the archway that led from the retail store back into the offices and shop. With the spots and floodlights that were left on at night, his sporting goods store soon became such a place of interest that many residents would drive by and get out of their cars just to look in at all of the animals.

Roy commissioned Henry Maravion to paint a mural of a typical African landscape on one entire wall of his new office, directly behind his desk. Spotlights in the ceiling above this wall highlighted the colorful scene.

The shop was also a large, roomy, well-planned area, and across the back of the property a 100-yard underground firing range was constructed. This permitted range firing and chronographing of his rifles to be done right there in the basement of his shop. The communities all around South Gate were so impressed with the sporting goods store and rifle manufacturing plant that, for several years, Boy Scout troops and school classrooms organized field trips to tour Weatherby's facility. In later years, many of these boys who had visited Weatherby's in their youth became owners of Weatherby rifles.

The total cost of the land and construction came to about $83,000. Weatherby had been paying only $450 per month rent for his smaller quarters on Long Beach Blvd.; he was now obligated to a $900 per month rent and a 10-year payoff, at which time title would pass to the corporation.

Just before the building was completed, Roy's mother died. She had been living with him for several years. She had eagerly watched each phase of the construction of the new building, and was very proud of her son and the name he had made for himself in the shooting industry in just five short years.

Setting Up Weatherby Dealers Nationwide

Beginning in the early 1950's, on each trip that Weatherby made he took time to call on gun dealers. There was no gun law at that time to prevent selling direct to the consumer, but Roy felt that his products should be handled in retail gun stores. As a result of his efforts several of the smaller shops were ordering Weatherby rifles to fill a specific customer's request, but very few of them were actually stocking his products. He *had* succeeded in setting up stocking dealers in several key cities across the country, such as Marshall Fields and Von Lengerke & Antoine (VL&A) in Chicago, Roos-Atkins in San Francisco, J. L. Hudson Company in Detroit, Oshman's in Houston, Withers & Company in Dallas, and Abercrombie & Fitch in New York.

Weatherby had been attending and exhibiting at the NRA annual meetings since 1948, getting great response and acceptance of his rifles. In 1955 Roy decided to make a major move, to exhibit at the industry's largest trade show, the NSGA. Sponsored by the National Sporting Goods Association, it was held each February in Chicago.

There were no large convention centers, so the manufacturers in the sporting goods industry took over an entire floor of the Morrison Hotel for their exhibits. Attendance was limited to sporting goods and gun dealers rather than the public and, in spite of the terrible weather that generally prevailed in Chicago in February, dealers from all over the country would converge at this show.

Roy had just hired an ex-Air Force colonel, Robert T. Smith (another former Flying Tiger), and he took him along to Chicago to help man the booth, answering the dealers' questions and writing up orders. By the time that 1955 NSGA Show closed Weatherby was elated. Not only

24

had they succeeded in setting up a number of new dealers across the country, they had also written almost $20,000 worth of dealer business.

Putting Salesmen On The Road

Weatherby was always his own best salesman. He continued to call on dealers, trying to sell them on the idea of stocking his rifles, ammunition and scope sights. His attendance as an exhibitor at the annual NSGA trade show in Chicago for the past two years had proven to be a very good move as he was able to establish new dealers at each of these shows.

In the spring of 1955 he sent his first two salesmen out on the road, specifically to set up new dealers. Knowing he would need assistance in manning his exhibit at the NRA meetings in Washington, D.C., he mapped out four different routes between California and Washington —two through the Central and Northern part of the U.S., and two through the South. Three weeks before the date of the NRA meetings he sent Bob Smith, the ex-Flying Tiger and retired Air Force colonel he had hired the year before, to travel the Northern route, calling on dealers all the way. Marty Noonan, an employee who had been with him in various capacities since 1946, was to travel one of the Southern routes doing the same thing. Both men, along with Weatherby, met in Washington, D.C. to work at the NRA exhibit. When the NRA meetings were over, each of these two men took a different route and three more weeks to return home, once again calling on dealers.

That experiment with "salesmen" revealed two things: 1. that the dealer trade liked having Weatherby salesmen call on them, explaining in detail the attributes and sales features of the rifles; and 2. that the company expense compared to the income generated was prohibitive.

The solution was to hire manufacturer's representatives who were already established working as independent agents, but carrying enough non-conflicting lines that enabled them not only to cover their expenses, but to earn a reasonable income as well. Finding the right man for each territory proved to be difficult.

By the end of the 1957 NSGA Show, however, Weatherby had contracted with five such reps who collectively covered 27 states. Three of these original five were excellent choices and represented Weatherby for many years: John Lutes, from Michigan, who covered six states in the mid-West; Ralph Strauss, from Maryland, who covered seven middle Atlantic states; and Marty Noonan, from California, his ex-employee who had left the firm to become an independent representative, who covered three Western states.

Weatherby soon became a coveted line, and for the past three decades there has been very little turnover of sales reps. Today, the firm employs 12 different rep firms, many of whom have associates working for them, giving Weatherby a total of 31 salesmen calling on the dealer trade in the continental United States. In addition, there are two representatives in Canada and two in Europe.

Influence Of Weatherby Magnum Calibers On The Industry

By 1957, long before there was any knowledge in the industry of the new Mark V action, the increasing popularity of the Weatherby Magnum cartridges was making the other arms companies sit up and take notice. As an example, Winchester had come out with some new magnum cartridges of their own: the .458 Winchester, the .338 Winchester and the hot little .264 Winchester. Jack O'Connor, in the March 1958 issue of *Outdoor Life,* referred to Winchester's new .338 and .264 calibers as follows: "These two new Winchester jobs will give shooters something to talk about…It wouldn't surprise me too much if they weren't scared out of the bushes by the Weatherby series…" Remington had also introduced their new 7mm Remington Magnum. There was no doubt in Weatherby's mind that he had been at least indirectly responsible for these advancements, and with production finally under way both in the US and in Germany of his Mark V action, he was determined to keep pace with, if not stay ahead of, these larger arms companies.

Although he had yet to receive a completed Mark V rifle from either of his manufacturing sources, he immediately started work on the design of a smaller version of this action, one that would have only six locking lugs instead of the nine, with the overall size scaled down accordingly. He had long felt that the .220 Rocket was on its way out in popularity. Consequently, he had never commercially produced ammunition for this caliber. Nevertheless, it was his opinion there was a definite market for a .222 caliber centerfire rifle. Although development of this smaller action was to take more than three years, in l962 the Weatherby Varmintmaster rifle was introduced, chambered for Weatherby's own *.224* - the only belted varmint cartridge in existence.

The "Weatherby Look" rapidly found its way into the lines of many firearms manufacturers, with that distinctive, high-lustre finish on high-grade, figured walnut stock. The Monte Carlo comb and the prominent spacers between wood and buttplate or pad, on the grip and on the forearm, are now integral parts of many rifles.

Weatherby, of course, added more conventional rifle elements to its lineup in recent years. Less expensive, less flamboyant designs made their appearance as "Weatherbys," and the South Gate firm even led the field by being first on the market with an over-the-counter fiberglass stocked rifle.

But the verdict is in. Roy E. Weatherby placed the Weatherby mark on the firearms/hunting fraternity, probably to be there for all time.

Government Defense Contracts

In 1951 Weatherby made a decision that would prove very costly. He knew the government was granting a lot of defense contracts for the building of missiles and other war material, and that the large firms receiving those contracts were subletting some of the smaller jobs out to independent machine shops. With the additional shop space he now had, he determined to go after some of those sublet contracts.

He felt there was also an opportunity to make money in the defense contract work. Since his first trip back east he had kept in touch with the contacts he made for gunsmithing and rifle building equipment. Now, he proceeded to slowly purchase additional pieces of used equipment, some of which would also prove useful in the building of his rifles.

Roy next hired Earl Wright, a man who had experience in this type of work, and who was purported to be knowledgeable in submitting bids. He also hired two outside salesmen specifically for the solicitation of this type of work, and paid them six percent of any job that materialized. By mid-July he had obtained several contracts, had hired enough men to operate two eight-hour shifts daily, and was performing work for companies such as Airesearch Manufacturing Company, Ferris Screw Products, Diversified Metals, Douglas Aircraft Corporation, Pacific Gauge, U.S. Electric Motors and several others.

Now he had 34 shop employees—machinists, gunsmiths, stock makers, a highly skilled operator for the Salstrom 18-spindle stock carving machine, and shipping personnel, plus six men for the retail store; and nine employees in the offices. His overhead was tremendous for the amount of work that was being done. And, in spite of the number of small defense contract jobs that came his way, the really large ones continued to escape him. There was little repeat business and, he was to learn later, some of the parts they worked on were rejected by the government for failure to meet the precise tolerances required and the extremely rigid inspections.

After several months it was obvious that his company was losing money on practically every job they took. Roy discovered that the experienced man he had hired to serve as foreman of the machine shop was a catastrophe as a bid estimator, despite being a very conscientious and dependable employee.

Once, after he had submitted a bid of $295 for a job on a missile project, the prime contractor personally visited Weatherby to caution him about the employee. He explained that he had received four bids for that job, with the highest being $1,300 and the lowest, except for Weatherby's, being $900. He was positive Weatherby could not do the job for $295, and convinced him to withdraw his bid. The company would surely have lost a considerable amount of money on this one project.

After about a year of trying to compete and operate a business about which he knew absolutely nothing, Weatherby got out of the defense contract business. He reduced his overhead by dismissing employees. He eventually sold several pieces of equipment at a substantial profit, since that type of machinery was difficult to obtain and in great demand.

Excise Tax

In May of 1951 Weatherby was visited by agents of the Internal Revenue Service, who advised him that the converted rifles and ammunition he had been selling were subject to an 11 percent excise tax, which he had not been paying. Weatherby was able to produce a letter which he had written in 1945 to the Department of Internal Revenue, advising them of exactly what his operation would consist of when he first went into business, i.e., repairing rifles, installing barrels, receivers and other mechanisms required to convert existing rifles to Weatherby calibers. In this letter he asked if these operations would require him to obtain a manufacturer's license for a fee of $25.00, or a dealer's license for a fee of $1.00. The Department of Internal Revenue replied to him that the $1.00 license was sufficient to cover his operation. Using this letter as a basis, Weatherby tried to convince the IRS that he was not in the same category as the larger arms companies, and, therefore, should not be subject to excise tax. He also argued that there were many other smaller gunsmiths around the country performing modifications on existing rifles similar to what he was doing who were not being assessed this excise tax.

To fight paying these back taxes, Weatherby hired George Zeutzuis, an attorney who specialized in such matters. He also attempted to enlist the support of the National Rifle Association, and wrote a letter to C. B. Lister, who was the top man at that time at the NRA. He contacted Roy Gradle, a well known local gunsmith, Alex Kerr, a champion skeet and trap shooter who operated a gun shop and sporting goods store in Beverly Hills, and P. O. Ackley, another well known gunsmith in Salt Lake City, and sent a mimeographed letter over the signature of these four men (Weatherby, Gradle, Kerr and Ackley) to thousands of independent gunsmiths throughout the country, urging them to join in the crusade not only to make the assessment of excise tax not applicable to the independent gunsmith, but also asking them to write their congressman in an effort to change the structure for the collection of excise tax. Weatherby felt it was unfair for this excise tax to be charged on the sale of guns and ammunition, which necessitated 11 percent being added to the cost of these products, and thereby increasing the price to the consumer.

Roy believed it should be charged on each hunting license sold so that the person who was actually hunting the game would be paying the excise tax. He argued that this would also simplify collection procedures for the government. Weatherby himself wrote many letters on this subject to his California congressman at the time, Cecil King. However, in spite of all of his efforts to get this ruling changed, he was unable to do so.

In the midst of his battles with the local agents, he received a letter from the Commissioner of Internal Revenue, advising him that it would now be necessary for him to obtain a $25.00 manufacturer's license in addition to the $1.00 dealer's license in order for him to continue operating his business as he was doing.

In the meantime, the local auditors were going through his books and by mid-August of 1951, he received a notice that he had five days to pay nearly $1,200 for excise taxes due on just the portion of the audit that had been completed at that time. By March of 1952, the department had completed their audit of Weatherby's books to date, and had determined that including a 25 percent penalty for late payment, Weatherby owed the government $16,000 for unpaid excise tax. Through his attorney he filed a protest stating that the audited merchandise included items not subject to excise tax, such as scopes and mounts. He asked for and was granted a 30 day extension, and during this time was able to prove his point on this matter at least. He, therefore, succeeded in getting the amount of back taxes reduced to $13,000.

Since that time Weatherby has been paying excise taxes on a quarterly basis, and has undergone a number of successful IRS audits.

Changes in the early 1960's

For several years prior to 1957 Weatherby had shown a slight profit, but 1957 and 1958 were loss years even though sales continued to increase. These losses were largely due to the research and development costs of the new Mark V action, the ever increasing interest charges due Herb Klein for his loans, and interest paid as floored inventory was withdrawn from a bonded warehouse. The year 1959 was extremely profitable because of shipments finally being made on the large backlog of orders for the new Mark V rifle.

The national economy slowed down in 1960 and gave Weatherby cause for concern. He didn't want to lose the momentum he had gained in 1959.

Roy took stock. He reviewed all phases of his operation to eliminate unnecessary costs and reduce expenses. Deluxe rifle production of excellent quality was arriving monthly from J. P. Sauer in West Germany. This meant that his carving machine was now idle too much of the time. He had discontinued offering semi-inletted stocks carved for the various actions of all makes, as it had become necessary to devote all available time on this machine to the carving of his own Deluxe rifle stocks.

Ken Bucklin, his employee who had been operating the stock pantograph equipment, decided to go into business for himself, but he didn't have the money to buy the Salstrom machine outright. Weatherby leased it to him, not only saving the salary of a highly paid, skilled employee, but also gaining some revenue from the lease payment. And, Weatherby had a source for the carving of custom stocks or any other special stocks as needed. Removing that huge piece of equipment also made room in the shop for receiving, inspection and any rework necessary on the rifles coming in from Germany.

Roy also reduced shop overhead by eliminating five other employees no longer needed for barrel making, rifle assembly, stock checkering and inletting. He determined that many of the services he had been

Herb Klein, a wealthy Texas oil man, became the angel Roy Weatherby needed. He was Roy's first partner, buying 100 shares of stock for $10,000 in January, 1949, and regularly provided additional funding when it became necessary. Klein hunted extensively throughout the world, and was the first recipient of the Weatherby Big Game Trophy Award. Here, he and Roy (right) examine a custom Weatherby rifle stocked with tigertail maple.

offering were not profitable enough to continue, and discontinued the hand loading of cases for consumers and dealers. Production of the .375 Weatherby Magnum caliber rifle was ended, since sales in this caliber continued to decline in favor of the more popular .378 Weatherby Magnum. He notified dealers that the sales of all standard caliber rifles, with the exception of the .270 Winchester and .30-06, which he would have Sauer produce, would be discontinued. He also stopped offering special barrel contours except on full custom rifles.

Roy was also working on an improved safety and trigger mechanism which would move the safety lever back onto the bolt sleeve for more convenient operation, and hoped to have it ready for 1961 production. He planned to send one of his employees to Germany as a full-time quality control inspector, to further reduce rework in South Gate. And, he continued development of the smaller Mark V action for a new .22 caliber.

Sauer made a request that Roy accept a 10 percent increase in their cost price, in spite of the fact that a contract had been signed at the agreed upon price of $66.30 per rifle for the first 10,000 rifles. He and Fred Jennie had worked so closely with them for the past two years that Weatherby was convinced they were sincere and honest with their revised cost figures. With Sauer never having made rifles before, he felt they had simply misjudged on several of their original cost estimates, especially in the area of the Weatherby stock design. Roy knew from building stocks in South Gate that the shape of his stock did not lend itself to mass production. The application of his high luster finish also required a great deal more hand work than the European style shotgun stock Sauer had been accustomed to producing. He, therefore, honored their request, although he knew this meant an increase in his selling price.

As a result of the many cost-cutting changes and decisions Roy made, and in spite of a sluggish economy for the first six months, 1960 ended up with the company showing a profit. Not a substantial one, but at least it was another year in the black.

Partners and Problems

After six months in business, Weatherby was barely keeping his head above water, operating with not enough money, inventory or space. He realized that it would be difficult to increase business and operate profitably without additional capital. He asked his attorney friend, Bill Wittman, if he would be interested in buying a half interest in his company for $10,000. He was and did. Bill was a silent partner, more interested in fishing than in hunting.

This new money allowed Weatherby to reduce his payables as well as purchase additional equipment for the shop. By now Roy's employees were four gunsmiths and two stock makers in the shop, plus two retail store salesmen, a secretary and himself. One of the stock makers was Leonard Mews, a highly qualified and nationally known custom stock maker. The other was J.D. Bates. The two retail store salesmen were close friends of Weatherby's from prior years, Wayne Glaze from Wichita, Kansas, and Marty Noonan, a youthful former hunting companion.

Weatherby/Klein Problems

For the first 10 years or so that he was in business, Roy Weatherby pretty much ran a one-man show. He was president, general manager, sales manager, advertising and promotion director, market and research director, etc. The only managerial assistance he had was from his accountant.

Although the net worth of the company continued to increase, so did the debt to Herb Klein. Most of the early years had simply produced little or no profit, even with increased sales. Ralph Maddox, Klein's business manager and right hand man in Dallas, had never been in favor of Herb investing his money in the Weatherby Company. In Roy's words, "Ralph doesn't like me, never did, and is a bad influence on Herb wherever I'm concerned. Without a doubt, he has convinced Herb that although I might be the world's greatest salesman and promoter, I don't know how to run a business. And, Herb is beginning to agree with him. After all, he's got hundreds of thousands of dollars invested, and we're not making any money."

In 1956 Maddox convinced Herb to hire his own general manager to assist Roy in running the business, and Klein sent Maddox to California to interview several applicants. He finally hired Bill Hanson and gave him the title of comptroller.

For a few months Weatherby worked very closely with Hanson, but before long it was apparent that there was a definite personality clash between the two men. Hanson was a very stubborn, strong-willed individual, and he disagreed openly with almost every suggestion or plan presented by Weatherby. It soon became obvious that Hanson felt he was in total charge of the organization, for he was making many changes without even consulting Weatherby.

One such change especially provoked Roy, when he learned that Hanson had arbitrarily switched insurance brokers in order to place all of the company policies with a friend of his at another insurance firm. When Weatherby learned of this, he told Hanson, "I would much rather we keep our policy with our original broker. Not only has he been kind, considerate and efficient over the years he has carried our insurance, but many times he has personally made some of our premium payments back in the days when I couldn't get the money to him on time. I can see no reason for us to change brokers."

Hanson's reply was, "I don't work for you. I work for Klein, and I have more to say about the operation of this company than you do!"

Weatherby, very upset, immediately wrote a letter to the insurance carrier authorizing them to continue with the original broker, thus rescinding Hanson's instructions. He then called Klein, explained the insurance fiasco and some of the other "Hanson" problems. Klein promised to straighten his man out, clarify with him his position and authority.

Things did run a little smoother for a while, but by the middle of 1957 Weatherby was convinced that hiring Hanson had been a mistake. Several department heads had complained, in memos, about problems they were experiencing with Hanson. They ranged from complaints from customers about mistakes in their account balances and payments promised to suppliers that were not made, to other daily problems simply due to forgetfulness and errors. He wrote to Klein detailing what he called "a deplorable state of affairs in the office."

Roy wrote: "The turnover of office help has been appalling—11 girls in the last seven months, indicating to me that Hanson has no ability or judgment whatsoever in hiring personnel. Also, last month I personally sent out the month end customer statements, and discovered over $30,000 past due, dating back to March or longer. No effort has been made to even send out second notices, much less collect these past due accounts. And, as for our payables, he issues checks without a thought as to who should come first, or which is the most important to be paid. Consequently, some of our most important suppliers are not being paid, which is affecting production.

"Any instructions given to him are generally lost in the pile of papers on his desk. Just one look at his desk shows how absolutely careless and sloppy he is. As far as getting along with him, I have no complaint. Since the day you talked to him on the telephone, he has been a changed person, but I must urge you to take immediate steps to dismiss Hanson. I believe it has now been proven without a doubt that this arrangement of hiring Hanson from your office, and giving him such drastic authority, was in error and I wouldn't like to see this repeated." Early in July of 1957, Hanson was dismissed by Klein.

Once again, however, Ralph Maddox was instrumental in hiring his replacement, Bob Morrissey. In Herb Klein's letter of July 30, 1957 to Morrissey, in which he outlined in detail what his duties as comptroller would be, he states, "We are looking toward you and Roy Weatherby to run the organization. You and Mr. Weatherby jointly will formulate all policies of the company." According to Roy, "Bob Morrissey was a completely different person than Hanson. He was a happy go lucky fellow with a terrific personality. Very friendly and easy to work with."

Unfortunately, it wasn't long before a problem with Morrissey surfaced, and by December, in a report to Klein, Weatherby wrote, "The situation with Morrissey is growing considerably worse. He is here in the office less each day. And, when he is here, he reeks of liquor. He generally has just enough to make him very happy, as he continually sees the world through rose-colored glasses. I am sorry about this turn of events because he does possess some very admirable qualities, but, whenever a person is this lax, it causes laxity throughout the organization." By the end of the year, Morrissey was also dismissed.

After these two unfortunate and costly errors caused by the intervention of Maddox, Weatherby was able to convince Klein that he should be the one to interview applicants and select a comptroller. He did just that and, with the aid and approval of his auditing firm, Weatherby hired Lyle Dale as his new comptroller. Lyle was very satisfactory and remained an employee for more than 11 years.

Weatherby was very much aware of the ever increasing amount of money Herb Klein was investing, and he also knew he was becoming impatient and dissatisfied with the company's inability to show profits. In a report to Klein in January of 1958, Weatherby states, "For the first time, we have gone above one million dollars in total sales for the year 1957. There is no question in my mind but what we have passed the most difficult, uphill climb. Therefore, I say we can't stop. We must go on—up and up. We must continue taking gambles. We can't recoup our losses in a 10 cent game when we lost them in a no limit game. Therefore, I feel we must go ahead full speed on a new Mark V action and rifle."

For a couple of years following the hiring of Lyle Dale, things ran smoothly between Weatherby and Klein. In 1961 Klein and Elgin Gates went on a hunt together into Hunza, north of Pakistan, for Marco Polo sheep. Their guide was John Coapman, a man Roy Weatherby had known since the late 40's. At that time John worked for the Coca Cola Company in Australia and, as a Weatherby rifle owner, had corresponded frequently with Roy and visited with him whenever he came home to the US. When he started his guide service in Hunza, he asked Roy to help by referring clients to him, such as Herb and Elgin. By then he had left Coca Cola and was working for a firm in Cleveland for six months out of the year while running his big game hunting business overseas for the other six months.

Herb was quite impressed with Coapman after spending time with him on this hunt, and by the middle of June 1961 he had convinced Weatherby they should hire Coapman as sales manager. Based strictly on Herb's and Roy's personal impressions of the man, and without either of them checking into his previous employment credentials, John Coapman moved to South Gate and became sales manager for Weatherby's in August of 1961.

Within six weeks Weatherby told Herb, "I'm sure we've made a mistake in hiring John. I feel I did everything possible to help him when he first came to work here. I helped him locate a place to live, loaned him money for rent, introduced him to my personal friends, and entertained him and his wife and family socially. Now that I have been able to observe him under working conditions, I find him to be very head strong and argumentative. He exaggerates the truth beyond all proportions. He jumps to conclusions before facts are known, and continually tries to put his point across and prove that he is right.

"As an example, I called him in on a conference with our advertising agency the other day, and he got into a most heated argument with the head of the agency as to the type of advertising we should be doing. He insisted we spend our advertising dollars on point of purchase sales aids for our dealers, which is what Coca Cola does according to John, rather than on media ads directed to the consumer.

"I finally had to break up the meeting to get him quieted down." Herb's reply was, "Let's not discourage the boy and criticize him for coming up with an idea or two. We all know that you and Fred (Jennie) are snowed under and must have some help, so let's evaluate his ideas, and if they are good, use them, and if not, let's drop them. It's just as simple as that."

Roy, however, definitely began to question Coapman's acclaimed accomplishments and abilities, and his many stories of successful ventures. He decided to check with Coca Cola and the Kellogg Development Company in Cleveland on John's record and work history with each of these firms. The owner of the Cleveland firm told Roy that John had left his employ voluntarily, but that he felt it was a good thing. He stated, "John wasn't like an average employee. Your first impression of him is fine, but he is very young and immature in many ways. He seems to have dreams of grandeur, and just can't come down to earth and face reality in the business world. We've only been in business about five years, and have always worked like hell as far as time and effort is concerned, but we just couldn't get any effort out of John. He feels he already knows everything and he won't take instructions." This previous employer went on to say, "If John can get the magic and fantasy out of his mind...if someone can strip him clean and get him on the right track, he might finally amount to something. I hope you can do this, Mr. Weatherby."

The references received from the Coca Cola Export Corporation, where John had worked for a number of years in India and Pakistan before being transferred to Australia, were very similar. "We were not particularly satisfied with Mr. Coapman's performance in India and Pakistan, particularly because of the difficulty in securing from him concise, full and accurate reporting. We personally found him to be a most charming individual and a good talker. However, he continually displayed an immaturity which resulted in a failure to perform as well as was considered necessary. It was because of this immaturity, and in an effort to increase his sense of responsibility, that we transferred him to Australia where he could receive more direct supervision and intensive training. However, these efforts to improve his value to our company were unsuccessful."

During one of Elgin Gates' visits, Weatherby asked him his impression of John, and Elgin replied, "It's none of my business, Roy, but I don't know what in hell you were thinking about when you hired

John for a sales manager. He's a regular fellow and a nice guy to go hunting with, but, as far as I'm concerned, he is full of bullshit. He asked me for a job and I turned him down. I don't think anyone will hold that guy down long enough to teach him anything."

All of these reports were forwarded to Herb by Roy in an effort to convince him that Coapman was not the right person. But, for some reason - whether it was because he knew that the hiring of Hanson and Morrissey had been costly mistakes on his part, or whether he was truly convinced of Coapman's abilities, Klein insisted that he be given more of a chance to prove himself.

One of the proposals made by Coapman was that a European office be established to serve as liaison between the South Gate office and the various Weatherby suppliers in Europe. And, of course, Coapman was to be the overseas Weatherby representative. Roy was not in favor of this for two reasons. First and foremost, he felt that the expense involved would not justify the end results, for he felt the working relationships he had already established with each of these suppliers were excellent and could be maintained through correspondence and occasional visits from either himself or his engineer. Secondly, he knew that one of Klein's commitments to Coapman when he hired him was that he would be allowed to take a three month's leave of absence during the year to return to India and pursue his profession as a hunting guide. Weatherby had not been in favor of this concession on Herb's part from the beginning, and after receiving the reports from John's previous employers, he felt that he was not qualified to handle the responsibility of an overseas office, and that Coapman had more to gain personally from his suggestion than the company did.

After Coapman had worked for four months, Weatherby had had enough. He was still getting reports from his department heads about Coapman's lack of abilities and the time he was wasting, not only his own, but other employees' as well. Herb Klein was on an East African safari at the time, but on October 30th Roy sent Herb a letter in care of his safari outfitters advising him, "The Coapman situation has turned out to be most ridiculous. This morning I asked John Coapman to resign, something I should have done some time ago. It is the only thing I think any sensible businessman would do, and what I feel you would have expected me to do."

When Klein returned from Africa, Roy sat down and had a long talk with him. "Herb, you have become one of the most unpredictable men

I have ever known," he said. "It's apparent you don't have confidence in me or my abilities any more. Otherwise, we would not have had to go through the costly Hanson era, at least $25,000 spent on Hanson and playboy Morrissey for nothing. Not only was their salary wasted, but look at the time it took Lyle Dale to get the office and our records into shape after all of their errors.

"You're probably thinking right now, who in the hell does this ungrateful bastard think he is? Well, brother, I am the first one to get down on my knees with prayers of humble thanks to you. You know how much I appreciate everything you've done for me. I have praised you time and again to your face and behind your back. I have gone out of my way to do things for you that money can't buy to try and show my appreciation. Not only to show my appreciation, but because I have always liked and admired you. You above all other people know this to be true.

"I have been asked on many occasions where in the hell would I be without Klein's money? My answer has always been the same. I don't know. Maybe I would be a much smaller organization or maybe I would be larger. But, there is one thing I am pretty damn sure of, if it had not been Herb Klein, it would have been someone else or a lot of someone else's. Believe me, I wasn't about ready to throw up my hands and bury my head if you had not put money into the company. I would have found someone else.

"I've made mistakes and I'll probably continue to make mistakes. As the years pass, it is so easy to stand on the sidelines and say, if you had done this you would be here instead of there. But, in spite of any criticism, we keep on growing, getting bigger and better just as fast as we can with the horsepower and fuel available.

"If one has but a gallon of gas in his automobile, and he has 20 miles to go to the next station, and he knows that at 20 mph he'll make it, he doesn't tramp down on the gas to get there more quickly for then he'll end up five miles short. I haven't been tramping down on the gas to get there more quickly when I knew that the gas wouldn't last me. I knew that if I obligated myself too much I wouldn't reach my goal. I would run out of gas.

"When you came into this business in 1949, we were doing in the neighborhood of $200,000. Today we are nearing the $2 million mark. I'll agree that I'm not making progress half fast enough, and I am not at all happy, but, there has been progress. Herb, I welcome your suggestions and try to follow them closely. I didn't even object too strenuously against Hanson until I saw what we had gotten ourselves into. You have since agreed that he was not the man for this organization, and since that time we have made considerable progress. This time with Coapman, I just couldn't stand by and see such a thing happen again. I would be more than happy to have some capable assistance in the management and operation of this business. How I wish it could be possible that you would be that person, and with your experience and particularly your knowledge of this business, and being here to know the day to day operation and problems, I am sure no two people could get along more harmoniously."

Thus, early in 1962, Klein decided to take a more active role as a partner. He accompanied Weatherby on a trip to Europe where they visited the Norma factory in Sweden, and Sauer and Hertel & Reuss in Germany, thus giving him firsthand knowledge of their overseas production facilities. Klein also attended the National Sporting Goods Dealers Show with Roy which was held in Chicago in February of 1962. It was at this show that he introduced Roy to his nephew, Lloyd Klein. Lloyd was a bright young man who had studied law and passed the bar, but was working with the Arthur Anderson accounting firm in Chicago as an auditor. Klein suggested that since he couldn't possibly devote his full time and efforts to helping Roy run the company, his nephew Lloyd might be just the person they were looking for. With Weatherby's blessing, Lloyd was brought into the company as assistant to the president. His principal duties were to develop long-range financial planning, cost analyses, and budgeting.

For several months things went along smoothly. However, before long it became evident that, while Herb Klein's and Roy Weatherby's interests and ideas in the field of guns and hunting were very compatible, their philosophies and practical application of business operating procedures varied considerably. Herb failed to see the need to have salesmen on the road, and felt that by eliminating them the company would be saved the expense of paying commissions. Weatherby was equally firm in his beliefs that the future growth of the company lay in having as many gun dealers as possible carry the Weatherby line, in order to satisfy consumer demand, and that the best way to accomplish this was through a nationwide sales force.

With his law background, Lloyd Klein was very helpful in drawing up the contract between Beretta and Weatherby for the manufacture of the Mark XXII rifle. He also prepared a new and updated version of the contractual agreement between J. P. Sauer and Weatherby. He organized an operating committee comprised of himself, Weatherby, Lyle Dale and Fred Jennie. Herb Klein was the fifth member of this committee, and although he was seldom able to attend the weekly meetings, if his vote was needed to break a tie on any issue he responded by mail. In conjunction with the operating committee, Lloyd established a "management guide," detailing the personal responsibilities and authority of each of the four working members. Under his system, each of the four members reported only to the operating committee as a whole. Weatherby's objection to this system was that there were now "four generals with no chief of staff."

Lloyd was adamant in regards to the line of authority, and at times this became downright ludicrous. As an example, the place was burglarized one night, with the burglars gaining access to the building through the roof in the shop area. After the burglary, a roofing company was called to repair that section of the roof. A day or so later, the company called to say that there were other sections of the roof that were also in need of repair. When the information reached Fred Jennie he replied, "What part of the roof? If it's over the shop, it's my department. Otherwise, give the message to somebody else!"

On another occasion, when Weatherby learned after the fact of a policy change Lloyd had made, he asked why he had not been advised of the change: "As the president and one of the stockholders of this company, I would like to be kept informed of what is going on." Lloyd told Weatherby that was not the way the management guide was written. According to Lloyd, Roy had nothing to say about anything within the organization with the exception of sales. That convinced Weatherby that Lloyd had usurped too much authority and felt that he had his uncle's backing in doing so.

At that time Klein's total investment in the company was more than $700,000: original stock purchase investment made in 1949, plus his loan for the purchase of the land and construction of the new quarters in 1951, plus the notes payable for the many loans he had made to the company over the years on which interest only had been paid. Weatherby was very much aware that his first 17 years in business had been an uphill struggle with very few profitable years. Yet he felt, justifiably so, that the phenomenal growth of the company, and the worldwide acclaim given his rifles, had been due to his operational methods, even though he knew that it wouldn't have been possible without Klein's financial support.

Roy also was convinced that his hardest years were behind him. He was very optimistic about the future, provided he wouldn't have to contend with any influences that might curtail and suppress his vision, ability to lead the company as he had done in the past. So, he asked Klein if he would sell his half interest. Klein agreed, but indicated he would want to realize a profit of at least $125,000 over and above his total investment.

Sale Of Klein's Interest To J. P. Sauer/Dynamit-Nobel

Weatherby immediately set out to find another partner. He recalled his good friend, Udo van Meeteren, who owned the J. P. Sauer Company, had often remarked during the five years he had known him that it was a pleasure to work together and how pleased he was with the excellent business relationship that had developed between their two firms. Van Meeteren's offices were in Dusseldorf, where he headed up the Michel Corporation, whose interests were varied. They owned several coal mines, oil fields and other interests, with but one of their holdings being J. P. Sauer & Sohn in Eckernfoerde.

When Weatherby contacted van Meeteren about buying Klein's 50 percent interest, he learned that Dynamit-Nobel in Cologne, West Germany, had recently purchased a half interest in J. P. Sauer. Dynamit-Nobel also owned RWS, the largest munitions firm in West Germany. In turn, Dynamit-Nobel was part of the Flick Group who also owned several banks, coal mines, and the Mercedes Benz auto firm.

Van Meeteren expressed a genuine interest in having Sauer become a partner of Weatherby's, but he explained to Roy that he would also have to convince Dynamit-Nobel of the soundness of his proposal since they now owned 50 percent of Sauer. In July of 1962, Weatherby went to Germany to meet with van Meeteren and Manfred Holzach, who was the managing director of Dynamit-Nobel, the managing director of RWS, and the new managing director of J. P. Sauer & Sohn. These two gentlemen reviewed all of the historical and financial data that Weatherby furnished them on his visit. They advised him they were definitely interested in pursuing the possible purchase of Klein's interest, but would need some additional time to study the market and the future prospects of such a merger. Within a month of Weatherby's visit, they sent their accountant plus a member of their own auditing firm to California to conduct a thorough review of the Weatherby Company and its financial status.

By the end of October, 1962 the sale was consummated, and Weatherby had two new partners—J. P. Sauer and Dynamit-Nobel, each owning 25 percent. Herb Klein recovered his entire investment plus a $125,000 profit, in addition to all of the interest he had been paid over the years. Neither Herb nor Roy allowed their business related differences of opinion to interfere with their long standing friendship, and they remained close friends until Herb Klein passed away in 1974.

Problems With The New German Partners

Almost from the beginning it was apparent to Weatherby that all would not run smoothly with his German partners. Udo van Meeteren was a very astute businessman, but was so involved in the many entities of his Michel Corporation that he did not devote much attention to Weatherby, Inc., despite being on the board. The other German board member was Manfred Holzach, managing director of both J. P. Sauer and Dynamit-Nobel. Completing the quorum of board members was Roy Weatherby, Bill Wittman and Lyle Dale, who was Weatherby's comptroller.

Language was not a problem as both Holzach and van Meeteren, and any of their colleagues who were involved in the partnership, spoke English fluently. Communication was the problem. Top management at Weatherby's found themselves inundated with almost daily correspondence from Holzach, who apparently felt he was also to be the managing director of Weatherby. At his insistence the board meetings were held in Germany, and in Weatherby's words, "These meetings were utter chaos. Holzach was a very suave, handsome man with a persuasive gift of gab, but he knew nothing whatsoever about running even one business—much less three."

The RWS Ammunition Company was one of Dynamit-Nobel's holdings, and within a year Holzach had canceled the Weatherby contract with the Norma Company to load Weatherby ammunition, and instructed them to send the Weatherby cartridge case brass direct to RWS for loading. Weatherby knew nothing about this move until he sent a cable to Norma requesting delivery information, at which time they advised him of Holzach's instructions. Weatherby was furious and immediately called Holzach.

"Why did you make this move without consulting me?," he asked, "Don't you know it's physically impossible for any company to tool up and load ammunition properly in less than a year's time? I have no objection to having RWS load our ammo, but you should not have discontinued the loading at Norma until the loading procedure at RWS has been perfected. We need ammunition now. We can't sell rifles without ammunition."

But the damage was done. Before the ammunition could be loaded, it even became necessary for Weatherby to charter a plane to ship 12,200 pounds of the correct powder to RWS from the United States. This move from Norma to RWS precipitated another acute ammunition shortage by Weatherby during the critical fall hunting months. By July of 1963, his inventory of loaded ammunition, as well as empty cartridge cases, was exhausted, and the first shipment of loaded ammunition from RWS was not received until December of 1963, and that only in .300 caliber. During this time repeated letters, cables and phone calls from Weatherby went unanswered. He attempted to have RWS send a quantity of empty cartridge case brass to South Gate for loading to relieve the shortage. His requests were ignored, and Weatherby once again suffered losses in both profits and reputation during the fall of 1963.

Van Meeteren remained pretty much in the background, with Holzach being the contact man between Germany and South Gate. And, while every attempt to promptly answer Holzach's numerous inquiries and requests was made by all parties in California, it was almost impossible to get any response from him on matters Weatherby wanted handled.

As an example, although the purchase of Klein's interest was consummated early in November of 1962, it was not until Weatherby's trip to Germany in May of 1964 that he finally succeeded in getting the Klein stock certificates signed and surrendered so that new ones could be issued to Sauer. Both Wittman and Weatherby had made repeated requests to Holzach through numerous letters, phone calls, and on their previous visits, that this technical part of the transaction be completed so that formalities with the corporation commissioner could be finalized and the corporate records be brought up-to-date.

Many other problems were encountered with Holzach during 1963 and early 1964 in connection with Weatherby rifle production at J. P. Sauer. During this time, the .224 Varmintmaster rifle and the .340 caliber Mark V were in the development and initial production stages. Many unnecessary delays were directly attributable to Holzach's management, or non-management. He also insisted that RWS, instead of Norma, produce both the cartridge case and the loaded ammunition for this new .224 caliber, but when shipments of the .224 rifles finally started arriving in South Gate there was no ammunition available. Weatherby had a tremendous backlog of orders waiting to be filled with this new model rifle, so dealers had the .224 rifle in stock for six months before they received any ammunition.

Included in the Weatherby/Sauer contract was a provision that the walnut stock blanks furnished from the United States by Weatherby were to be used only on Mark V rifles shipped to South Gate, and that less expensive, lower grade walnut blanks, to be procured by Sauer, would be used on the Mark V rifles sold on the European market. However, with Holzach as managing director of J. P. Sauer, this was not being adhered to, and Weatherby was receiving rifles with very plain stocks while the fancy wood was appearing on the European models.

In spite of monthly reports being sent to the Sauer factory upon receipt and inspection of each rifle shipment detailing the minor manufacturing faults that needed correcting, little or no attempt seemed to be made to improve the quality. Rework expense on Mark V rifles shipped to South Gate amounted to nearly $14,000 over an 18 month period from January of '63 through June of '64. It finally became necessary for Weatherby to send one of his gunsmiths, Fred Meyer, as a full time quality control inspector at the plant in Eckernforde.

When Roy went to Germany in May of 1964 he discovered that most of the letters he had written to Holzach were never put into the company files. Holzach didn't want anyone but himself to see them, and that was the last straw for Weatherby. In the meeting at Dynamit-Nobel, attended by Weatherby, Wittman, van Meeteren, Holzach and others from both J. P. Sauer and Dynamit-Nobel, Weatherby created quite a ruckus when he revealed all of these problems, which he felt were due entirely to Holzach being in charge at both Sauer and RWS.

"The conditions under which we have had to work since becoming associated with Sauer and Dynamit-Nobel have been unbearable," he said. "I personally feel if this man is left in charge he will break not only our company, but yours as well. He has left me with no choice but to bring suit against RWS and Dynamit-Nobel for the loss of sales and reputation we suffered just because of his mishandling of our ammunition program last year."

Although everyone present appeared to be surprised and shocked over Weatherby's accusations, the discussions that followed reinforced his statements. Before the meeting ended Dynamit-Nobel offered to pay $10,000 to Weatherby rather than have him bring suit against them. At this, Weatherby got up to leave and said, "Don't even talk to me about $10,000. It wouldn't begin to cover my losses."

One of Roy's partners from 1966 to 1974 was Leo Rothe, left, shown here with Roy examining a Weatherby Regency shotgun. In 1968, Rothe sold half his interest to John Allyn.

As Roy was gathering together his papers, Wittman kicked his foot and whispered, "You'd better take what you can get." Weatherby looked down at him, and in a loud voice said, "You don't need to whisper. I'm not interested in $10,000." And with that, he walked out of the room. The next day they offered Weatherby $25,000 and, although he also felt this was too little, he accepted their offer. He knew that he still had to work with this company, a 25 percent partner. But before he left the meeting he let them know in no uncertain terms, "The damage this man has done to my company is almost irreparable. As I see it, you only have two choices, put in more money as a capital investment or let me find someone to buy out your interest at whatever price I can get."

Van Meeteren confided to Weatherby that he was equally disgusted with Holzach, feeling that because of his mismanagement he had also placed Sauer in a very critical position. Less than a month after Weatherby's visit Manfred Holzach was dismissed by both Sauer and Dynamit-Nobel.

Buying Out His German Partners

The firing of Manfred Holzach resolved most of the difficulties and problems with his German partners, and things went along smoothly for the next year or so. Because of the losses sustained by the Weatherby Company in 1962 and 1963, however, and despite the sizable profit shown in 1964, the German partners were unwilling to supply any additional working capital to Weatherby. Roy was determined to buy out their 50 percent interest, and both J. P. Sauer and Dynamit Nobel were just as anxious to terminate the partnership.

In August of 1965 they gave Weatherby written approval that they were willing to sell their half interest for $687,000, even though they had paid $841,000 for Klein's interest just three years earlier.

Weatherby began to investigate the possibility of a public stock offering, with him retaining 60 to 62 percent of the stock and putting the rest on the market. If he could get a definite commitment from a brokerage firm on the underwriting of a stock offering, he believed, he would then be able to go to a lending institution and borrow the necessary funds on a short-term basis to buy out his German partners. However, a number of underwriters advised him to delay going public for at least another year or two, until his company had a better earnings picture to present.

At a 1966 meeting of the Shikar Safari Club International in Mexico City another opportunity presented itself. The year before he had sponsored for membership in this elite organization a friend, Leo Roethe, who owned NASCO Industries in Fort Atkinson, Wisconsin. Leo and his wife had dinner with Roy and Camilla one night in Mexico City during the conference, and Leo, an avid hunter and a real Weatherby enthusiast, asked, "Do you suppose, Roy, there's some way I could buy into Weatherby?"

"Why, I suppose there's a possibility," Roy answered. "Why don't we set a date for us to get together and we'll talk about it."

When they got together a short time later Roy told Leo the past history and problems of the company, including all of those with the Germans, the losses he had incurred in '62 and '63 and the reasons for those losses. He showed him the financial statements for the previous two years, which had been profitable ones, and then said, "Leo, six months ago the Germans were willing to take $687,000 for their 50 percent share, but I have a pretty good idea that by now they might be willing to sell for around $500,000. If you want to put up $500,000 I'll give you 10 percent of the company and pay you back all of your money plus interest." Leo jumped up from his chair, ran across the room, shook Weatherby's hand and said, "That's a deal!"

Weatherby was right about the Germans being anxious to sell. When Weatherby, Roethe and Wittman went to Germany in April of 1966, the German firms agreed to sell their Weatherby interest for $490,000 to Leo Roethe, who signed a letter of intent and agreed to have the funds available by June 30th.

Upon their return home Weatherby wrote to Roethe, "The main reason for this letter is to thank you for going to Germany to help me get the deal straightened out with the boys over there. Of all the trips I've made to Europe, this one was more fruitful than all the others combined. I feel I have a new lease on life now. Thanks again a million times. I think we came out of that deal smelling like a rose!"

As Weatherby was soon to learn, however, nothing ever came easy for him. As the date of June 30th drew close, Leo's alibis began. Although Roethe was a wealthy man on paper, he was over- extended financially and had been unable to come up with the money. In desperation, Weatherby and his attorney, Bill Wittman, flew back to

In this February 1956 photo Roy is shown with Robert A. Kleinguenther and his family, just arrived from Austria under the refugee program. Roy hired this talented gunsmith and stockmaker three years earlier while in Germany arranging for manufacture of scope sights, and sponsored his entry into the United States, but a three-year battle was necessary before visa clearance was granted. Years later Kleinguenther left Weatherby, moved to Seguin, Texas, and began building his own KDF rifle. He was the second to come to South Gate under Roy's sponsorship, following German stockmaker Robert Brosch, who arrived in 1954.

Milwaukee on the day the money was due in Germany (or else the deal was off), and along with Leo Roethe the three of them went to nearly every bank in Milwaukee, to no avail until they visited the Midland National Bank.

As luck would have it, the president and another officer of this bank were not only hunters, but both of them were also great Weatherby fans. After listening to the story they advised they couldn't loan Roethe the money based on his own collateral, but if Roy would be willing to put up his 50 percent of the Weatherby stock as Leo's collateral, they would loan Roethe the money. Weatherby realized he was being pushed into the corner, and his original offer of 10 percent ownership to Leo had now become 50 percent. But he felt this was no time to be choosy, as time was running out on Roethe's agreement with the Germans. In order to meet the deadline, the $490,000 was forwarded by cable on June 30th to his German partners, and once again Roy had a new partner.

Several years later Roy reminisced, "Leo was a good friend and a helluva nice guy. He was always vitally interested in all aspects of our company and yet he offered no interference, and let me run the company any way I wanted to. But he was also a great problem, because he was *always* in financial trouble. For the first two years of our partnership he spent much of his time and mine trying to sell either his half interest in Weatherby's or the entire company. He nearly drove us all crazy out here by having prospective purchasers or finders going through our books all the time on behalf of somebody he felt was an interested buyer."

Over a 12-month period during 1967 and 1968, Weatherby was approached by more than a dozen different parties expressing a genuine interest in acquiring his firm. He afforded each one of them the courtesy of investigating the company thoroughly, and he provided them with complete financial information and future growth plans. Among the more noted of these interested parties were the Leisure Group, who had just acquired High Standard; the Walter Kidde Company, who bought Harrington & Richardson; Laird & Company, who had acquired Ithaca; Colt Firearms, and the Shakespeare Company of fishing tackle fame. A couple of them even got as far as drawing up the legal documents for the purchase, but Weatherby's gut feeling that his company would some day be worth many times more than he was being offered kept him from selling.

Roethe, meanwhile, was being pressured continually by the Midland National Bank in Milwaukee for payment of his $490,000 loan. To meet this demand he sold one-half of his 50 percent interest in Weatherby to John Allyn, the owner of the Chicago White Sox baseball team, for $250,000. Thus in 1968 Roethe was able to pay off his note. Roy Weatherby's stock, which had been held as security by the Midland National Bank, was returned to him. He now had two partners — Leo Roethe with 25 percent interest and John Allyn with 25 percent interest.

The Weatherby/Roethe/Allyn Partnership

After buying out the German partners in 1966, the Weatherby firm had profitable years in 1967, 1968 and 1969. It was a constant struggle, however, for during this period there was no infusion of any additional capital. Roy made many trips to Europe and Japan in search of suppliers for both existing and new products. Although he had renewed his contract with Beretta in Italy to continue producing the Mark XXII rifle, he was also looking for a source to have this rifle manufactured in Japan. Not only did he need to improve the delivery situation, but his costs from Italy kept rising. Also, with the German economy and inflation on the rise, his costs for the Mark V rifle from J. P. Sauer were continually increasing, so he was also investigating the possibility of moving Mark V production to Japan. And, in 1966 he had entered into an agreement with an Italian firm in Brescia, Angelo Zoli & Sons, to produce the Weatherby Regency over and under shotgun—his first entry into the shotgun market.

By 1967 he had contracted with a firm called KTG in Japan to produce the Mark XXII rifle. He was also negotiating with Howa Machinery, Ltd. to produce the Mark V rifle. These plans were finalized late in 1969. During 1970 Howa worked on the necessary tooling and development of this project, and actual production began in 1971.

For the first two years of Japanese production Weatherby ran dual manufacturing operations, receiving rifles from both Sauer and Howa. He felt this was a precaution he must take in order to insure a continual flow of quality merchandise, just in case Howa might encounter some unforeseen problems in the initial stages of their production.

51

In 1968 Leo Roethe started talking to Roy about the possibility of his firm, NASCO Industries, buying Weatherby. NASCO was founded in Fort Atkinson in 1940 as the National Agri-cultural Supply Company, a firm that provided education aids, instructional material and equipment in agricultural science, home economics and arts and crafts. Roethe proposed that the three Weatherby partners—Weatherby, Roethe and Allyn—exchange their Weatherby stock for NASCO stock in the equivalent of two and a half million dollars. NASCO stock was then selling over the counter at $23 per share.

Roethe assured Roy that his firm would be operated separately as a wholly owned subsidiary, with Weatherby in control. Such a merger would make Roethe and Weatherby the largest shareholders in NASCO, giving Roy a position on the parent company's Board of Directors.

Weatherby was reluctant to make this move for the same reason he had backed away from the many offers presented to him for such mergers or outright purchases in the past. He believed that within the next few years his company would be able to double its sales volume, project a better earnings picture, and undertake a successful public stock offering on its own. Discussions as to the pros and cons of merging with NASCO went on for well over a year, with pressure being applied by both Leo Roethe and John Allyn.

Weatherby/NASCO Merger

For the first time in the history of the Weatherby Company four new products were scheduled for introduction in the same year, 1970: the Vanguard bolt action rifle, the Regency over/under shotgun, the Sightmaster spotting scope and the Mark XXII 4X scope. Roy was extremely concerned about the tremendous amount of operating capital it would take to adequately promote and advertise these four new products. So were Roethe and Allyn, who as a result felt even more strongly that a merger with NASCO would be beneficial. In order to convince Roy of the soundness of such a move, his partners came up with a plan whereby they would each sign over to Roy 5 percent of their Weatherby stock, thereby reducing their ownership to 20 percent each, giving Roy 60 percent.

After much deliberation, Weatherby finally agreed. When the Weatherby stock was exchanged for NASCO stock, he would receive 8,400 shares of preferred and 72,000 shares of common stock for his 60 percent; Roethe and Allyn would each receive 2,800 shares of preferred and 24,000 shares of common stock for their 20 percent interest. Although there was to be no cash transaction connected with the merger, they each assured Weatherby that within the first year they would individually purchase from him $250,000 worth of his NASCO stock, thus giving him a much needed $500,000 in cash. Roethe also assured Weatherby that NASCO would be in a position to assist the Weatherby firm financially with additional capital.

In February 1970 Roy Weatherby and his son Ed, who was 18 at the time, and his attorney, Bill Wittman, flew to Fort Atkinson, Wisconsin to sign the papers and complete the merger. The board of directors and shareholders of NASCO Industries voted to change the name of the parent company to Weatherby/NASCO, Inc.

Upon his return to California Roy wrote the following letter to Leo Roethe:
"Dear Leo:
I won't be forgetting February 5, 1970 very soon. I don't know for sure whether it's a day to be celebrated, or whether it will be a day to mourn. The die is cast, Leo, and I don't know if I have done the right thing or not. I think I have, but only time will tell."

Weatherby's Divestiture From NASCO

During the four years he was connected with NASCO, Roy faithfully attended the board meetings of the parent company, participating actively in all policy-making decisions. As President of Weatherby/NASCO, Leo Roethe spent a great deal of his time seeking out companies that were "ripe" for acquisition, and was able to convince the shareholders and board members in a number of instances to complete such acquisitions. A majority of the seven or eight firms that were acquired were not very productive. Some ended up in bankruptcy. Others were such a drain on the parent company that *they* got the funds Roethe had promised would be available to Roy. Neither did Roethe nor John Allyn fulfill their promise to purchase from Weatherby some of his NASCO stock.

In 1971, however, Earl Jordan, a friend of Roy's who was also a long time shareholder and member of the board of Weatherby/NASCO, bought 5,000 of Roy's 8,400 shares of preferred stock for $250,000 cash. Earl was the General Agent for Massachusetts Mutual Life Insurance Co. in their Chicago office and, as a fellow hunter, had for several years been a close friend of both Roethe and Weatherby.

By the end of 1973 Weatherby believed that NASCO was wrong in continuing to pursue the acquisition of other companies. He decided it would be in his best interest to divest his firm from the parent company. In February of 1974, therefore, he presented a request to the board of directors and received approval for a corporate separation of his firm from Weatherby/NASCO. Although this became a very time-consuming project, requiring a great deal of legal consultation and applications in order to conform to all of the SEC regulations, the divestiture was completed in June of 1974.

Weatherby, John Allyn and Earl Jordan each surrendered their shares of Weatherby/NASCO stock in exchange for their proportionate shares of Weatherby stock. Leo Roethe's Weatherby shares were encumbered, however, as he had pledged them on one of his acquisition transactions. Since he was not in a financial position to redeem them, nor did the party holding them desire to become a part of the Weatherby Company, Roy convinced another good friend, Jim Blankenbaker, a vice president with Minnesota Mining & Manufacturing Co. in St. Paul, Minnesota, to buy those shares.

The 2,405 shares of Weatherby stock that had been delivered to NASCO Industries in 1970 in exchange for NASCO shares were returned to the four shareholders of Weatherby, Inc. in 1974 as follows:

Roy E. Weatherby - 1,127 shares
John Allyn - 599 shares
Earl Jordan - 367 shares
Jim Blankenbaker - 312 shares

Once again, Weatherby, Inc. was a privately owned company and Roy Weatherby had three new partners.

John Allyn died April 29, 1979. When his estate was settled in 1981 Roy bought Allyn's 599 shares from his heirs. One year later, redemption of the remaining shares belonging to Jim Blankenbaker and Earl Jordan was approved by the Weatherby Board of Directors.

In 1982, 37 years after he first started in business, Roy Weatherby became the sole owner of his thriving and profitable company.

At the time Roy stated, "It's a wonderful feeling, after all these years, to know that you own 100 percent and have complete control of your company. I will be forever grateful to John Allyn, Jim Blankenbaker and Earl Jordan, for if they had not assisted me in my efforts to de-merge from NASCO, this may never have come about."

3

Weatherby: The Man

Celebrities

Roy Weatherby and famous folks were drawn to each other, and the advantage was mutual. Such relationships had their beginning because of two factors: 1. the juxtaposition of Roy's South Gate plant and "Hollywood;" and 2. the fact that many stars of stage and screen were avid shooters and hunters. Weatherby's low-key personality was tailor-made to develop friendships with prominent people.

Cataloging all of the famous and near famous people with whom Roy Weatherby became acquainted in his lifetime isn't possible, but many come to mind. The first one was Gary Cooper in 1946, and he and Roy spent much time together talking about guns and shooting at the range.

In the late 1940's Burt Lancaster's studio wanted some publicity for him in connection with a movie he was making. They called Roy and set up an appointment for Burt to visit and have pictures taken.

At the time Lancaster was a little-known but up-and-coming star, and the studio wanted to make a big game hunter out of him in the public's mind. Weatherby set up a bridge table outside the rear of his shop, camouflaged it a bit, and loaded some blank cartridges. The camera-men stood out in front and took photos of Lancaster as he fired the blanks.

When the picture appeared in the movie magazines, the caption stated that Lancaster was sighting in his rifle at Weatherby's "shooting range." But the day of the photo shoot, when Weatherby started talking hunting with Lancaster, Burt confessed that he didn't do any hunting at all. That was a rare exception. All the other celebrities with whom Roy became acquainted actually sought him out, on their own, as real hunters interested in his product.

Arthur Godfrey, immensely popular on both radio and television in the '40's and '50's, was an early customer of Weatherby, and had several custom rifles built. Roy and Arthur became quite good friends. They both had young daughters the same age, so they had something in common. On New Year's Day, Godfrey was one of the commentators on national television for the Rose Parade. When the float from the City of South Gate passed in review, he commented on the air, "Oh, there's the float from South Gate. That's where my good friend, Roy Weatherby, makes those wonderful rifles."

Howard Keel, a popular movie star with a beautiful singing voice also visited the Weatherby plant in the early 50's. Another singer, Mel Torme, visited Weatherby's about the same time, to be fitted for a custom rifle. So did Jane Powell, whose husband was a big game hunter. He brought his diminutive wife to Roy's establishment one day to order a rifle for Jane for an upcoming hunt.

Robert Taylor made several trips to Weatherby's and he and Roy also became good friends. At that time, Winchester had just named him their Sportsman of the Year. He confided in Roy that most of his shooting had been with a shotgun and he'd like to become more adept with a rifle.

Roy offered to help, and took Bob to the range one day with several rifles. Bob started shooting with a .300 Weatherby Magnum, and on the first shot the scope almost hit him in the head. Weatherby told him, "Bob, you've got to get farther away from the scope. If that scope hits you it'll leave a nasty cut. You make your living with that face of yours, so don't get your eye so close next time."

Bob moved farther back on the stock but not quite far enough, for on the next shot the scope got him right above and beside the right eyebrow. Blood trickled down the side of his face. But the cut wasn't deep, just crescent about a half inch long. Weatherby pulled the wound together with a Band-Aid and advised Taylor to check with his doctor about the possibility of needing stitches. He continued shooting for

Walter O'Malley, owner of the Brooklyn and Los Angeles Dodgers baseball team, accepts delivery of his .300 Weatherby Magnum from Roy. In keeping with the "Dodger Blue" tradition, O'Malley ordered his rifle with a light blue laquer finish in place of the usual natural wood, high lustre finish.

another hour or so with no problem, and later that night called Weatherby to tell him that the doctor said no stitches would be necessary.

Roy Rogers and Andy Devine, both avid hunters, became good customers and very good friends with Roy Weatherby. Other noted film stars who became Weatherby rifle owners and friends of Roy's were John Wayne, Gene Autrey, Lorne Green, Cornell Wilde, Earnest Borgnine, Chuck Connor (who was the Rifleman on the T.V. series of the same name), John Russell (of Lawman fame), Robert Stack, Mike Connors, and many others.

Not only movie stars, but many important personalities in other walks of life were customers and friends: Walter O'Malley and his son Peter (of the Los Angeles Dodgers baseball team); General Nathan Twining, who was Chairman of the Joint Chiefs of Staff; General Curtis Le May; Ed Quinn, then President of the Chrysler Corporation; Dr. Heinz Nordhoff, President of the Volkswagen Company in Germany;

John Wayne with one of his most prized possessions, his custom made .300 Weatherby Magnum rifle.

Henry Timken, of the Timken Roller-Bearing Company; W.K. Whiteford, President of the Gulf Oil Company; Bob Waterfield, the famous U.C.L.A. and Los Angeles Rams quarterback; Wilbur May, of the May Company stores; Brigadier General Robert L. Scott, Jr., one of the original Flying Tigers; and Lieutenant General Hamp Atkinson.

Most of the astronauts enjoyed hunting, and Wally Schirra, Gus Grissom, Jim McDivitt, Jim Lovell, Joe Engle and many of the other astronauts made frequent visits to the Weatherby plant in South Gate. Some of the space modules that were used in the early space flights were being assembled at an aircraft plant in the nearby city of Downey, and when NASA sent the astronauts to Downey they invariably spent time with Weatherby, either at his home or at his office talking hunting.

Weatherby could count not only movie stars and industrial giants as customers and friends, but also heads of state from a number of foreign countries. In the mid-50's, Weatherby built several custom rifles for the Shah of Iran and his brother, Prince Abdorreza Pahlavi, with all of the details being handled by correspondence. When the Shah was to make a visit to Washington, D.C., however, one of his requests was that his itinerary include a trip to Weatherby's in Los Angeles.

Roy received letters of instruction from the State Department giving him protocol guidelines. An entourage of Iranian generals and body-guards, along with American Secret Service men arrived in black limousines at the South Gate factory. The Shah, with all of his body-guards and others following him, was given a tour throughout the plant, after which Weatherby led him back to his office. As Roy stepped aside for him to walk into the office, the Shah closed the door so that none of his people could follow them in. He and Weatherby sat in the office for at least an hour, talking about guns and hunting.

In 1962, the Shah's brother, Prince Pahlavi, was the recipient of the Weatherby Big Game Trophy Award, with Andy Devine making the presentation to the Prince. Three years later, the Prince himself made the presentation of the Big Game Trophy to the 1965 winner, Francois Edmond-Blanc of Paris, France.

The King of Nepal was another member of royalty who visited Los Angeles in the early 1960's. A luncheon was held in his honor at a Los Angeles hotel, and he made the specific request that Roy Weatherby not only be invited, but that he be seated next to him at the head table. Two days later, he also visited the Weatherby plant in South Gate with a similar lineup of bodyguards and black limousines.

Five custom Weatherby rifles were built for Miguel Aleman when he was President of Mexico. One of these was built at the request of the State Department and was presented to President Aleman by our President Dwight D. Eisenhower, with an engraved gold plate com-memorating the occasion inlaid in the buttstock.

General Jimmy Doolittle, the Flying Ace of "30 Seconds over Tokyo" fame, was a good customer and frequent hunting companion of Roy Weatherby's. Another famous World War II ace, Joe Foss, who went on to become the Governor of South Dakota, later the Commissioner of the American Football League, and still later President of the National Rifle Association, was also a very good friend of Roy Weatherby's. Joe Foss presented the second annual Weatherby Big Game Trophy to Jack O'Connor in 1957.

Throughout his life, Roy Weatherby was extremely proud to ac-knowledge having such distinguished personalities as his customers,

Roy's proximity to Hollywood and his flair for public relations brought him access to celebrities in all walks of life, as well as politicians and world leaders. He became good friends with many of them, and their use of Weatherby firearms was enormously helpful in promotion. Clockwise from upper left, Roy is seen with actress and singer Jane Powell, the Shah of Iran, movie and television actor Gabby Hayes, movie and television actor Andy Devine, the King of Nepal, and singer and actor Roy Rogers (with Elgin Gates).

but he was equally as proud of his thousands of patrons who were not so well known. He felt that all of them, large or small in name, were discriminating buyers who wanted the finest in firearms.

Roy Weatherby and Jack O'Connor: A Strong but Stormy Friendship

When Herb Klein first became associated with Weatherby, although he was already an accomplished big game hunter, he had never been to Africa or India and was certainly not the renowned hunter he was to become later. Klein was well aware and a bit envious of Roy's close alliance with most of the outdoor writers, and one time when he was visiting Roy in South Gate their conversation touched upon Jack O'Connor, who was living in Arizona at that time.

Herb said to Roy, "I'd sure like to meet Jack. Why don't you call him and see if we could fly to Tucson tomorrow so you could introduce me to him?" Roy made the call and Herb paid the round trip air fare for the two of them to fly to Tucson and back the following day, solely for the purpose of visiting with Jack O'Connor. O'Connor was equally impressed with getting to know this multi-millionaire, and as a result of that meeting Klein and O'Connor visited, hunted together, and corresponded frequently thereafter.

O'Connor was a very gruff, outspoken individual. Although Jack was a staunch supporter of the .270 Weatherby caliber, Roy often was miffed at his writings. It was not always about his published opinion of Weatherby products, but rather his interpretation of some of the things Weatherby, the man, was accomplishing. Consequently, the two of them were often at odds and kept up a running feud, in spite of maintaining a lasting friendship.

Herb Klein also became involved in this ongoing controversy by frequently writing to O'Connor, berating him for some of his expressed written opinions regarding Weatherby. One such instance was when Weatherby introduced the Weatherby Imperial Scope. In one of his columns Jack wrote, "Weatherby is importing a new line of German scopes."

Upon reading this, Weatherby wrote a letter to Jack complaining about his choice of words. He had personally informed Jack some months earlier that he was introducing an entirely new scope of his own design, and had explained in detail his innovative ideas that would be incorporated.

Jack wrote a sarcastic letter in reply, "I didn't know, Roy, that in addition to all of your other attributes you were also an optical engineer. I thought I'd been doing quite well by you, but I guess I haven't, so I'm sending back the rifles and scopes you've sent to me."

Roy replied, "It's too bad you can't take criticism, Jack. You sound like a little boy that just lost all his marbles in a game. And if you send the rifles back you'll just have to pay the freight both ways, for I won't accept them." Roy sent Herb Klein copies of Jack's letter and his reply.

By this time, O'Connor had moved to Lewiston, Idaho and, on one of Roy's visits to the Speer Cartridge Company, he had dinner with Jack and his wife at their country club. After dinner the two men went to the restroom and Jack, in his loud, rough voice said, "Weatherby, why in the hell did you send Herb Klein copies of those letters we wrote?" Roy replied, "Why shouldn't I? Look how insulting you were to me in your letter. I wanted Herb to know the situation."

Jack wouldn't let the matter drop and continued to berate Weatherby, telling him, among other things, "It seems to me you're getting pretty damn big for your britches." Then Roy said, "Jack, there was a time when I needed you, but I don't think I need you like I used to and I'd appreciate if you'd not write anything more about any of my products." Jack came back with, "I'll write about any product I want to and say whatever I want to say."

This was just one of their many tiffs. O'Connor went on to write many fine reports on Weatherby products. Proof of their underlying friendship was shown many years later when Weatherby named O'Connor to the selection committee for the Big Game Trophy Award.

Roy did take exception to some of the accounts in Jack's last book: "I don't think anybody knew Jack much better than I did and he sure got some things kind of mixed up in that book. He lambasted the Big Game Trophy dinner. He gave it hell. He didn't tell the truth. When I made the first presentation to Herb Klein there was no committee. There were no nominees.

Ken Niles and I were invited to Herb's house, and we both went down and made the presentation.

"Jack said he was asked to be on the voting committee. Hell, I didn't ask Jack to be on the voting committee. I didn't know who to give the trophy to in the beginning because I didn't know anybody. Then, I

Ken Niles, a popular radio emcee in the 1940's and 1950's, gets a laugh from Roy and Jack O'Connor (center) during a visit to Jack's home in Lewiston, Idaho. Weatherby and O'Connor argued frequently, but remained friends.

was trying to improve my business, get in with people to write nice things.

"After Herb got the first trophy, I asked him to serve on the awards committee, so then it was Herb, Ken and me. There were three of us. I knew that Jack had done a hell of a lot of hunting, so we just chose him for the next one. Jack says that he told me that it shouldn't go to arms editors, but he never said a word to me.

"Herb said that the 1953 trip he made to Africa with Jack cost *Outdoor Life* $5,000 for a two month trip or something like that. He asked me, "Roy, do you think if I take Jack to Africa with me and pay his way he'd give us a little more publicity in his magazine?" I said "I don't know whether he will or not. He just doesn't like high powered rifles." And so Herb Klein paid for that whole trip. In the magazine Jack talked about the Shah of Iran and the Prince, but I'm the one who introduced them to him.

"Early on Herb thought I was the greatest guy because I could build these pretty rifles, and he wanted to meet Jack O'Conner. Jack was a very popular arms editor, and so I introduced them. I went on a hunting trip in 1947 and took Coleman Jonas and a few people. I took Jack along, paid his whole way, and he wrote a story about it, talking about Ken Niles and Coleman Jonas. Then he added, incidentally, Roy Weatherby was on the trip, too. I knew Jack real well."

Hobbies And Interests

Roy Weatherby was a perfectionist. In business he enjoyed tackling problems and licking them. But once they were licked, he lost interest and moved on to something else. The same pattern applied to his hobbies. They absorbed his interest and energy while they were in the development stage, but once they became routine he was through with them.

One of his first hobbies, long before he got into business, was taxidermy. It was about the only one he was not able to perfect, probably because he tried to learn it on his own, with only textbooks as a guide. His first and only attempt was to mount a pigeon. After carefully skinning the bird and following all the directions as closely as possible, the finished product didn't remotely resemble a pigeon. The experience convinced him that, should he ever collect any trophy animals, he would turn them over to a qualified taxidermist for mounting.

Photography was one of Weatherby's most steadfast hobbies throughout his lifetime, beginning long before he began building guns. He continually upgraded his camera equipment, buying only the finest, and thoroughly enjoyed taking pictures wherever he went—prints, slides, movies, and, later, videos.

By the late 1940's a Leica was his 35mm still camera, and he had advanced from a Bolex 8mm movie camera to the more sophisticated Bolex l6mm. He developed and enlarged prints in his own darkroom. He spliced and edited all of his own movie film, then had magnetic tape installed so he could add his own narration to each reel.

This hobby not only served his personal needs, but was invaluable in the early days of his rifle business when he prepared his African films for public showing.

By 1956 Roy and Camilla's family was complete, with two girls and a boy: left to right, Roy, Ed, Diane, Connie and Camilla.

When his oldest daughter, Diane, was five years old, Weatherby bought her a toy train for Christmas. In teaching her how to operate it he became so fascinated that he started reading every magazine he could find on model railroads. Soon he had accumulated a locomotive kit, some roadbed and track. In less than a year his three car garage looked like the Santa Fe railroad yards.

Once he had completed his vast, intricate layout, and spent a number of weekends over the next few years enjoying this hobby, his interest waned. Soon everything was sold intact to another railroad enthusiast, with the exception of one steam engine that he kept and placed on a mantel in his den.

Becoming a "ham" radio operator was another passion of Weatherby's in the late '40's and early '50's. After getting his amateur license he spent hours at a time, during the evenings and on weekends, huddled over the mike in front of his sophisticated shortwave radio equipment. From the den of his home he talked with other ham operators all over the world. He made many friends over the years that he never met in person, but whom he knew very well by their voices. He delighted in being able to "patch" phone conversations from different parts of the world to anywhere in the Los Angeles area whenever he could accommodate such a request from another ham operator.

Not long after the model railroad equipment was sold, Weatherby became interested in lapidary, and rock polishing wheels and machinery were installed in his garage. He started attending swap meets on weekends in search of rare and unusual rough stones. He would take his family and drive out to nearby desert areas to look for such stones. Roy realized a great sense of accomplishment in creating beautifully polished pieces from the rough unsightly chunks. After cutting and polishing, he frequently made up cufflink sets, tie stickpins and necklaces and, he enjoyed giving away the finished products to his friends and relatives.

By the time Ed was a young boy, Weatherby's interest had turned to building remote-controlled model airplanes. Some of these were enormous, with wing spans of from three feet up to eight feet or more. As he completed each kit and had a new plane to try out, he and Ed would go to the playground of a nearby school to put the plane in the air. Using the remote controls, they would see how high they could fly the plane before maneuvering it into performing rolls and loops. Being able to put the plane into a stall and bring it out of it before hitting the ground was a challenge he couldn't resist. When he failed, he ended up with a banged up airplane, but this only meant he had to spend more time restoring it to flying condition.

One of his most expensive hobbies, but one on which he usually came out ahead of his investment, was the buying and restoration of old automobiles. Most were resold after the restoration was complete, and Weatherby had his fun driving them around. The earliest pieces he collected were a '30 four door air-cooled Franklin, a '31 Marmon and a 1939 Graham automobile. He subscribed to magazines and newsletters that kept him abreast of the value and available sources for antique and classic automobiles.

In the early '70's he bought a '54 Packard Caribbean model sedan, and at one time had a 1959 Silver Cloud Rolls Royce. He also did something few car collectors are able to do: repurchase one of his own automobiles that he had bought when new. One of the subsequent

Roy shows his specially built and equipped Buick station wagon to Brig. Gen. Robert L. Scott, Jr., the author of God is My Co-Pilot. *The sliding drawer held 10 rifles.*

owners, in tracing the ownership of a 1956 Chrysler Imperial, contacted Roy to ascertain if he was indeed the original owner. When Weatherby found out the caller was willing to sell it, he immediately bought it from him, almost 20 years after his original purchase.

Roy often attended car auctions in Southern California, when they first got started, whether or not he planned to do any bidding. He just wanted to view the cars on display. Once he got carried away, bidding on a 1948 Lincoln convertible. When the bidding reached about $4,000, with Weatherby the last bidder, he heard the auctioneer cry out "Sold" and realized he was the buyer. Turning to Dean Rumbaugh, one of his employees who was also a car enthusiast, Roy said, "What have I done? I didn't really want that car!"

Roy went to the man who had been bidding against him and sold it to him on the spot. Later, he frequently told the tale that he was the owner of a '48 Lincoln convertible for about 15 minutes! At that time, he already had in his collection a '65 Lincoln Continental four door convertible, as well as a 1966 Lincoln convertible. Two cars that he always dreamed of being able to own, but was never able to find at the right price, were a Duesenberg and a Hupmobile.

Roy's interest in automobiles was not limited to the classic or antique vintage, but included new models as well. One of his rifle customers, with whom he had become good friends, was Ed Quinn, president of the Chrysler Division of the Chrysler Corporation. In 1956 Weatherby ordered an Imperial 4-door South Hampton hardtop automobile from the Chrysler-Plymouth dealer located next door on Firestone Blvd. His order was loaded with extras such as radio, heater, air conditioning, autronic eye, the "new" 3-speed automatic transmission, 4-way power seats and electric windows, white sidewall tires, and a clock in the steering column.

Ed Quinn learned of his friend's order, and decided to add some further touches that would make this what he later termed "the most elaborate Imperial ever produced," and the only car like it in the world. The interior was upholstered in tan leather and trimmed with zebra hide on the seats and door panels. The exterior had a special two tone paint job, very unusual at that time. This snazzy car caused a great deal of comment wherever Roy took it.

Several years later, in the fall of 1961, through the efforts of Roger Kyes, another good customer/friend who was a vice president of General Motors, Weatherby was personally presented with a gift of a specially built, beautifully wood-panelled Buick station wagon. It also had zebra hide as part of the upholstery. In addition, each of the inside front door panels had an oversize diamond inlay of beautiful contrasting woods, an exact replica of one of the Weatherby Custom stock inlays. The center console between the front seats was built to position and display a Weatherby rifle. With the back tailgate open, a specially constructed drawer pulled out from under the floor of the wagon. This drawer had 10 compartments, each fitted with rests to support a Weatherby scoped rifle. This tempting merchandise was concealed when the drawer slid back into place and the tailgate was closed. Both General Motors and Weatherby, of course, received a lot of valuable publicity when this unique Buick was used by Weatherby and some of his salesmen to make dealer calls.

Along with the above more unusual type hobbies, Weatherby at one time or another also enjoyed stamp collecting and coin collecting, and he considered writing to be one of his hobbies. Over the years, especially in the early days when he started in the rifle business, he was successful in having a number of his articles on ballistics or stories on hunting experiences published in the outdoor magazines.

"I have a number of other personal desires that could very easily be called hobbies," Roy once said. "I would like to take up piano playing if only I had the time. At one time, in my younger days, I could sing quite well, and I'd like to practice voice again. But either of these two would be very time consuming, a commodity which I don't have right now.

"Another hobby is public speaking. I've done quite a bit and, although it's tiresome, I like it. I remember well my first audience of about 75 people, and how nervous I was. Now that I have given hundreds of talks on hunting in Africa, and on ballistics and guns, I hardly realize there is an audience out there.

"There's a certain satisfaction in entertaining people right there in front of you. Yes, you could say that public speaking could be called a hobby...if you don't make your living doing it."

Weatherby: The Promotional Man

Roy Weatherby was the consummate promotional man. Public relations and promotion and advertising and exposure were as natural to him as was breathing, and his temperament and talents were perfectly mated in this direction. He was a good writer and a good photographer; he was great at public relations; and he understood advertising.

Roy never missed an opportunity to publicize the company and his message about high velocity. This dedication to marketing eventually made Weatherby a household word among hunters.

In 1955 Weatherby's was selected as the subject matter for the weekly television show "Success Story." The half-hour program featured successful businesses in the Los Angeles area. It covered the entire Weatherby facility, from the retail store with its numerous mounted game trophies on display, to a tour through the shop area where every phase of operation in manufacturing the Weatherby rifle was shown step by step.

"You asked for it"

In the early fall of 1954 Roy Weatherby appeared on "You Asked For It," a national TV show, where he displayed several of his beautiful custom rifles. He expounded at length on the theory of lightweight bullets traveling at high velocity, comparing them to slower-moving, heavier bullets that had been touted for so long by gun experts and the larger, old line eastern firearms firms.

That appearance was a bonanza of exposure for the Weatherby Magnum rifle. The resulting benefits—increased correspondence and orders from customers—were felt for years.

"Impact"— A 30 Minute Commercial Film

Weatherby had been showing movies of his African trips to sportsmen's groups all over the country ever since 1953. The audiences loved

On the "You Asked For It" show, Roy even got the host, Art Baker, to demonstrate a Weatherby rifle (here seen during rehearsal).

his talks and the films. Each year he received more requests for appearances, to the point where he couldn't accept them all. Roy recognized the importance of the publicity to be gained from these presentations, however, and decided it was time to have a promotional film produced by a commercial photographer. Up until then he had done all of the editing and narrating of his African movies himself.

When Weatherby made another trip to Germany, in October of 1958, he arranged for a commercial photographer to film the Sauer and Hertel & Reuss plants, showing various stages of the manufacturing processes of his Weatherby rifles and scopes. This footage, along with Weatherby's hunting films, was turned over to a film company in Los Angeles. From those, a 30-minute film entitled *Impact* was pro-

Lorne Greene, star of the popular television series **Bonanza** *(and twice a presenter at the Weatherby Big Game Trophy Award ceremony), Robert Petersen of Petersen Publishing Company, and Roy Weatherby, at surprise 40th anniversary celebration in 1985. Greene was the emcee of this Los Angeles affair.*

duced. Radio announcer Ken Niles, Roy's good friend, did the narration.

Prints of this film were distributed nationwide, free upon request, through Modern Talking Pictures, an educational film distributor. Although Weatherby continued to appear personally whenever his schedule permitted, now he was able to offer a substitute program if that wasn't possible. For almost 10 years this film was in constant demand, shown to thousands of sportsmen's groups, service organizations and schools throughout the United States.

Benefits From Other Advertisers

For the first 15 years Roy was in business his primary shipping carrier was Railway Express. A representative of Railway Express called on Roy and explained that his firm wanted to use someone from private industry in a testimonial-type ad. They had narrowed their choice to either Firestone Tire & Rubber Company or Weatherby, and finally selected Weatherby.

Roy appeared in their ad holding one of his rifles, with the caption reading, "For dependability we ship Railway Express." The ad copy further identified him as the builder of the powerful Weatherby Magnum rifles. It was another marvelous promotional coup, and was the beginning of something good for Weatherby, being selected as part of national ads for several companies not directly related to the arms industry. Such exposure was a block-buster adjunct to his own advertising in the outdoor publications.

Later, when he switched to Timken steel for his rifle barrels, this major firm in Canton, Ohio ran a full page ad showing a lion charging across the page and a Weatherby rifle across the top. The ad copy read, "Not only does Timken manufacture roller bearings, but we also provide the barrel steel for the world famous Weatherby rifles."

A Trans World Airlines pamphlet featured Roy and his rifles, and was another instance that afforded him an untold amount of publicity and free advertising. He was very flattered and grateful for each of these unsolicited assists to his own advertising campaigns.

NRA Annual Meetings

In 1948 the National Rifle Association had incorporated into their annual meetings a display of commercial exhibits so that the public and the NRA members could view in person the various products that were offered in the industry. The Weatherby company was one of the exhibitors at this first such display, along with Bob Brownell of Brownell Industries in Montezuma, Iowa and Al Freeland of Freeland's Scope Stands in Rock Island, Illinois and many other firms. As this is being written more than 40 years later, these three firms are the only original exhibitors with continuous attendance over the years.

"Tomorrow's Rifles Today"

From the very beginning, Weatherby utilized his promotional talents in a variety of ways. He prepared all the copy and artwork for his national ads, no matter how small or large they were. He cultivated the friendship of well known personalities both in and outside the shooting industry, and never hesitated to use these contacts whenever possible to obtain much needed publicity.

The second year he was in business he produced a 10 page catalog that he entitled "Tomorrow's Rifles Today." It contained complete information on Weatherby Magnum rifle conversions on the four calibers then in existence—the .220 Rocket, .257, .270 and .300 Weatherby Magnum. It included complete loading data on both formed and unformed cases for each of these calibers. It also included a price list covering the conversion of any other rifle to his calibers; the cost of loading dies, including inserts required for sizing the .300 H&H case down to the .257 and .270 calibers; the price of Buhmiller or Ackley barrel blanks; custom stock work; scopes and mounts that were on the market at that time such as the Weaver, the Lyman Alaskan, and Stith; the price of various bullets, powder scales and other loading components; and books that would interest shooters, such as Phil Sharpe's *The Rifle in America* and *Complete Guide to Handloading.* The second, third and fourth editions of "Tomorrow's Rifles Today" were all published while he was in his original location.

Shortly after moving into his new quarters on Firestone Blvd., an 84-page fifth edition of this booklet was printed. Although it was all black and white photography, the fifth edition contained many photographs of actual operations involved in the building of his rifles, as well as ballistics and reloading data on not only the original four Weatherby calibers, but on two additional ones he had now brought out—the 7mm and .375 Weatherby Magnum. This issue also contained an article written by Weatherby entitled "Velocity Versus Bullet Weight," in which he described many of his experiences from his own African safari. There were testimonials from users of Weatherby rifles.

Throughout his years in business, Weatherby continued to produce this catalog, with a new edition coming out every two or three years. Each issue was enlarged and improved. Although the first 10 page edition was given out as a free promotional piece, Weatherby eventually found it necessary to place a minimal charge on the book to cover the cost of printing. By the late 1960's, the photography throughout the book was in beautiful color, and the name of the publication was changed from "Tomorrow's Rifles Today" to "The Weatherby Guide."

Trans World Airlines

Another interesting piece of promotional work accomplished by Roy Weatherby in 1952 was a folder that he prepared for Trans World Airlines on East African safaris. It was distributed throughout every TWA office in the United States. In addition to being a very colorful folder, with the names of both firms, TWA and Weatherby, Inc. appearing on the cover, it contained a wealth of valuable information on how to prepare for an African safari. It included the names and addresses of a number of professional white hunters to be contacted; how to go about obtaining the necessary passports, visas and health certificates; the types of cameras recommended to be taken, along with other gear and personal clothing suggested, and the calibers of rifles and ammunition recommended for the taking of various game.

A map of the colonies of Uganda, Kenya, Tanganyika and Zanzibar was included in the pamphlet along with the licenses for each type of game that was required in the various colonies, which all of these were at that time. Lastly, complete shipping information was given along with baggage allowance, the cost of air fare for two people, and the various routes that could be taken. There was a photograph of Roy with one of his African trophies, and the small brochure ended with the following message: "To all who fly to East Africa on safari, we wish

In 1952 Roy hit a promotional home run when he got TWA to put his display in the TWA downtown Los Angeles office window. The window promoted Africa and Weatherby rifles.

good luck and good hunting, (signed) Roy E. Weatherby, Builder of America's Finest and Most Powerful Rifles, South Gate, California." This pamphlet, needless to say, did a great deal to promote the use of Weatherby rifles by hunters throughout the world who were going on African safaris.

In addition, TWA arranged for Weatherby to prepare a window display in their Los Angeles office at 6th and Grand - one of the busiest corners in downtown Los Angeles. Roy himself made up the display using one of his lions, a leopard, a hyena and some smaller African animals. Prominent in the display was a Custom .257 Weatherby Magnum rifle, the colorful red and black TWA pamphlet that Weatherby had prepared, and one of his own books, "Tomorrow's Rifles Today." Two large posters stated that anyone going to Africa should fly TWA and use Weatherby rifles. It was a most spectacular display, another great piece of publicity that cost Weatherby nothing.

Roy and Elmer Keith, one of the most colorful gun writers, at Keith's Salmon, Idaho, home, were friendly adversaries throughout their lifetimes. Keith was a proponent of the big bore calibers utilizing heavy, slow-moving bullets, as opposed to Weatherby's strong belief in the effects of high velocity and flat trajectories obtained with lighter weight bullets.

"Lucky Bwana"

Throughout his first few years in business, Roy Weatherby himself wrote many articles covering subjects ranging from his high velocity concept to his own experiences on various hunts. Some were published; others never got into print. In addition, he was able to get millions of words of free publicity in magazine articles written by others because, let's face it, he made interesting reading.

After Herb Klein made his first safaris into Africa and India, he also began to have some of his hunting stories published. Herb was very personable, and possessed a flair for transposing his wit and humor into the written word in a modest but interesting fashion. One of his first stories, entitled "Hunting Sheep With Royalty," appeared in *Outdoor Life* magazine after Klein, Prince Abdorreza Pahlavi and his brother, Shah Mohammed Reza Pahlavi, had hunted sheep and ibex together in the Elburz Mountains of Iran. Klein had taken along on this hunt a gorgeously engraved, inlaid and decorated .300 Weatherby

Magnum rifle, which he gave to the Prince as a gift. When the Prince was presented the gun, he murmured, "This thing did not come from a gunsmith...it must have come from a jewelry shop."

In 1953, Herb Klein wrote and had published a book entitled, *Lucky Bwana,* describing his adventures on safari in British East Africa. Liberally sprinkled throughout the book were photographs taken by Klein. In most of them, of course, his Weatherby rifle was prominently displayed along with his trophy animal. Frequent reference to the Weatherby rifles in various calibers that he used on this hunt was also made in each chapter.

I Knew Roy

Roy Weatherby knew thousands of people in just about every state and in many foreign countries. Among them were leaders of commerce and industry, of politics, of sports and of the firearms and hunting business. But also among them were many just plain Joe's, the rank-and-file hunters and shooters across the land who were either Weatherby rifle owners...or aspired to be.

We asked some of the more prominent men who knew Roy well to reminisce, to remember Roy.

JOE FOSS: Former Governor of South Dakota; Marine Pilot Ace in WW II; Holder of the Congressional Medal of Honor; Former Host of television series "Joe Foss: Outdoorsman."

The first thing I think of when I think of Roy Weatherby is a guy who started with nothing and is the manufacturer of guns. He went through hell and high water to produce a rifle that is very popular.

I used Weatherby rifles on my first trip to Africa, when I was doing The American Sportsman television series. Roy was a very dear friend of mine.

When he first came up with the idea to have the big game trophy, I thought it was an excellent idea, too. He asked if I would be one of the judges, and I said, "Sure, I don't qualify, but I sure know champions when I see them." I'm still on the committee.

As I said, Roy was one of my very, very dear friends, and I've known Eddie since he was a little bitty boy. I've hunted with both of them, had some great times.

Roy was a quiet man. I would describe him as a guy who wanted to do a lot of good things, but didn't want any particular credit for it. He was sort of an introvert.

And he really backed his own product, I'll tell you that. On one of our hunting trips, to the Black Hills of South Dakota, his guns didn't get there. Rather than use some other brand, and give the other 36 hunters on the trip something to heckle him about, he just didn't hunt. He pretended he had a bad hand and couldn't shoot, and spent the whole hunt being a deer driver instead of a hunter.

When we got back to my home after the hunt a guy who worked for me said, "Say, Joe, about two weeks ago a box came and I put it down in the basement. Forgot to tell you about it." It was Roy's rifles.—*Joe Foss*

FRED HUNTINGTON: A legend in his own right in the hunting and firearms community, Fred Huntington is best known for RCBS, the reloading tool manufacturing company he founded and ran for many years.

Roy was a pretty complex guy. When I first met him he lived on California Street and was selling AAA memberships, insurance and the like. But about that time Roy and a fellow named George Fuller, who was a very good mechanic and did some gun work, were getting interested in the big, high velocity calibers.

"I've got something here I want to show you," Roy told me one day. It was a 300 Weatherby, one of the first experimental models. Roy, George and I went out to the rifle range, out between the South Gate store and where he lived east of there. We shot that thing and it was like shooting a cannon.

Roy had a tough time, just about didn't make it a couple times. Then he'd find somebody like Herb Klein down in Dallas who'd put up $50,000 or $60,000 and he was in business and going like hell again. Herb told me one time, "I don't think I'll ever get my money back, but I've had fun." And that wasn't much money for him, so he really enjoyed it. Roy was a super salesman. That was his strong point.

I hunted with Weatherby calibers, but actually preferred the 300 Weatherby shrunk down just a bit, so it wouldn't be quite so dangerous if you messed up and got a full charge in it. We had what we called a 300 Kodiak, which was a full-length H&H case with about a 26 degree

Roy and his aide, Marty Noonan, preparing to show Weatherby's African films at one of his many speaking engagements.

shoulder. It would do almost what the Weatherby would do and was a bit more tolerant to overloads.

In all due fairness to Roy, he put out some data in the early days that was a bit dangerous. His first rifle and first data was pretty bad. He finally realized that and changed the data, backed off another 150 feet or so, and then it was much safer.

Roy Weatherby will always have a place in the gun world because he was the first to really come out strong for the high velocity calibers. His "300," of course, became very popular, and still is.

As for that flashy stock design, high gloss, spacers and the like, he really stuck with them. People liked those hot styles and many still do. And you do see a lot of "Weatherby" in many other guns today.

Roy was really a super salesman. He made friends readily. And he sorted out the people in the movie industry who liked guns, shooting and hunting, and spent a lot of time with them. It paid off in enormous publicity for Weatherby rifles.

Ed is running the company now, of course. He moved his family up to Templeton, about four hours from L.A., and will be moving all the offices up there, too. I'm not sure about that move, but he and his wife like the country. God, they have four really fine-looking boys and girls. What a nice family.—*Fred Huntington*

JACK LEWIS: Editor/Publisher of *Gun World* Magazine; Movie stunt man; book author ("Tell It To The Marines," etc.)

Roy Weatherby, at first, was a man ahead of his time. No doubt about that. He was coming up with things that people are still adopting today, by a different name, and calling it something new.

He was very good at promoting Weatherby on his own. Didn't need an entire staff and corporation t'do it. He was a helluva good promoter. He would come up with an idea, make it work, then go out and sell it practically by himself.

He had a lot of help, of course, from people like Elgin Gates, Roy Rogers and some of the other Hollywood stars. But it was Roy who sold the rifle and turned it into a minor legend.

I've hunted a lot with Weatherby rifles. Shot any number of animals along the way. Got my first bear with a .270 Weatherby, and several trophies in Africa with the same rifle. It's a good, flat-shooting caliber, a fine medium game rifle that will do what it's supposed to do. One shot kills, for the most part, and you can't say more for it than that.

The .300 Weatherby is a little more versatile in some respects. Elgin Gates always carried a .300 in Africa when he was there.

The Weatherby set-up where they sell the whole package—rifle, scope, mounts and all, a complete package—was and is ideal. That works well.—*Jack Lewis*

LARRY THOMPSON: Avid hunter and former Weatherby employee.

The first thing that will come to mind, when people think about Roy Weatherby a few decades down the line, will be high velocity, tremendous energy. Whether they believe his theory that high velocity kills faster than something going slower doesn't really matter, there'll always be contention over that, but it and Roy will be lumped together from now on.

Roy was really an interesting guy to work for—I was with Weatherby for 14 years, and I thoroughly enjoyed traveling with him. We'd share the same room, and usually stayed up past midnight just talking. About guns, of course, and hunting, but also about cars...well, just about anything. He had some tremendously interesting stories.

He had excellent hunting experiences in Africa, and that was back in the days when limits there were very liberal. It was a perfect situation for him to field test his Weatherby calibers.

It was a privilege working for him and traveling with him.

Describing Roy isn't easy, but one thing is certain: he was an innovator. He changed the firearms industry. The Weatherby rifle was the most criticized and copied rifle on the market.

The higher ballistic performance that Weatherby offered simply set a trend, and now that's being copied by other manufacturers. And they're offering Weatherby calibers in their rifles, which is a nice compliment to Roy. I wish that had happened before he died; he'd have gotten a kick out of that.

As for the "Weatherby" stock design—we call it the Hollywood Rifle, here again it has been widely copied. It doesn't appeal to everybody, but it is a unique feature of the Mark V Rifle. For some it does reduce recoil a bit, and I like the Monte Carlo stock.

Weatherby's bread-and-butter cartridge is the .300 Weatherby Magnum, and it's my favorite. In addition, I hunt with the .270, .378 and the new .416...Weatherby, of course.

Weatherby owners are like no other gun owners. They cherish their rifles, and can't handle a ding in the stock or a missed shot, whatever. They're very special people. Weatherby and Weatherby lovers have our own little niche in the industry, and we like that.—*Larry Thompson*

BOB FULLER: Hunter, shooter and long-time star of television, including feature roles in such series as "Wagon Train," "Laramie" and "Emergency."

Roy was a very gentle man, but he was a tough businessman. Seeing him behind his desk at the office you saw a different man from the one out in the field, sitting in a duck blind for hours. Two different people.

I knew Roy for 25 to 30 years, and hunted with him during the One-Shot Antelope Hunt in Lander. He was a very easy man to know, and had a great sense of humor. We spent a lot of time together at the Hunt with Gen. Jimmy Doolittle and Wally Schirra.

He was great with youngsters, and very good to my sons Patrick and Rob. They shoot Weatherbys, naturally. I have a .300 Weatherby that I've had for 30 years, and it's an incredibly gorgeous gun.

Roy was surrounded by celebrities. He didn't use them in any sense of the word. They loved Roy, and they both gained from that experience of being with each other. They wanted to use his rifles, which was great for Weatherby. When he was with them, he was the celebrity. He was outstanding.—*Bob Fuller*

BUD BRANHAM: One of the premier hunting outfitters in America, Bud is particularly famed for his Alaskan operations. He has operated extensively in Africa, as well, lives in Utah, and is a very successful booking agent for hunts around the world.

In my considered opinion, the rifles that Roy Weatherby engineered and made in the beginning, and that his company still makes, are probably the best in the hunting world today. They are probably the most prestigious guns in the world today, too.

The 7mm Weatherby that I own (which I am giving to my grandson David) has done exemplary work for me. I have taken some 50 or 60 animals with it, from the very small to animals the size of Eland, and have never had a malfunction. Mike (Bud's son, a veteran hunting guide in Alaska, Africa and Mexico) has one exactly like it and has experienced the same great results. Roy Weatherby was a man of exemplary character and integrity. Although not a man to make close friends, Roy was certainly one of the most human people I have met and his solicitude for his family, and those things that were close to him, was exemplary. Roy didn't seem the type of man who would really want or could have intimate friends, perhaps because he felt he didn't need them. Nevertheless, he did make many friends who were genuinely fond of him, and certainly I was one of them.

I knew Roy Weatherby almost since he began his business and have been an invitee to the Weatherby Big Game Trophy Dinner every year since it started, which I believe was in 1956. I have attended all of them except for one or two when I was on safari in Africa and I think three or four when I was in the hospital when I was injured in 1982. We have been close friends all of these years. I have never asked Roy for a favor that he didn't grant, nor have I ever recommended anyone to him that he did not give consideration. He was a keen shot and a thoughtful man, especially when those that he was fond of were concerned. He was always that way with me and I revere his memory.—*Bud Branham*

BERT KLINEBURGER: Guide, Outfitter, Taxidermist, Author, Adventurer, and Hunting Consultant, Bert has tremendously wide experience in hunting throughout the world.

I was one of Roy's closest friends and knew him for one hell of a long time. He was always in our party for the One-Shot Antelope Hunt and the Carlsberg goose hunt. Elgin Gates was also a great friend, and the three of us would often get off alone and talk about the good ol' days.

Roy was a pioneer in the firearms business, of course, and did a lot for hunting by his advertising and promotion. He was a sociable type.

Roy Weatherby (left) introduces President Gerald Ford to Bert Klineburger at the 1986 Mzuri Safari Club Conference in San Francisco. Klineburger and Weatherby were close friends for many years.

He did get out and see people and promote and he was one of the pioneers of modern hunting rifles. He stimulated other gun companies. The .300 Winchester Magnum obviously was a caliber to compete with his. And so he did a lot for hunting because of that.

His establishing of the Weatherby Trophy was, in his words, origi- nally more of a publicity thing, but then it became a very serious award. It was a very good thing for the sporting world.

Roy didn't hunt much in his later years, and I think I arranged his last safari when I was a director of Mozambique Safrique. Ed was on that hunt. Adelino Pires was their professional hunter.

One day I got an urgent message at our Fairbanks store to meet the plane from Kotzebue. Roy Weatherby would be on board and needed to see me. I did, and he had a huge polar bear he'd just taken. It was something special, the largest taken that year, 1959, and in body size one of the largest we ever mounted. I did the work personally, and Roy had it on display in his store for years.—*Bert Klineburger*

Letters From and To Roy

Roy was a prolific letter writer, and the contents of many of those letters from and to him reveal much about the man.

April 27, 1951
Mr. Edwards "Pete" Brown
Associate Editor, *Sports Afield*
Minneapolis, 1, Minnesota
Dear Pete:

Well, we finally got moved in and half way straightened around. Brother, what a job it was! But, honestly, it is worth it—this is the prettiest doggone place I've ever seen; in fact, I've never seen a sporting goods store in my life that even half way comes up to this one. It's really spectacular.

We have our new LaPointe broach too and now we can broach all of the rifling in our barrels, but friend, that darn thing costs $15,000. That's a lot of money to pay for broaching barrels.

I've talked to you several times about sending you some of my rifles to shoot and check over. Tell me which one you would like to have me send first and I'll see if I can't get out from under this pile of orders and get one made up and send it to you. I'd like you to try them out and then tell me which one you like best.

Yours very truly,
Roy E. Weatherby

The hunting of jaguar was legal, of course, when Roy hunted them in Mexico and wrote the letters about his hunt.

March 13, 1972
Mr. Juan Naude Cordova
Mexico
Dear Juan:

Words cannot express my deep gratitude and thanks to you for your gracious hospitality.

As I have mentioned to you before, I have never been jaguar hunting but have always had a keen interest to get a jaguar. It was so nice of you to invite me last year to hunt with you. I am sorry I had to decline but I just couldn't decline this year's invitation and I want you to know I enjoyed every minute of the days that I spent with you in your beautiful country.

I only regret that you and I do not speak the same language but through our good friend, Oscar, making it possible for us to communicate through his excellent translation, it was almost like speaking directly to you.

I want you to know, Juan, how much I appreciate your asking Oscar to come along with us for it gave me an opportunity to get better acquainted with him also.

Of course, the jaguar was the climax but I want you to know that I thoroughly enjoyed the opportunity of really getting acquainted with you. I feel now that I know you so much better and a finer man I have never known.

It was so nice of you to take so much of your time to be with me on this hunt. I really enjoyed being with both you and Oscar.

Alvaro is such a personable fellow, and both he and his crew I felt were very outstanding. They all worked so hard to find a jaguar for me and without them and those dogs, I would have not been successful. It was a thrill to hear those dogs when they found the trail and to see the happy expressions on everyone's faces, especially, yours, Oscar's and Alvaro's, when the jaguar was finally ours. Of course, I realize that you have made all of this possible and without the efforts and hard work put forth by Alvaro and his men, well actually, I should take little credit for bagging a jaguar for it was their efforts that made it possible.

Honestly, Juan, no one has ever been a greater host than you were and I shall always remember this as one of my hunting highlights.

I just hope that somehow, some day, I may be able to repay you for your kindness.
My very best regards.
Roy E. Weatherby

March 13, 1972
Mr. Oscar Brooks
Mexico
Dear Oscar:

It was so wonderful of Juan to invite me jaguar hunting. I enjoyed it immensely. But there was one person who made it so much more enjoyable and that was a nice fellow known as Oscar Brooks.

It was very nice of you to take your time to come along with us. Without you, it wouldn't have been the same. You added so very much to the hunt.

Never having hunted jaguar before, I really didn't know just what to expect. I can see now it takes a lot of work and especially for the guide, his men and dogs. They are the ones who make it possible and much easier on the hunter.

Actually, Oscar, this was a particularly enjoyable hunt for it gave me an opportunity to get to know both you and Juan better and I just want you to know I found both of you fellows to be extraordinary nice people. I'm so happy I had this opportunity and so thrilled that collectively everyone was successful in making it possible for me to finally get a jaguar.

Let me thank you again for the important part you played by just being with us.

My best regards.
Sincerely,
Roy E. Weatherby

Mexico D.F., April 10th, 1972
Mr. Roy E. Weatherby
Dear Roy:

Your letter of March 13th was about the nicest letter I ever received. Thank you, Roy, I can assure you that I enjoyed the hunt immensely, more than anything because I had an opportunity to realize what a marvelous person and fine sportsman you are.

I wished very hard for you to get your jaguar, so you will realize how elated I was the way things worked out. Even though everything was extremely enjoyable in our first camp I admit I was disappointed at the negative results and I had my misgivings as to the ultimate result because, as everybody knows, jaguars don't come easy.

My last trip into the same area was a complete failure and several friends of mine have flopped too, so you will understand how happy I was when you placed that shot between the jaguar's eyes. I was more thrilled than if I had shot it myself.

I repeat that it was a treat to me and I consider it a great privilege, that you accepted my invitation to come hunting with me and I do hope that the future will give us many opportunities to hunt together.

We in Mexico have a very special concept of friendship. We feel that true friends are forever.

Please convey my family's kindest regards to your charming wife and warmest wishes to both of you.

Sincerely, your friend

Juan Naude

March 13, 1972

Mr. Alvaro Zuno Arce

Guadalajara, Mexico

Dear Alvaro:

I am so happy that Juan made it possible for me to hunt with you and that great team of fellows you have and those dogs. It was a memorable event that I shall never forget.

I didn't quite realize what a thrill it was to hear the beller or howl of the dogs when they finally found the Jaguar trail. The excitement and anticipation and finally the thrill of finding the elusive Jaguar was something I shall never forget.

I realize this is only a part-time hobby of yours when you are able to get away from your office, but I want you to know I don't think you could have done any better if this was your full-time profession.

You are such a vivacious, personable fellow, and I want you to know I truly enjoyed your company. Let me thank you again for making it possible for me to get my first and only Jaguar.

My best regards.

Sincerely yours,

Roy E. Weatherby

October 11, 1985
Mr. Sam Fadala
Casper, WY 82602
Dear Sam:

It was nice to get your letter of October 3. As for the new catalog, it still won't be out for perhaps another three or four weeks. I will leave word to send you one as soon as it comes off the press. The one you have now will give you some testimonials on the .257 that will probably be about the same as the new one. The catalog won't have much more in it as far as the .257 is concerned than what you now have.

It is difficult to give you an exact date of the .257 beginning but when I went into business in 1945, I already had the 220 Rocket that was on the Swift case which I later dropped. I had the .270, also the .257 and .300; I'm sure it was sometime in 1944. Sometime in 1945 or early 1946 I brought out the 7mm Magnum. Then I made an improved .375 but I dropped that in 1953 when I brought out the .378 Magnum and a little bit later the .460 Magnum. Sometime later we brought out the .340 and later yet the .240. The .224 Varmintmaster came sometime in the early 1960's. The .257 was one of the originals and has always been my favorite rifle for almost everything. I have shot animals up to as far as 300 yards with dynamic success. We all know that most of our game is shot within 100 to 200 yards.

It is true that you can load any of our cartridges to greater velocities, but we never load over 55,000 psi. I would think that if you printed an article with some hotter loads, we would have a lot of people out there using them; it's a little different for somebody who knows guns, ballistics and pressures like you do. When one gets to these top pressures, it doesn't take much more to get into dangerous pressures. There are just too many handloaders out there who don't realize the dangers of excessive pressures.

When we were testing the Mark V action to see how strong it was, we took a .300 cartridge case, filled it clear to the mouth of the case with 4350, then compressed a 180-grain bullet—no problem. We put a 180-grain bullet in front of this round and still were able to open the bolt by tapping on it—no damage to the gun. We had to load a 220-grain bullet in a completely full case and insert a 220-grain bullet in front of that, then the receiver ring blew but no gasses came back through the bolt sleeve. We did this by remote control, of course. The

Mark V will take more pressures than the average gun but we have thousands of all of our calibers on the market that were made on the FN Mauser action.

There were no chronographs on the market in 1943 and 1944, therefore I had to make one. It took about two men and a boy to operate the damn thing and about 15 to 20 minutes to get the reading on one round. After I received my first chronograph in about 1950, we found that the loads we had chronographed with the home built one was almost on the button but I had no way of checking pressures. Since 1953 our pressures have been checked by Norma and double-checked by H.P. White Laboratories.

I note in my letter of September 24, I gave you some of my experiences with the .257 and I still say I use it a great deal. Incidentally, with the .257 I always use the-100 grain bullet.

I have found that the 100 grain does more damage than the 117 within reasonable ranges. On the .270, I use the 130 grain. With the 7mm I use the 139 grain and the 150 grain in the .300 almost exclusively. I remember the first elephant I shot back in 1948. I used the 220-grain full patch in the .300 because you are shooting them between the eye and ear for a brain shot, and there is a lot of bone to penetrate. I don't use full patch bullets on much of anything except shooting elephant or if I am after a small antelope like a Tommy for camp meat where I don't want to destroy any meat, then I use the 220 grain. I am one who wants that bullet to completely disintegrate inside the animal's body. It seems to do more damage, by far, than just normal expansion.

I hope I have been of some help to you. But if I can be of any other assistance to you, let me know.
Sincerely,
Roy E. Weatherby

J. P. Sauer & Sohn
Eckernforde, West Germany, June 29th, 1972
Mr. Roy Weatherby
Dear Roy,
A sad event is today the reason for writing to you. We have shipped the last two containers with the last 156 weapons to you to-day.

Herewith ends an important part of our co-operation.

Beginning with autumn of this year the Weatherby-production at Sauer's is completely run out.

These are very difficult days for us, Roy, but I hope that at least for Weatherby, the decision to transfer the production to Japan, will turn out right. The new rumours about the devaluation of the Japanese Yen give reason for apprehension.

In this letter I would also like to take the opportunity to thank you and your gentlemen for a long and positive cooperation. Our cooperation in Europe and Canada will last, at least until the end of the year 1973.

Hoping to hear soon from you I remain,
Rolf Murmann

August 1, 1972
Dr. Rolf C. Murmann
J.P. Sauer & Sohn
West Germany
Dear Rolf:

Thanks for your letter of June 29th. I want you to know that we are very sorry that our long business relationship is coming to an end, but we are sure you can understand the circumstances. However just because we may be ending most of our business transactions, I sincerely hope it will have no effect on our long friendship. We feel very close to all of you people over there. I only wish it had been possible for J.P. Sauer to have continued the manufacturing and sale of our guns.

Incidentally, I saw a picture of your new centerfire rifle in one of the European publications the other day and would like very much if you could send us a brochure and price list.

Fred will contact Howa relative to the existing rifle parts you have on hand and rest assured we will do everything possible to assist you.

Again, I want to tell you it has been a pleasure doing business with you and your people all of these years, and even though we may be ending some of our business transactions, I want you to know we will always try to help you in every way possible. We feel that both our companies should be in a position to help each other.

Very truly yours,
Roy E. Weatherby

June 25, 1974
Mr. Leo W. Roethe
Nasco, Inc.
Dear Leo:

I have your letter of June 10th, and believe me, my friend, I do wish it had been possible for you to have converted your stock so that you could have been a part of Weatherby, Inc. - just like Earl and John for I would have enjoyed having you with me.

I want you to know, Leo, how much I appreciate your coming into this company in the first place by buying out the Germans and also your belief and trust in me and this company by wanting it to become part of Nasco. These things I will never forget.

Leo, let me say the same as you said in your last sentence. I, too, think you're one "helluva guy." I like you, admire you, and always will think you're one great guy and I hope we'll always be friends. All either of us can do now, is keep our fingers crossed and hope that Weatherby, Inc. and Nasco prosper. I want you to know that I wish you all the success in the world. You've worked hard and deserve a great reward.

The main thing, I always want to be a friend of yours for I think you're a great guy.
Sincerely,
Roy E. Weatherby

April 16, 1980
Mr. S. Miyoshi
Howa Machinery Co., Ltd.
Shinkawa-Cho
Near Nagoya 452, JAPAN
Dear Mr. Miyoshi:

I am enclosing a copy of a telex that is self-explanatory and wish to thank Mitsui for their endeavors in trying to help us locate a source for wood. We have been working feverishly for many months, attempting to obtain wood from different sources. In fact, we have contacted practically every source of wood in the United States. What makes it so difficult for us is that we are after a fancier grade of wood than the other manufacturers use.

Unfortunately, walnut trees only produce a very small percentage of fancy wood, particularly black walnut, which grows in the Midwest and East.

I have personally contacted both sources mentioned in the telex; however, I am happy to inform you that we have been able to purchase some very suitable wood that will be on its way to you very shortly. In fact, our men are in Oregon this week on a wood-buying trip that we feel will result in a sizable purchase.

While attending the National Rifle Association Meeting in Kansas City, Missouri, last week, I personally made a trip to southern Kansas to an unknown wood source and found they have a very good supply. However, it will be the latter part of the year before they will have blanks cut and dried.

In the interim we are attempting to purchase wood from any source available at almost any price in order to keep Howa in production. We are running very short on some calibers in Mark V, and we are completely out of other calibers and in a backlog condition.

I want to apologize for this delay in getting stock blanks to you. It is very unfortunate that our main supplier of wood, Calico, has begun selling to so many other companies, both here and in Japan, to the point that it has affected their supply of wood to us. Calico also had an unfortunate happening when they had two of their large kilns go bad on them, and thousands of blanks were ruined. These were the type they sell us to ship to Howa.

You may rest assured we are working very diligently and will continue purchasing wood every place possible. We would be able to obtain all the wood necessary if we used the type of wood like the major gun companies use. But since we cannot economically compete with Winchester, Remington, etc., we must have a fancier grade of wood on our rifles.

Very truly yours,
Roy E. Weatherby

MEMORANDUM
FROM: Mr. Weatherby
TO: Max Salisbury/Chuck Murray/Stock Department
SUBJECT: Masking Tape

We are buying $45.00 worth of masking tape *every three months*, which seems prohibitive. The masking tape I am speaking of is not the type that is used for masking the bolt handles in the bluing room, but the type used on rifle stocks.

Each roll has 60 yards or 180 feet. With an average production of 80 to 100 rifles each month, it does not seem logical that we could possibly use this much tape. It may be a small item, but it is a combination of these small items that loses money for the organizations.

May I ask your cooperation?

bn for REW 3-10-56

(From:)

Sports Afield

Minneapolis 1, Minnesota

July 30, 1947

(To:)

Weatherby's Rifle Conversions

8823 Long Beach Boulevard

South Gate, California

Gentlemen:

You will be interested in knowing that *Sports Afield* is starting a full page, four color campaign in *Life* magazine.

First advertisement of this series appears August 11th.

Sports Afield's circulation has hit an all time high of 750,000!

Now, more than ever, the world's number 1 sportsmen's magazine!

Sincerely

R.F. Gardner

MEMO TO: Roy Veale, Roy Burt, Herb Ludwick, and Bob Smith

FROM: Mr. Weatherby

I can see no reason why you people do not keep the fan turned off on the shooting muffler in the basement. Those fans are almost worn out now from continuous running. They need only be on when somebody is range firing rifles.

The light pit is on also every time I go to the basement, and the fan in the basement runs almost continuously.

I do hope that it is not necessary for me to caution you people again.

bn 8-11-55

Beverly Wilshire

Beverly Hills, California

July 12, 1948

Dear Roy:

I just wanted you to know that right now I am terribly jealous.

I went out to your joint last Thursday just to see how things were going in your absence, and everything seems to be just fine. The boys have completed all three of my shotguns and they sure are beauties. Mr. Mews will finish my .300 Weatherby in about a month he says so that will be perfectly ok.

Miss Fields had sent me a copy of your diary up to the 15th of June and I had left Dallas before it got there, so I had it forwarded and I have just finished reading it for the fourth time and every time I read it my blood pressure goes up 5 points. So that's why I'm seeing a little green right now!

I know you are having a wonderful time and I sure wish I were there with you, but better luck next time. Don't shoot all the Big Stuff but leave just a few for me in case I happen to get over there sometime.

I will be here until the 28th I think, so if you should happen to get home by that time be sure and give me a ring here at the hotel. I would enjoy a little visit with you before I go back to Texas.
Lots of luck,
Herb Klein

"We are so fortunate to live in a country where a man can climb as high as his ability will let him. For me there is no stopping for tomorrow. As long as I am physically and mentally capable I will keep on climbing, bringing out new products, entering new fields. I don't believe I'll ever sit back and say, 'I have accomplished my goal,' for I keep setting my goal higher with every passing year."
Roy E. Weatherby
July 26, 1960

September 9, 1980
Mr. Grits Gresham
Natchitoches, LA 71457
Dear Grits:

I have just read your article in *Sports Afield* on Tony A'costa, and I thought you did a magnificent job telling the story. I think you told it just as it is, and, as you mentioned, if that smooth bore is going to lessen the friction of the bullet in the rifleless part of the barrel, why doesn't it increase velocity with regular factory ammunition? The theory of the gases squirting past the bullet and pushing the air away, as far as I'm concerned, Grits, is nonsense.

Another comment that I thought appropriate is where you mentioned that the arms companies, with their sophisticated ballistics laboratories, claim the peak of pressure is at the breach end of the barrel, but after all these years, Tony has found differently. In fact, I remember years ago, before I was in business, when I visited Aberdeen Proving Grounds, talking to some of the ballisticians there, finding out how little I knew, they explained that peak of pressure very thoroughly to me; showed me, without any question, that the peak of pressure is immediately in front of the cartridge case. Naturally, there is a slight variation, depending upon the burning rate of the powder. Normally speaking, we say, the peak of pressure is in the first 3/4" of the barrel.

When we tested a gun that he made up for us, our results showed the same as you report. We found the cartridge case was difficult to extract, and there were definite signs of pressures; also, we could find no improvement in accuracy.

When he was out here visiting us, we told him that there was no way to determine the pressures to obtain his velocity with his handloads without sophisticated pressure equipment, and we recommended that he contact H. P. White Laboratories or someone else with pressure equipment, to determine what pressures he was creating to achieve those velocities.

I thought the article was very well put and very interesting.

Very truly yours,

Roy E. Weatherby

March 30, 1981
Mr. Jim Dumas, Sr.
Chowchilla, CA 93610
Dear Mr. Dumas:

I want you to know how terribly sorry I am that you have had difficulty with one of our rifles. I had my office check through our files, and they just can't find any of the past correspondence, so I'm at a loss to know just what the trouble may have been, other than what you had in your letter to Mr. Gresham.

We do our very best to build the finest rifles in the world, but of course, I suppose sometimes something could go wrong. You mentioned there was something wrong with accuracy. Let me mention, that with a light weight barrel, it is the first three shots that count, because after the light weight barrels begin to warm up sometimes they have a tendency to warp a little. But I note you mention that your first shot was accurate and then your second shot was way off. This even seems too much to be a bedding problem due to stock warpage. It could be, of course, from a loose scope mount screw, or the scope itself, but you may rest assured that all of our rifles are shot before shipment, and they all must do 1 1/2" or less at 100 yards.

I just want you to know that I am terribly sorry that your experience with our gun was not to your liking, and hope that sometime we will get you back into the family of satisfied Weatherby customers.
Sincerely,
Roy E. Weatherby

July 21, 1986
Dear Adam:

Ten years ago today you made your grandfather very happy for you were my first grandchild with the name "Weatherby." Had your dad not had any boys, his would have been the end of our Weatherby name. Now I even have a backup for you and that's Daniel.

When are we going to get together and play with out remote-controlled cars?

Have a happy birthday, Adam! I love you very much.
Grandpa

(From:)
Bozell, Jacobs, Kenyon & Eckhardt
January 26, 1987
(To:)
Mr. Roy E. Weatherby, Chairman of the Board
Weatherby, Inc.
Dear Roy:

I have heard through the shooting fraternity you are retiring. Congratulations and best of luck to you on your well-earned rest.

Although we did not have the opportunity to work together very long, I wanted you to know that I have a profound admiration for your achievements. After almost 35 years in the advertising business in the West, I've had the opportunity to meet, worth with and known many of its pioneers and entrepreneurs—Elliott Handler at Mattel, Norton

Simon with Hunt-Wesson, Bob Peterson, Ernest Gallo, Walt Disney, and Roy Weatherby. All of them had something in common, all entrepreneurs, all geniuses, all made quality products, and all have a unique and personal way of doing things. You are no exception and your 40-year record of accomplishment speaks for itself.

I am sure Ed will carry on in your tradition. I am proud and honored to have known you and worked with you. I wish you good health and happiness in your retirement years.

Sincerely,

Cy Schneider, Chairman

October 31, 1987

Dear Roy:

I phoned Betty the other day and she said you were out of intensive care. You continue to inspire us who are lucky enough to know you.

I was just thinking this morning of some of the treasured opportunities you have provided me. Aside from a 15 year livelihood for which I hope I have communicated my appreciation, you are responsible for countless other valued experiences in my life. Like shaking hands with Gen. Jimmy Doolittle, Ken Niles, Ted Williams, John Connally, Joe Foss, etc., not to mention General Bob Scott who, in effect, brought me together with you. Now, for a boy who grew up on a 40 acre farm in Idaho that's an enviable list of acquaintances!

And, probably, were it not for you I would never have seen McCormick Place, the Houston Astrodome, New Orleans, Atlanta, or Indianapolis. My world has broadened because of you.

My opportunities for leisure activities expanded from my association with you and the precision products you produce. My counsel was sought after by people in the trade, and this opened the door for hunting opportunities that would surely have not occurred otherwise.

Roy, I guess the most outstanding residual of my relationship with you is the feeling of belonging to the "family" of Weatherbys. I say that in quotes because it not only includes your immediate family, but extends to Betty, Marty, Dan Thimmer, Larry Thompson, ad infinitum...those who make up the most cohesive cadre anyone could hope for in a company. That loyalty can exist only because of your strong leadership.

I share the happiness of your many friends in your recovery. Now hurry and get out of there, and get back to writing that book on your life.

Respectfully yours,
Harry S. Bane

January 6, 1988
Mr. Harry S. Bane
Phoenix, Arizona
Dear Harry:

Harry, your letter was one of the nicest I have ever received. I want to thank you very much for all the compliments you paid me.

It was interesting to read how you grew up on a 40 acre farm in Idaho. I grew up on 160 acres in Kansas, but it wasn't very good land. We had an awful time making it.

It's true, Harry, you really do belong in the Weatherby family.

It will be quite some time before I'll be returning to the office even on a partial basis, but I won't have anything to do with the operation of the business. This last operation was just about too much for this 77 year old man. I think I just about didn't make it.

Thanks again, Harry, for such a very nice letter.

Sincerely,
Roy E. Weatherby

(Roy died three months later, April 5, 1988)

Roy, the Writer

Roy was quite a good writer, a prolific one, and wrote several articles over the years in addition to copious letters, memos, diaries, and directives. Here is a feature of his, written in collaboration with Sam Shepherd, that was published in *Sports Afield* Magazine, the November 1953 issue.

The Bigger They Are

By Roy Weatherby
and Shep Shepherd

I had come to Africa with a pet theory about killing an elephant with one bullet. I was warned against trying it out. The next thing I knew, here came the elephant charging at me.

Dawn broke crisp and clear on that morning as we started our third week on safari. To the west, lofty Mt. Kenya stabbed its snow-capped, 17,040-foot peak through a roof of billowy white clouds. We were hunting the plains to the east, a section broken occasionally by wooded areas, ravines and valleys. We had taken virtually every species the district had to offer. All but our chief prize—the elephant.

Starting today we are going to hunt elephant and keep on hunting them until we find them. In the past two weeks we have been continually distracted and led off on tangents by waterbuck, impala, topi, eland, zebra and even lion. Now it's elephant or nothing.

I have a special reason for wanting an elephant. They are reputed to be, and I guess there's no argument about it, the hardest to kill of all big game. They are the supreme test for any new theory on firearms. And I have a theory. I have it built into the rifle I'm going to use on the first elephant I see. The theory is that a small caliber bullet can kill anything under the sun if it has enough velocity. To prove it, I have a rifle with me that hasn't yet been fired at a living target. It's a .378 caliber that will propel a 300-grain bullet at 3,100 feet per second, and has a muzzle energy of 5,600 foot-pounds!

African white hunters state flatly that nothing less than the big English double rifles of .475 or .500 caliber, firing a 500-grain slug, can kill elephant or rhino. Yet even now I have an interesting wager on with my white hunter. His bet is that I can't kill an elephant with what he calls "that little rifle." I've given him odds that I will not only kill an elephant, I'll do it with one shot!

We have two white hunters with us. Pitcairn Holmes and Bunny Rey. Holmes outlines a plan for the day. We drive about 10 miles to a valley he knows, then another 10 miles up the valley to where we may find elephant. We reach the valley and are bouncing across the ant hills and boulders when one of the boys suddenly yells, "elephant!" He points to our left.

101

Pit lifts his glasses and scans the valley half a mile away. He looks at me with a grin. "There's your target," he says. I grab the glasses and look. A bull. The tusks will go 80 or 90 pounds each. "Okay, Pit," I say, "let's get him."

The huge pachyderm is walking across the valley through the grass and scrub trees as though he has a destination, but plenty of time to reach it. I follow the tracker. Pit follows me. Then comes Bunny with the movie camera. Behind Bunny come half a dozen natives. Surely, I think, the elephant will hear this mob, but no one speaks as we walk quietly but rapidly. It's all I can do to keep up with the tracker, who isn't really needed since we can see the elephant all the time.

I feel sure the bull will see or hear us. Though we are moving fast, he seems to stay the same distance ahead of us. We walk for half an hour before we begin gaining on him. We walk as silently as nine men can. The bull keeps going steadily on. He stops occasionally to pick leaves from the trees. These short halts let us close in a bit.

The trees and brush thin out. Now we are about 200 yards from the elephant, but he is going directly away from us. I'm sure not going to try to kill an elephant by shooting him in the rear end. After all, this .378 is only a shoulder weapon.

Then the bull stops to gather more leaves. "Now?" I ask Pit. "He's turned so I can get him in the side of the head."

"No," he says, pushing my gun down, "he's too far."

"Not for this rifle," I whisper. "We're taking a chance on losing him every minute we wait."

All the time we move forward. We cut the distance to 150 yards. Again the bull turns sidewise and I shoulder the rifle. Pit almost knocks it out of my hands. "No!" he says, "we'll get still closer."

This method of hunting doesn't fit in with my plans. I step out ahead of both Pit and the tracker. I suppose I am breaking all sorts of rules, but I am getting anxious. We have been going at a fast pace now for 45 minutes, and I am puffing and perspiring. My mouth and throat are dry and my heart pounds, but the sight of this biggest living target in front of me spurs me on.

Now I am 50 yards ahead of Pit and the others. He thinks I'm a fool, of course. But I'm sure I know what I'm doing and I'm not going to let this elephant get away. I can travel more quietly alone. So, I take the chance.

Two of those people back there have big bore rifles, cocked and ready to shoot. Their purpose is to protect me, but I don't think I'll need it. I'm as sure as I can be that one shot from this rifle in my hands will bring down that elephant.

Now he is 100 yards away. I run to the leeward side. That lets him gain a little. He turns his head again and I see a chance. I raise the gun—too late—he's going straight again! I run as fast as I can. I'm 20 yards to his left and 80 yards behind. I look back and see I've left the others by a 100 yards or so. Now the bull angles off to one side. My heart sinks. There is heavy brush ahead of him. This is my last chance!

I stop and bring up the rifle. The grass is too high to let me drop to one knee. I aim at a point between the eye and the ear. I hold my breath to stop the trembling. I pull the trigger. The report rolls across the valley as I watch the bull. Instantly, he crashes to the ground and the red dust rolls away in clouds. He never moved one step after that slug hit him!

I haven't stopped trembling yet when the others run up. I know by the look on Pit's face that he is wavering in his belief that all Americans are crazy and that only big bore rifles can kill big game. He hadn't expected to get an elephant, so we have to send back to camp for tools to cut out the tusks and take the lower legs for wastebaskets and a piece of hide for a table top.

The natives are exuberant. They sing all the way back to camp. They always sing when there is fresh meat.

Two days later we start south to the Masai. The move takes three days of slow travel. Our goal here is rhino. These big, armor-plated, horn-snouted African brutes, more often than not, are harder to kill than elephant. At the same angle from the same distance the elephant, of course, is tougher.

On the second morning in our new location, Pitcairn leaves camp in one of the trucks about 5:30, going out to look at some lion bait and scout for rhino. Bunny and I leave as the sun comes up at 6:30. We turn north down a little winding trail. We have no particular goal in mind.

It is a beautiful morning, crisp and clear. We drive along several minutes and cross a ravine. As we churn up the other side, we notice rhino spoor. Two rhinos, one walking in each car track. These are fresh rhino tracks too, for they have been made since Pit passed this way an hour ago.

103

We keep going up and around the rise, and the tracks keep going right ahead of us. Excitement begins to build up in me through we don't know if we'll ever see the rhinos. They may turn off at any minute and go into the brush. We have a good chance though, for the brush is at least a mile away. And around us are open plains studded with thorn trees. The nearest timber is a mile to our left. It's probably five miles north, or straight ahead to the next timber and it's almost that far to timber to the east. So the rhino can go only one way to cover.

We reach the crest of the ridge. And there, 300 yards ahead of us, walk two rhino. Now what?

We can't shoot them from the car, but if we leave the car we will never catch them. If they get our scent they will either charge or be off to the timber. They haven't heard us yet. We look through the glasses. We see one is a cow and the other a bull—and what a bull! One look at his horn starts me trembling. I've had an eye out for rhino since we started on safari.

I reach behind into the truck and get my .300 Magnum and a half dozen rounds of ammunition. Three of these cartridges are special ones made for me by the Norma Company in Sweden to try out for penetration. There's no better test than this rhino.

I get out of the car and start running, as quietly as possible. Bunny trails me. The rhinos are now about 250 yards away. They walk about as fast as I can run. Then they become aware of us, stop, turn completely around and stand there looking our way with their tails up in the air.

I have been told that rhinos have poor eyes and can see no farther than 40 yards. But is that true? They sure seem to be looking straight at me. I slow down a little. The bull runs back and forth twice, getting our scent. Bunny is about 25 yards behind me. He is armed with a .375.

The two rhinos snort, their tails go up again and they start towards us. Now what in hell am I going to do?

They are 250 yards away and the car is 300 yards behind me. The big bull keeps turning his head from side to side, apparently he's having a little trouble holding our scent. I make a decision and shoulder the rifle. When the bull turns his head I aim for his shoulder and fire. Even as I pull the trigger I know the distance is too great. At that yardage I lose all the high velocity advantages I built into the .300.

I hear the plunk. The bull stumbles and goes down. He gets up again and stands still, swinging his head. The cow turns and heads for the timber. But the bull gets our scent and charges.

As he thunders toward me, I run as fast as I can to the left to try and get a better target, hoping he will keep coming downwind on our scent. He does.

Don't ever let anyone tell you that a rhino can't run! By the time I am 20 yards off the trail he has cut the distance to 150 yards. When I gain another 20 yards he is shaving a 100. I detect a limp even in his earth-shaking stride and I know he's hurt—and mad.

I can hardly take my eyes off that tremendous horn. It gives the impression he is running behind a post. I look quickly over my shoulder to see if Bunny is covering me. He's standing in the trail with a camera—taking movies!

I turn back and line the rhino up in the scope. I get the cross hairs on a point behind his eye, aiming for the head on the theory that a miscalculation will still get him in the neck or shoulder. He is now 80 yards away.

I fire. Several thousand pounds of galloping rhino fold up and a dust cloud rises. When it clears, we find the rhino dead. I go for the steel tape in my kit on the truck. That horn measures 30 inches! It isn't a record by any means, but it's big enough to be talked about in the record books.

I sit down on the rhino's leg and lecture Bunny about something the white hunters have always said: That you must have full-patch or solid bullets to kill a rhino, and that you must even then be within 50 yards. I've known hunters who have fired a dozen rounds from a .470 into one of these fellows and still have had to trail him for a day in the brush.

Maybe I was just lucky, but I got this rhino with 180-grain expanding bullets.

Bunny stands very quiet, fingering one of the empties from my .300 Magnum. I think the expression on his face means I have another convert to high-velocity.

4

The Weatherby Big Game
Trophy Award

In 1955 Weatherby conceived the idea of giving a magnificent trophy to the hunter who had made the greatest accomplishments in the hunting world, not just for someone who might have been lucky enough to get a record head. It was to go to the hunter who not only hunted worldwide, collecting the rare and difficult-to-obtain animals, but one who was also actively involved with game conservation so that the sport of hunting would continue for years to come.

He knew of no one who had done more hunting at that time than Herb Klein. And, perhaps as a way for him to thank his friend and business partner for believing in him and assisting him financially for nearly 10 years, there was no one on whom he would rather see such an honor bestowed. Roy set up a selection committee consisting of General Nathan L. Twining, Chairman of the Joint Chiefs of Staff; General Robert L. Scott, author of *God Is My Co-Pilot*; Joe Foss, Governor of South Dakota; Coleman Jonas, a famous taxidermist from Denver, Colorado; Jack O'Connor, the arms editor of *Outdoor Life*; Warren Page, arms editor of *Field & Stream*; Pete Brown, arms editor of *Sports Afield*; and Ken Niles of radio fame. All of them were big game hunters themselves. He talked to each member of the selection committee, and they all agreed that they couldn't possibly find anyone who had accomplished more than had Herb Klein.

How to keep these plans a surprise and when to present the trophy was something Roy had to work out. A new home that Herb was building in Dallas, one that would include a den of nearly 1,700 square feet where he planned to display more than 100 trophy animals, provided the answer. Herb set a date in July of 1956 to host a "house warming" open house, and invited not only his local friends but some from all over the country.

The only members of the selection committee that were not on Klein's list of guests were General Twining and General Scott. Roy wanted Twining to make the actual presentation, and arranged to have them invited.

The trophy was spectacular. Its base and center pedestal were of walnut and shined with the same high lustre finish that Roy applied to his rifles. One of Weatherby's Custom rifle stock inlays, made of contrasting exotic woods, graced the face of the center column, and below that was a brass plate appropriately engraved with Herb Klein's hunting accomplishments. Another brass plate across the base of the trophy had the names of the selection committee engraved on it. Placed atop this handsome walnut base was a beautifully crafted cup inscribed "Weatherby Big Game Trophy" and the year 1956. The cup itself supported a brass world globe with a winged angelical sculpted figure atop the globe. On either side of the center walnut column a brass figure of a majestic ram stood on a riser of an eagle with swept back wings. This most impressive trophy stands almost four feet high.

Roy had connived with Herb's wife, Florence, to keep the trophy in a closet out of sight until the time came for the presentation. In the middle of the evening, Ken Niles upstaged his host by asking for everyone's attention. Acting as emcee for the first of what was to turn out to be 30 consecutive years for this annual affair, Ken amused the guests with a humorous repartee of some of Klein's hunting experiences. He then introduced General Twining, who proceeded to extol the virtues and accomplishments of Herb Klein. Herb couldn't quite comprehend just exactly what was going on, but about that time the trophy was brought out and General Twining made the presentation. To add to Herb's confusion, there were also newsreel cameramen and a reporter from *Life* magazine present.

With this nine-man selection committee in place, guidelines were established for the selection of future award winners, ones which have been strictly adhered to in awarding this coveted trophy through each

The first Weatherby Award gathering was a precursor of things to come, attracting an array of prominent people from many walks of life. Here, from left to right: Pete Brown, Arms Editor of Sports Afield magazine,; Gen. Nathan F. Twining, Chairman of the Joint Chiefs of Staff; Jack O'Connor, Arms Editor of Outdoor Life magazine; Ken Niles, radio emcee; Herb Klein, Texas oil man, Weatherby partner, and first recipient of the award; Roy Weatherby; Coleman Jonas, founder of Jonas Brothers Taxidermy in Denver; Col. Robert L. Scott, Jr., WWII flying ace and author of God Is My Co-Pilot; and an unknown attendee of the presentation in Dallas in 1956.

of the successive years. Potential nominees can be submitted by anyone, including themselves, with a limit of only six nominees being presented each year to the selection committee for their final vote. The name of the award winner is not revealed until the night of the presentation.

In 1957, at an invitation-only stag affair held in Denver, Colorado, Jack O'Connor became the second recipient of the Weatherby Big Game Trophy Award. Governor Joe Foss made the presentation. The next year the awards dinner was held in Washington, D.C. That was the first year wives and girlfriends were included in the invitation, a custom which has been followed ever since. Warren Page was the recipient of the 1958 Big Game Trophy, and General Twining once again made the presentation. For the second year in a row, Washington, D.C. was again the site of the awards banquet in 1959 when General James Doolittle made the presentation to Berry Brooks of Memphis, Tennessee. In 1960 the affair was held in Beverly Hills,

109

Jack O'Connor was the second recipient of the Weatherby Big Game Trophy Award, and is shown here with Roy in Denver in 1957

California, with General Doolittle once again making the presentation, this time to Elgin Gates, then of Newport Beach, California. Elgin was only 38 years old at the time he won this award—the youngest winner ever. In 1961, once again in Beverly Hills, Governor Joe Foss made the presentation to Julio Estrada of Cuernavaca, Mexico.

The award presentation had now become an international event. Although the event has been held in several cities over the years, including Las Vegas, Phoenix, Los Angeles, Beverly Hills, Washington, Newport Beach and Denver, the Los Angeles area has been its home for the past decade.

Roy and his wife, Camilla, clowned it up with one of their African friends at the 1960 awards presentation.

A highlight of each award presentation, in addition to revelation of the winner, is the presenter himself. That list includes a star-studded field from television, movies, politics, sports and science.

Through the years the high level of dignity with which this annual event is conducted has effectively improved the public image of hunters and hunting. Since his death in 1988, the Weatherby Big Game Trophy awards banquet has been sponsored and perpetuated by the Roy E. Weatherby Foundation*, a non-profit organization established in honor of its founder.

* The Roy E. Weatherby Foundation was formed in 1988 as a memorial to Roy Weatherby. Its objectives are expressed in the following statement of Mission:

"The education of the public on the values to society of wildlife and the beneficial role of ethical sport hunting in wildlife conservation.

"The promotion of the preservation of wildlife and its natural habitats for the enjoyment of future generations."

Raising an endowment fund of $1,000,000 is the initial goal of the Foundation. Income from this endowment will be applied to the aims of the Statement of Mission, concentrating in the early stages on public education on the values and benefits of ethical sports hunting.

Levels of membership:

Honorary Director for Life $25,000

Life Member $10,000

Charter Member $5,000

Founder $2,000

Patron $1,000

The Foundation is a tax-exempt organization under Section 501(c)(3) of the Internal Revenue Code and contributions are deductible.

In 1984 James Henrijean became the first and only Belgian to receive the Award. From the left, Roy and Ed Weatherby; presenter Mike Connors, actor; Henrijean; Elgin Gates; and Steve Ferber, Publisher of Aqua-Field magazines.

Elgin Gates, center, received the Award in 1960, shown here with Roy and Gen. Jimmy Doolittle, who made the presentation.

Joe Foss, WWII ace and later governor of South Dakota, presented the 1961 Award to Julio Estrada of Mexico City and Cuernavaca, Mexico.

Weatherby Award Winners: 1956-1990

Year	Recipient	Presenter
1956	Herb W. Klein, TX	Gen. Nathan F. Twining, USAF
1957	Jack O'Conner, ID	Gen. Joe Foss, USMC
1958	Warren Page, CO	Gen. Nathan F. Twining, USAF
1959	Berry B. Brooks, TN	Gen. James H. Doolittle, USAF
1960	Elgin T. Gates, CA	Gen. James H. Doolittle, USAF
1961	Julio E. Estrada, Mexico	Gen. Joe Foss, USMC
1962	H.I.H. Prince Abdorreza Pahlavi	Andy Devine, Actor
1963	John B. LaGarde, AL	Robert Taylor, Actor
1964	Dr. Frank C. Hibben, NM	Capt. Wally Schirra, Astronaut
1965	Francois Edmond-Blanc, France	H.I.H. Prince Abdorreza Pahlavi, Iran
1966	Dr. W. Brandon Macomber, NY	Lorne Greene, Actor
1967	Dan W. Maddox, TN	Cornel Wilde, Actor
1968	Weir McDonald, Ariz.	Dr. Wernher von Braun, Physicist
1969	O. J. McElroy, AZ	Gov. John Love, CO
1970	George Landreth, TX	Capt. James A. Lovell, Jr., Astronaut
1971	Juan Naude Cordova, Mexico	Sen. Barry Goldwater, AZ
1972	James R. Mellon, II, PA	Gov. John Love, CO
1973	Basil C. Bradbury, CA	Dennis James, Actor
1974	Dr. Lenneth W. Vaughn, CA	Roy Rogers, Actor
1975	Not held	
1976	Rudolph Sand, Denmark	Hon. William B. Saxbe, Cong.
1977	Madariagay Oya, Spain	Chuck Connors, Actor
1978	Arthur Carlsberg, CA	Ernest Borgnine, Actor
1979	Dr. Robert Speegle, TX	Gene Autry, Actor
1980	Watson T. Yoshimoto, Hawaii	Robert Stack, Actor
1981	Dr. Carlo Caldesi, Italy	Dennis James, Actor
1982	Glenn Slade, TX	Lorne Green, Actor
1983	Mahlon White, CO	Gen. Chuck Yeager, USAF
1984	Jacques Henrijean, Belgium	Mike Connors, Actor
1985	Thornton N. Snider, CA	Stewart Granger, Actor
1986	Hector Cuellar, Mexico	Richard Anderson, Actor
1987	Dr. James Conklin, PA	Jameson Parker, Actor
1988	Robert W. Kubick, AK	Steve Kanaly, Actor
1989	Donald G. Cox, MI	Jack Youngblood, NFL
1990	Robert K. Chisholm, KS	Patrick Duffy, Actor

5

Weatherby's Hunting Trips

Despite the time consuming challenges and frustrations of starting a business and keeping it going, Roy hunted as often as possible. Not only was making such trips virtually a prerequisite for a rifle manufacturer, particularly one advocating a radical new concept, but he really loved hunting.

In addition to pitting himself and his Weatherby rifles against game, Roy hugely enjoyed experiencing the varying environments that were the site of hunts. Not only was he a keen observer of details on his trips, with an excellent memory, but he was meticulous in recording facts and impressions on recorders, in notebooks, and with both still and movie film.

Here were a few of his more memorable outings.

1947 British Columbia Hunt

In 1947, Weatherby arranged with an outfit in British Columbia to take a group of seven or eight people on a big game hunt, which allowed him to go at a greatly reduced rate, amounting to practically nothing. By this time, Weatherby had met another celebrity by the name of Ken Niles. Ken was the announcer for the Amos & Andy show, the Eversharp show, etc. He and his brother, Wendell, were the most popular radio announcers of the day. Ken and Roy became the best of friends and were to develop a friendship that lasted for over four decades.

The hunt into British Columbia was to include Ken Niles, Jack O'Connor, the hunting and shooting editor for *Outdoor Life*, Sheldon Coleman, of the Coleman Company in Wichita, Kansas, Dean Olds, the chief design engineer at Coleman, three other hunters and Roy Weatherby. Originally, Gary Cooper was to be included in the group but he had to cancel because of filming commitments. At the conclusion of the hunt, Jack O'Connor wrote a glowing report of this B.C. hunt for *Outdoor Life*, singing the praises of his .300 Weatherby Magnum rifle. Weatherby benefited tremendously from this type of publicity.

Jack O'Connor, Sheldon Coleman and Ken Niles were among the hunters accompanying Weatherby on a hunt into British Columbia in 1947. O'Connor and Coleman are in the back row, left and middle, respectively. Niles and Weatherby are on the front row, right and second from right.

1948 African Safari

As a result of their successful hunt in British Columbia, Jack O'Connor and Weatherby decided to organize a party of hunters to go on an African safari. Jack agreed to contact a number of potential hunters if Roy would organize and handle all the arrangements for the trip. The first thing they had to do was find an outfitter. It wasn't like it is today. Now there are agencies throughout America booking for outfits all over Africa, but in those days, Kerr and Downey, and a few other professional white hunters, were about the only ones anybody had ever heard of. In fact, there weren't too many sportsmen in 1948 who had even been to Africa.

Utilizing his promotional talents, Weatherby contacted British Overseas Airway Corp. and arranged for special fares. Included in his planned itinerary were stops in London, Paris, Cairo and Khartoum, and then to Nairobi for a six-week safari. The fee of $4,500 that Weatherby charged each hunter took care of their total expense, from New York and back to New York, and included hunting licenses, safari outfitter...everything. Weatherby was a novice in the business of running safaris or tours, and unplanned-for expenses caused him to lose about $5,000 for the whole trip. It was money that he didn't have to lose in the first place, but the trip was his dream of a lifetime.

The group departed for London on May 27th, 1948. This hunting trip was to be the first time in history that small caliber high velocity rifles would be used for the largest African game. Included in the party were Dr. Ed Nickelsen, owner of the Portland General Hospital; Dr. Curt Von Edel, a plastic surgeon from Oklahoma City, Oklahoma; Walter V. Storm, owner of the Western Brass Foundry in Los Angeles; A.J. Pejsa, owner of the Champion Brass Foundry in Los Angeles; Merrill Porter, developer of the City of Avalon, Catalina Island; and Robert K. Johnston and his son, from Oklahoma City, Oklahoma. Weatherby wanted this African trip not only for the adventure, but for the publicity and for the education he would gain.

Outdoor Life wouldn't let Jack O'Conner accompany the group to Africa. They felt that an article covering an African safari would not have that much readership appeal, for in those days there were too few that could afford to go to Africa.

In 1948, British East Africa had a Game Control Department and some large game preserves had been established. But the natives had always lived there and they felt that this was their land and their animals. To reduce poaching by the natives, the government wouldn't allow them to own guns, so they shot their game with bows and arrows, using poisoned arrows. They would shoot an elephant and then follow it for days, waiting for it to die. They would then take the tusks into Nairobi and sell them to the Indian merchants. Herds of Cape buffalo were killed just for their tongues. Rhinos were killed for their horns. Wildebeest were killed for their white tails which were sold as souvenirs.

Seeing a need for selective hunting for the control and thinning of game, the Kenya Game Control Department began issuing very liberal hunting licenses in the late 40's to foreign sportsmen. Their safaris brought money into the country, and since they were led by local white hunters, selection of the game that was shot could be regulated.

Into this British ruled colony of Kenya Roy Weatherby arrived with his hunting party, which included seven Weatherby-built magnum rifles of various calibers, handloaded Weatherby magnum cartridges,

Gen. Jimmy Doolittle, Weatherby, Walter Karabian and Elgin Gates, all past winners of the annual Cal-Pines Honker Hunt in Northern California, pose with the rotating trophy awarded to the best goose shot.

and great expectations. Weatherby was like the kid in the candy store, the fox in the henhouse. This was his chance to realize a long-time personal dream and to prove a highly speculative theory: that high velocity would kill more surely and humanely than high caliber.

The hunting bag limits were unbelievably liberal, such as three Cape buffalo, 20 zebra, one elephant per hunter. One hunting license included everything, with the exception of an additional $100 fee if you wanted to shoot a second elephant.

In addition to his rifles, ammunition and photographic equipment, Weatherby also took a Dictaphone with him into the wilds of Africa. Prior to his departure, he had reached an agreement with a local Los Angeles newspaper that he would keep a daily diary and send parts of it home when he could. The newspaper ran the diary as a serial. Weatherby sent his Dictabelts relating the events of each day home to his office, where his secretary transcribed them and furnished them to the newspaper.

When Weatherby got home he spent many hours in the darkroom of his garage, personally editing and preparing a thirty minute film on his African safari. From then on he was in great demand as a speaker for the various service organizations, schools, Rod & Gun clubs and the like. Many times people paid to see his films and hear him speak, with the proceeds going to charity. This film did not have a soundtrack and he would give a live narration during each showing. He always ended his presentation with a stirring talk comparing the benefits of living in the great land of America as compared to conditions he was able to personally observe in every other country that he visited.

Weatherby's Second African Safari

Ever since his first safari to Africa in 1948, and the publication of his diary, hunters from all over the country had contacted Weatherby for advice about planning their own hunt over there. The pamphlet he later developed in conjunction with TWA also resulted in more inquiries from hunters. Because of this connection with TWA, and the amount of business that he was able to send their way from hunters, Weatherby was given a free airline ticket around the world by TWA.

He had also sent so many clients to the various professional white hunters that several of them had offered him a free hunt in appreciation. He was also able to take advantage of a savings to his company in

On hunts, Roy was meticulous in documenting everything that happened, with notes, tapes, still photographs and movies.

airfare by combining this safari with his European business trip, where much was accomplished. So, once again the struggling entrepreneur used his promotional talents to reduce expenses.

In preparing for this safari, Weatherby arranged for a companion, Colonel Robert L. Scott, a man whom he had come to greatly admire, to go along. At the time Col. Scott was the U.S. commanding officer at Furstenfeldbruk air base in West Germany, and was quite a hunter. He joined Roy in Rome where they flew on to Africa together, and had a delightful and very successful month long hunt. When the African hunt was over, Col. Scott returned to his base while Weatherby and the third member of their party, Joe Shaw, vice president of the Bechtel Corporation in San Francisco, went on to India to hunt tiger.

Scott had been one of the original Flying Tigers who flew the China-Burma-India hump before the U.S. was actively engaged in World War II. He was already the author of a best seller, *God Is My Co-Pilot,* about his experiences as a Flying Tiger. He later wrote another book, *Between The Elephant's Eyes,* which was the story of his and Weatherby's African safari. It was another good bit of free publicity for Weatherby and his Magnum rifles.

Weatherby flew home from this grueling two month long sojourn via Japan, where he visited some of the optical companies that had expressed an interest in producing his scope.

With his near professional knowledge and skill with a camera, Weatherby had taken about 4,000 feet of 16mm movie film during his African and Indian safaris. He sold some of it to be used on a popular TV series, Ramar of The Jungle, and for years when the Weatherby family watched that series they saw his pictures in the background.

At the time of Weatherby's around-the-world trip in 1953 the jet airplane was not in widespread use at all. Most commercial flying was still being done in propeller-driven aircraft. However, BOAC had just put their Comet One jet into service on a flight from Beirut, Lebanon to Karachi, Pakistan, and Roy arranged to experience his first jet plane ride on this leg of his flight to India. The Comet One was a relatively small jet, holding only about 60 passengers, and was very noisy. Weatherby recalls the pilot announcing they had reached an altitude of 40,000 feet and were flying at 640 miles per hour, a speed unheard of prior to this. He felt as if he were participating in a bit of aeronautical history!

Kodiak Bear Hunt With Roy Rogers

In May of 1957 Roy Rogers and Roy Weatherby flew to Alaska on the first leg of a trip to hunt Kodiak bear. The famed Western film star attempted to keep his first vacation in 10 years a secret, but word of his arrival leaked out. He was besieged by autograph fans as he stepped off the airplane in Fairbanks. He was dressed from head to toe in Western regalia, although his fancy silver tipped cowboy boots and wide brimmed Stetson were set off by an Alaskan touch, a parka.

At Terror Bay on Kodiak Island they were met by Kris Helgason, who proved to be an excellent Alaskan guide and camp host. After several days of hunting, and almost freezing on the boat, Weatherby

121

Roy Rogers scans the shoreline of Kodiak Island for bear activity while Weatherby warms up with a cup of coffee. The two Roys hunted Kodiak bear in 1957.

was becoming discouraged, beginning to think there was nothing on the Island except female bears and their cubs.

Luck changed on the fourth day out, when Roy spotted a bear. At about 250 yards away and higher up the mountainside, the bear looked awfully big. But the 150-gr. Hornady bullet from the .300 Weatherby went right through him and he just rolled down the mountainside. It was a nice trophy measuring almost nine feet.

Roy to Roy. Weatherby congratulates Rogers on his Kodiak bear.

Alaskan Polar Bear Hunt

In May of 1959, Weatherby and Elgin Gates embarked on a seven-day hunt for polar bear in Alaska. Their guide was Tommy Thompson. Weatherby and Gates had each hunted the world over, but later both men agreed that polar bear hunting was entirely different than any other, and very exciting.

Polar bear hunting was always done with two airplanes, a safety precaution in case one should be forced down or become disabled. Weather was often a problem. The first four days of their trip were spent at their base camp in Kotzebue, an Eskimo village about 200 miles north of Nome, waiting for suitable flying weather.

But, according to Weatherby, it was the arctic ice as well as weather conditions that made his hunt so difficult. Terrific pressures build up under the ice causing it to crumble and be forced upwards, forming ridges as high as a house, thus offering few good smooth landing spots for the small Cub airplanes.

Weatherby got his bear on the fifth day, using a 180-grain bullet in his .300 Weatherby Magnum, about 200 miles west of Kotzebue and only about 30 miles from the Siberian border. Having just crossed the international date line and shooting west across this imaginary line, Weatherby maintained that he shot at the bear on Friday but hit him on Saturday!

123

Roy took this huge polar bear out of Kotzebue, Alaska, during a 1959 hunt with Elgin Gates, a good friend who was the recipient of the Weatherby Award in 1960, and who later founded the very successful International Handgun Metallic Silhouette Association.

Upon spotting his bear, Weatherby and his guide landed on a rough piece of ice, making it impossible for the other plane to land beside them. Then, by the time he got out of the plane and climbed over a couple of these pressure ridges the bear was hundreds of yards, too far to shoot. It actually took four landings before he could get a shot.

The next day Weatherby and Gates flew about 700 miles and passed up at least a half dozen bears without finding one suitable for Gates. They flew as far north as Point Barrow, and back down along the coast to Kotzebue with no luck. On the seventh and last day of their hunt, however, they flew south of Kotzebue, just north of the Diomedes, and Gates got a bear almost the same size as Weatherby had shot two days earlier.

Elgin had a much easier shot and as he and his pilot landed Weatherby's plane circled while Roy took photographs of this kill. The bear jumped into one of the open leads, and eventually gave Elgin a 50-yard shot when he climbed back on the ice.

Roy thought that one of the most difficult things about arctic hunting was skinning the bears. Gloves had to be changed frequently to keep hands from freezing, and the hide usually froze before the skinning could be completed. The weight of Weatherby's bear was estimated to be about 1300 pounds. The skin measured more than 11 feet long, and the skull was 28-3/4 inches, which at that time was only about 3/4 of an inch smaller than the world record.

Upon his return, Weatherby had his bear mounted by Bert Kline-burger in an upright position. It made a beautiful mount standing more than nine feet tall, and was displayed in his retail store.

Roy's African Diary

Roy Weatherby was a meticulous note taker and memo writer, which is very fortunate for the sake of Weatherby records. He was also a very avid, prolific writer, quite good, and this is a fascinating diary Roy kept during his first safari to Africa, to Kenya, in 1948. Read it and you will get the flavor of Africa, the sounds and sights of a safari, brought to you by a man who was a keen observer.

This was a very long safari, and the diary itself is long, rambling, and sometimes repetitive. It's valuable from several standpoints, particularly in that it describes the awe with which a first-time visitor viewed Kenya. Keep in mind that this hunt took place more than 40 years ago when very few Americans had ever hunted Africa. The impressions and predictions of a young Roy Weatherby are even more interesting when viewed from that perspective.

Most readers will not want to read the diary straight through at one sitting, but browsing through portions of it on long winter nights will transport us into a hunting world that has been drastically changed by the intervening decades.

My African Diary

by
Roy E. Weatherby

1948 This is a day-by-day diary of my recent trip to Africa. The diary was written mostly as the things where happening—it gives fresh impressions just as they came to me.

The first of the diary of the African safari

I can't help reminiscing over the past two weeks— the flight from New York to London, over the North Atlantic; our stop at Gander, Newfoundland; our next stop in Ireland— then to London—the Pilot of our Constellation flying low over Windsor Castle. An hour or so later we were on our way to the city of Paris. We boarded the French Airlines and across the Channel—Paris came in just a few hours—then all we had heard, seen in pictures and read about began to unveil before our very eyes—the old buildings, lots of trees, the very old taxicabs, the Follies, the Night Clubs, the girls on the streets—a trip to Versailles—all of this and more—This was Paris! Even though it was grand, I was disappointed, seemed as though they were so far behind the times—my impression of Paris was not good.

Back to London—London seems to be more reserved, sedate and dignified—the buildings are so old. It rained two days and was quite cool. We stopped at The Savoy Hotel—old but lovely. We saw the city, the bombings and it was terrible. So many buildings still remain in ruin—London is having a hard time and one feels very sorry for the people.

Then on to Tripoli—stayed overnight there. Camels, Arabs, desert— all very interesting. Next morning at 4 o'clock we were on our way to Cairo—a three hour stop and trip about the city. Words cannot describe this fascinating desert metropolis— the great Nile River—the Pyramids—and all of ancient history in front of our eyes—it's all hard to believe!

Then on to Khartoum, where we spent the night. Bought rugs and hides from the rug peddlers, looked at the great Nile and early next morning on our way again to Nairobi. Now we find ourselves in the heart of Africa—a dream few ever realize.

Here we are in Nairobi—we flew from Khartoum directly to Nairobi, the capital of Kenya Colony. The nearest city of any size is Mombasa, which is the seaport for East Africa. If you remember your geography, the elevation rises at the Indian Ocean to approximately 5,000 or 6,000 feet, then levels off and stretches over the great plateau of East Africa. It then drops down into the Riff Valley but on this plateau one will find Nairobi. The population there is about 60,000 with 40,000 of people natives or blacks and 20,000 Europeans or white people. It is a much more modern town than one would expect to find in Africa.

Addis Ababa lies 750 miles north of Nairobi and Mombasa about 200 miles southeast.

The temperature is very moderate the year around—never hot and never cold, even though Nairobi lies almost on the Equator. The town has very many modern buildings such as we would find in our own country in a city of like population, with gas, water and telephones. Of course they are not nearly as far advanced as we are in the United States.

From the airport we went to the Norfolk Hotel where we had previously made our reservations. This hotel is several blocks out of the main part of the city, in a very quiet and beautiful setting. We spent a few days in Nairobi before going out in the field, getting our licenses and various hunting permits. The elephant license costs $200 and general license costs between $200 and $300, depending where one is going to hunt.

June 7th:

Ten days ago we left New York—ten days of exotic excitement—every day, every hour something new and different, but today is it. This is the "D" day of our hunt. We left the Norfolk Hotel at 5:00 this morning—a lorry and a truck—all loaded with gear. We traveled until 6:20 a.m. over a hard surfaced road—but rough. There is very little twilight here, and one has a feeling of excitement which is hard to describe.

Soon it became daylight—altitude 7,500 feet—it was very cold. I had my down jacket and how welcome it was—we came to the Great Riff Wall—there you look down into the Riff Canyon, a great expanse of valley—thousands of feet below you—there the game abounds by the millions—this is really spectacular—on down into the Riff and off on a small narrow dusty trail, for miles. Our first game to be seen was three giraffe, then a mile or so further came a lone giraffe—then a herd of

127

Grant's gazelles— now a herd of Thompson gazelles—on and on we see different species of antelope—here is a Secretary bird—a greater bustard— Oh, this is out of this world! The farther we go, the more game we see.

At 11:30 a.m. we get to the District Commissioner at the native village of Narok. We have to check in with him. Oh, these people— they are the Masai tribe, tall and slender, wearing just a hide over their shoulders—they live more like animals than people. You see them along the road herding their cattle and goats, the tall men with their spears— they almost frighten a person. We stopped to take pictures of some on the road—the women cover their faces and hover over their children so you couldn't get their pictures—a superstition I guess.

At this village Merrill Porter took a box of Wrigley's Chewing Gum and gave it to the natives. I took pictures of this— they just didn't know what to do with it—they all stood about in a huddle, chattering and tasting the gum.

We left the village and started West—mile after mile—more game than before, herd after herd as far as one could see—zebra, giraffe, gazelles, ostrich, wildebeest, eland, etc., then, as for those birds and animals classed as "vermin"— jackal, hyena, mongoose, hawks, crows, great huge birds, half the size of an ostrich—many with a spread of over seven feet.

My first kill in Kenya was about 5:00 p.m. on June 8th— I shot a jackal. He was only about 40 yards away—this was the first time our guns cracked in Africa. I shot him with my .270 Weatherby Magnum. We turned off the road to go to a special spot the Hunter knew of where there should be lion, buffalo and elephant. First, let me tell you, for miles you travel over a trail with your truck and safari cars, over plains dotted with flattop thorn trees—then you come into higher grass and thicker trees. You get into almost a jungle—you see monkeys and baboons scampering from limb to limb—a topi jumps up in front of us— we pass over huge elephant tracks—we see beautiful birds and beautiful flowers—everything is so green. The turnoff into the semi-jungle was almost disastrous—rocks, hidden in high grass.

It rained, darkness came, we got stuck in the marsh with both of our vehicles. Finally we had to camp for the night. Grass was wet and the ground was wet, but we managed after many tries to build a fire. We ate dik-dik for dinner— forgot to tell you—we came upon three of them under a tree—we stopped; I took the .270 Weatherby Magnum, aimed and missed. The animals were not over 30 yards distant. I had to hit him in the head or neck so as to have meat for our dinner. A dik-dik is the smallest of the Antelope family, not much larger than a large jack rabbit. Well, I didn't know just how or where to hold the rifle for a close shot like that, but the little devils—they didn't even run after I had shot. I took a different aim and let go again—this time I hit it in the neck—so, dik-dik we had for dinner—-and may I say it is good— very good.

After dinner, at 10:30 p.m., the boys had our cots all up, sheets and blankets—this wasn't bad. Mosquitoes weren't either, but we used our mosquito nets nevertheless. The sky was beautiful— the stars so bright, the Milky Way so clear— the howl and laugh of the hyenas just outside our camp, the cry of the night birds—and all the other night noises, gave one a feeling hard to describe in words—so this is darkest Africa! Not long after we had gone to sleep, in spite of the hyena and jackal noises, came a sound most terrifying—a lion. I awoke, sat up in a half stupor with a fearful feeling. I soon realized where I was and what it was, and went back to sleep. Another time, before morning, he woke me again with his growl and semi-roar. I turned over and went back to sleep, with a firm, undisputable conviction that this is Africa and that there is not another place in the world like it. It's easy to forget all else. This is so fascinating!

JUNE 9th:

Wednesday, 8:00 a.m. We are waiting for the boys to prepare our breakfast and we will then be on our way for another adventure, new and different from yesterday. We had a bad rod on the Chevrolet truck—our Hunter had to repair it. While they worked on that, we men, with one of the natives, took out for a bit of a hunt. We hadn't gone 500 yards until we came upon three warthogs—well, Merrill shot one with his .257 Weatherby Magnum, and I shot another with my .270 Magnum—as the third one ran through the tall grass, I shot it too, so we bagged three warthogs. They make nice, but ugly, trophies. No sooner did we have them skinned out than the buzzards appeared.

This is a beautiful day, but on the warm side. It rained last night and humidity is high this morning. Everywhere we go, every place we turn, we see game—thousands upon thousands of head. The ground is soft, the grass is tall. This is a place that no one can believe until they are here to see and hear. It has looked like rain all day—dark clouds in the West. About the middle of the afternoon, after passing thousands of all kinds of game, we came upon a waterbuck with a very good head, according to my White Hunter. He said "You better shoot this one, he's a good one." I jumped out of the lorry, ran down through the timber and let him have a shot from my .270 Weatherby Magnum— one was all that was necessary, and down he went. Yes, he was a beauty—horns 27 inches—the record is 30 inches—this was my first big kill, a waterbuck. I had shot a dik-dik, two warthogs, but this was a real trophy. Pictures were taken; 30 minutes later our skinners had the head and hide on the truck and off we went, and none too soon for the sky was black. You could hear the rain behind us, as well as see it, and it was coming faster than we were traveling. Remember, there is no road here— we're just bouncing along over the plains. Soon the rain came—we must get to our camp site in spite of the record trophies. We did come near to a reedbuck—our hunter told us we should shoot this one as the head was a good one. In spite of the driving rain, I jumped out, shot three times at that leaping reedbuck as he ran across the plain—he was a good 250 yards and better than 300 when I fired my last shot. Too bad. Can't hit every time.

Soon we came to a river—the Mara River— a beautiful jungle. We're at the end of the road and this is our camp—this is where we will make our home for weeks and weeks—no one could ever find us—I don't know where we are myself, except that we are some place in Africa— way back in Africa. This is a beautiful jungle—monkeys in the trees by the hundreds. Parrots and all sorts of beautiful tropical birds. Of all the jungle noises, one never heard the like—all kinds of sounds—how I wish I had brought a recording machine. These sounds would be invaluable to a lover of nature or for sound pictures.

It's still raining slowly. Our camp is up now—the men worked hard and in the rain. We have our tent—a bed or cot for Dr. Nickelsen, Merrill Porter and myself, as well as Harry, the photographer from B.O.A.C. We have a cook or dining tent—then the White Hunters have theirs. The Negroes have theirs also.

This is a safari camp—a real one. We have hot water in front of our tent in a canvas basin, very good meals and we sleep between sheets. But we must have mosquito netting—the mosquitoes are not bad, no comparison to those in the North Country of the United States.

With bag limits amazingly liberal back in those days of 1948 when Roy made his first African safari, he shot dozens of animals and carefully recorded the effects of the shots from his Weatherby calibers—good and bad.

However, these carry malaria and yellow fever—they are dangerous. In spite of my protection, they chewed on me plenty last night.

JUNE 10th

Morning came—it's daylight—this is it, another "D" day. This is what we have waited for. Today we are going HUNTING—we're going to look for elephant and buffalo—but now it's bacon and eggs for breakfast—our guns in preparedness, we're off for the day! I'm going to use my .270 Weatherby Magnum. Merrill Porter is using his .257 Weatherby Magnum and Doctor is using my .300 Weatherby Magnum. I can't see why we don't shoot some of the many herds of animals we pass but our White Hunter is looking for **big stuff** and only "records" in the game on the plains.

We drive for an hour or so and come upon a herd of zebra. Our first zebra—it's Doctor's first shot—he misses— can't see why, he is only 200 yards from the animal. So, the next zebra I shoot with my .270 Magnum—a shot in the shoulder put him down in 20 yards. He is dark brown and white. While we were skinning him out, Doctor walked some 300 yards and shot his with my .270 Magnum—one shot and the 700 to 800 pound zebra was dead. While the two zebra are being skinned out we have time to waste. Merrill and I walk a few hundred yards away and stalk a nice "Tommy"—that's the Thompson gazelle—a

131

cute little animal—wonderful eating. Merrill shot his with my .257 Magnum, at some 250 yards. Mine I shot with my 300 about 200 yards distant. We will eat them for dinner tonight. The head of mine will decorate my den some time this year and with it will remain a memory hard to forget. This is my fourth trophy. Now it stands a warthog, waterbuck (a beauty) a zebra and a Tommy.

The sky is clouding up—it's beautiful, and rain is coming we know but we keep on and on, passing countless game on all sides—a lone giraffe, and topi by the thousands—more than any other game. We won't shoot any now, we can get them any time. Soon it began to rain again, but we're nearing camp—we stop in the rain to shoot a topi, for lion bait—but while they were hanging the game we spotted a large hyena. Merril, Doctor and I started slipping up on it—we arrived— Doctor shot my .270 Weatherby Magnum and down went the hyena— some 200 yards away—broke his back, but he wasn't dead—it took a shot from my Colt to put him out. A hyena is a large, ugly animal— must weigh about 100 to 150 pounds—this one was a mangy looking fellow—it was our first one. His hide was so bad we just couldn't take him in with us.

We arrived at camp about 1:00 p.m.—now for lunch—we're hungry too. This afternoon we must sight in everyone's rifle again. I spent the entire afternoon sighting in all the shootin' irons. At 4:00 p.m. our Hunter goes out for lion bait— Merrill goes along. Dr. Nickelsen fishes in the river with a line, a hook and a stick. Tonight we eat fish, and it's good. It really didn't rain today but it sure looked as though it was going to. There is plenty to keep one busy here—have I been that way since I left that day, May 23rd. There isn't any use trying to tell you how wonderful Africa is—the pictures I have, the game we see—it is all unbelievable. This morning when we came out of our tent we saw in the top of a tree, just in front of us, more than 50 parrots—beautiful—a stork in the top of another tree—a monkey in another—that is Africa.

Night has fallen—it is 8:45 p.m. We are finishing our dinner of Doctor's fish and our Tommy gazelle—Oh, what a dinner—ending with stewed prunes. I'm going to bed early tonight with the thought in my mind that I've seen more game in the past three days than there is in the entire North American Continent. One cannot believe or comprehend—without being here in person—it matters little whether or not we get a full bag—the trip is worth a million to any true sportsman.

JUNE 11th:

Today is Friday—I had a good night's rest— retired at 9:00 p.m.—the night was cool and very comfortable—each night we sleep under mosquito netting. We were awakened by the Negroes at 5:00 a.m., long before daylight—to hear the silence broken by the baboons, monkeys, parrots and other African bird and animal sounds—it nearly makes one think they are in a large bird sanctuary. It was quite cool, I didn't want to get up very badly— but remembering we had put out lots of lion bait last night gave me added strength. Tea was brought to our tent, and before daylight we had our gear in the Lorry and ready to go. No lion but we saw almost everything else under the sun. White, fleecy clouds dotted the sky—beautiful it was—no wind, just right. I shot a Tommy that had nice horns.

We came back to camp for breakfast at 8:00 a.m.—to leave again before 10:00. We had gazelle liver, then off again to roam the great expanse of these African plains and jungles—baboons and monkeys, by the thousands, frolic and chatter in the trees everywhere—at any time you can look up from camp and see them—you just can't miss seeing them.

This afternoon Merrill shot a nice impala with a beautiful head—with his .300 Magnum, using a 180-grain Corelokt bullet. About 250 yards away with one shot. It ran about 75 yards— the only explanation being that the Corelokt bullet is so heavily constructed that it did not break up—it expanded well and passed on through, but if it had been a bronze point expanding bullct, it would have caused much more damage, I'm sure.

We passed herd after herd of zebra, giraffe, topi, wildebeest, a few warthogs, hyena, bat eared fox and jackal, and stopped under a tree out in this great wonderland for a bite of lunch. The sun comes straight down here and it's quite warm, but not over 80 degrees—it was 50 degrees this morning. While we were under the trees cleaning out some of our game that we had shot, Merrill Porter kept eying an eland off about a mile or so—he figured he could walk out to the windward side of it and possibly get within a few hundred yards. We all thought it rather folly, but he went ahead. We watched through binoculars with the greatest of interest. The eland looked the other way—he was completely unaware of the danger creeping up on him. Merril slipped up behind the only tree between himself and the animal, which he estimated must be about 400 yards away. Suddenly the eland sensed danger and rose to his feet—instantly Merril aimed, and crack went his rifle—the eland ran—Merril fired a second shot as the animal collapsed one shot went into the shoulder and one in the rump— Merrill was using his .300 Weatherby Magnum and 180-grain Corelokt bullet—he was 357 yards away when he shot—an eland weighs between 1200 and 1400 pounds—they are the largest of all the antelope family— they are really huge. No sooner did we have this fellow skinned than thousands of buzzards, vultures, maribou stork appeared for the clean- up—in less than an hour there was nothing left but bones, every last vestige of meat was gone. Tonight the hyena and jackal will come and carry off the bones—tomorrow the ground will be bare—this is Africa—a sight one can never forget. I took motion pictures of this great phenomenon.

We hadn't gone far until we came to a herd of about 40 or 50 giraffe—you can come to within 75 yards of the herd and I acquired some outstanding pictures of them. It wasn't 30 minutes later that we came upon a hyena that I'm sure weighed upward of 180 pounds— large and ugly. I shot him with my .257 Magnum, hitting in the front legs only, high toward the shoulder—he didn't die until he ran 10 yards—then just fell over—nothing can withstand the shock of high velocity bullets, even when not hit in a vital spot.

A short while later we came upon 3 lion—this was our first glimpse of lion—a lioness and two almost full grown cubs—you drive the Lorry within 30 yards of them—they just look at you, then turn around and saunter off into the tall grass—again I remind you that these things are only seen one place in the world, and that is Africa.

We just keep looking for record or near record animals—it isn't a question of getting your game—for you could shoot a thousand head of animals in one single day—if you chose to.

It's 6:30 p.m., Friday now—we're back in camp—I'm sitting here without a shirt, writing this—the temperature is about 70 degrees—the sounds of the birds and monkeys are very stimulating and won't allow one to forget he is in Africa, in a country where few white men have ever traveled—we haven't even encountered any native villages here—

Roy on his first African safari. Note the big shortwave receiver on the table.

I'm lost—but I guess our White Hunter knows how to find his way back. Tomorrow we are going to look for buffalo and maybe elephant.

JUNE 12th:

Saturday is here. It is cloudy this morning. We were awakened by our boys with hot tea as usual—this comes each morning about 5:30. We go out to inspect our lion bait—we are back for breakfast about 9:30—we didn't see any lion at all—saw two hyena and scores of other animals. Merrill stalked and shot a beautiful waterbuck—with 27-inch horns—as I have said before, the waterbuck is a very handsome animal, so well formed, so sleek looking, they weigh about 400 pounds. Merrill shot him with the .300 Weatherby Magnum, using 180-grain Corelokt bullet, at 280 yards—the bullet passed through his shoulder and stopped just before it passed through the skin on the other side. The Buck went down—the bullet had lost a lot of velocity by the time it reached the animal—Merrill is very proud of this beautiful specimen and rightly so he should be.

For breakfast this morning we had cornflakes, bacon and eggs— "Tain't bad at all!" By the way—I must say a word about our table waiter, who is really a character. He wears a white, full length coat and a green vest and green fez. Nice fellow. None of these blacks speak or

135

understand English—they speak Swahili. We are learning some Swahili, but very little, however we have over a month to stay in here. It looks like rain today, but nevertheless it's a beautiful one—temperature is 65 degrees.

As I sit here at the table, the anvil birds keep sounding off—they sound exactly like a blacksmith's anvil. It is now 6:00 p.m. and our day is nearing an end—every day different and exciting—we were looking for lion again today, but didn't see any. Early this morning, Dr. Nickelsen shot an impala—a beauty, too—with 28-inch horns, but he really had a time. The Doctor is using one of my rifles—the .270 Weatherby Magnum, with scope sight—he isn't used to the rifle, his first shot was almost a miss—the impala ran away—we all trailed that animal until we found him—this was the first one we didn't get in his tracks. Well, that's the way it goes. We passed hundreds more, herd after herd of them, but we're looking for one with a big spread. We passed up six warthogs today—none of them with record tusks. Saw two hyena but we didn't want to shoot them because of scaring other game around—however, the animals of Africa seem to pay little attention to gun shots.

It rained a little, but not much—it has been cloudy most of the day—never got over 75 degrees. We saw several giraffe, and thousands of topi—these topi are everywhere, they are a very excitable animal—as soon as you approach them, trying to get in range of a huge eland, they snort, lunge, stamp and stampede, scaring all the other game. We are allowed three of them but we can get them any time, just a few minutes walk from camp. There must be millions of them in Africa. They say there are more zebra than any other animal, but in this district I think the topi and Tommies are first—these little Tommies are cute little fellows—We're allowed nine of them—I'm bringing home four with me—two of most everything else. It isn't a question over here of "if" you are going to get them—you know in advance you are going to get them, for they are here for the shooting.

This afternoon we came upon a most pitiful sight—we saw an animal raise its head some 50 yards to our right—we turned the Lorry over in that direction and slowly rose a hyena with the entire top of his head bitten or chewed off—his vertebrae were showing—the flies had taken their toll—it was alive with larvae—his rear end was badly torn and bitten—how he was still able to live is beyond comprehension. He was able to half run from us—we put him out of his misery with my .257.

On closer examination, it made one turn away, it was simply unde-scribable. A bit farther on we found a dead zebra, killed by a lion we suppose, but the buzzards were cleaning him up. The hyena had either been in a fight with a lion or some of his own kind. At the end of a day, it is hard to go back and reconstruct the day's experiences for it seems a lifetime of experience happens in each day—I can't forget the hundreds of baboon scampering to the timber as we came to within 50 yards of them—the motion pictures we are taking will be more than interesting when we return.

Last night the hyena awakened us just outside our tent—not over 50 yards distant—with their undescribable howl and high pitched laugh.

It is now 6:00 p.m.—temperature is about 60 degrees—we are listening to the Zenith short wave radio we have with us—the United States is hard to get—last night we picked up New York and heard part of a ball game. Dinner is over—the men are all around the table, talking over the day's experiences.

JUNE 13th:

Sunday—it's now 3:00 p.m.—back in California it is only 6 o'clock in the morning, but our day here is coming to an end—we will be sleeping soundly before Californians have their noonday lunch. Tried very hard last night to get an American station on the short wave radio—but just couldn't—reception is poor. We get London, South Africa, China and all of Europe, but not America. I'm hungry for some news from home—we'll be in here weeks yet before we even get out to get mail—that is the life of an African safari.

The boys brought up tea again this morning—you drink it too—for a sorta waker-upper—before daybreak. We're off again to inspect our lion bait. At one bait there were five ugly hyena—at the other bait nothing but buzzards—but at the third bait, the lion has been there—we had a huge waterbuck that we had shot the day before, high in the tree—but the lion got it—they jump for it and sometimes we don't have it high enough—they got it down and dragged it for 25 yards— then apparently carried it. Now a waterbuck, with his head and hide gone, will still weigh about 350 pounds, but they had to carry it, as there were no signs of anything being dragged through the grass any further than about 25 yards.

This afternoon the boys are out to put up another kill—maybe tomorrow we will be more successful. This morning I shot another impala—at 175 yards with my .257 Magnum—one shot, that's all, and they just fold up. So now I have my two nice trophies. We came back to camp, had our breakfast, caught up on some writing. We're going out of here in another week to pick up mail and to mail our letters at a native village—it will take a man all day and maybe two days to get out and back—no one could ever find us I'm sure, for I guess God only knows where we are—I'm sure I don't—all I know is that we are in the most beautiful country I've ever seen in my life. The Doctor and Porter, as well as the B.O.A.C. photographer, are out this afternoon again, but I just had to stay in camp and get caught up on some odds and ends—things happen so fast, one has little time to spare.

It is now about 4:00 p.m.—the sun is shining, a few beautiful white clouds float in the sky—the native boys are all busy with their duties—they afford the birds competition with their constant chant as they work—one of them is ironing clothes—two of them are skinning out heads of our trophies—the cook is busy preparing our dinner—there are seven of them here in camp now; about 75 yards from where I sit are the skinners—and about 20 yards from there sit about a dozen vultures and buzzards ready to pounce on every scrap the skinners leave.

As I look west across the river, I can see three monkeys and two baboons sitting high in the top of one of Africa's fig trees—these trees are as large as any elm tree I ever saw—in fact, they are very large with heavy foliage—beautiful trees too. This morning when coming back to camp, I counted 73 baboon, not over 50 yards from our Lorry, scampering back to the dense jungle—now and then, one would sit on top of one of the smaller ant hills to look us over—sometimes it's hard to tell them from the natives—except for their size.

By the way—back home one hears a lot about these ant hills—well sir, you should see them—when the big black ants make them they start out small, end up 10 to 12 feet high and perhaps 20 to 30 feet in diameter at the base—during the rains, these hills green up with the rest of the terrain and they make fine "lookout" points.

It's rather lonesome here in camp alone—these natives can't speak my language and I can't speak theirs!

In a continuation of his research on the effectiveness of his Weatherby calibers, Roy took this rhino on safari in Africa in 1978.

It's 6:30 p.m. now—Merrill and the Doctor just came back from hunting—Doctor shot at a waterbuck but apparently it was not a good shot as the animal ran away.

JUNE 14th:

7:30 a.m.—We had a good night's rest—in spite of the hyena. We are out after our bait again—again no lion, but the devils have carried away our waterbuck that we had hanging in the tree and they carried away a zebra that we had in another tree—that proves they are here all right. We hunted all day today for buffalo and lion. Doctor shot his waterbuck, a fine one, too, with my .270 Magnum, about 150 yards. The waterbuck went down with a shoulder shot. When we skinned this fellow out, one could hardly imagine an animal being able to move after being shot the way he was with that .270 Magnum—he was torn up inside terribly. Later on in the morning, Merrill shot his first topi at some 150 yards, with his .300 W. Magnum—down and dead in one shot. In the afternoon Doctor went out with the assistant White Hunter and shot another impala, with the same .270 Magnum. Late in the afternoon we came upon a herd of eland—this is a very wild animal and it is very difficult to get close to them. I crawled on hands and knees for 200 yards, came up by a clump of thorn trees—then behold, I couldn't see them for the grass and tree limbs around me—couldn't make out the big horns—they saw me first, and off they ran. We passed herd after herd of giraffe and zebra.

We saw a very interesting sight on the way into camp—a female impala with a little calf ran down our road in front of us, the little fellow following closely behind. She soon realized she couldn't run fast enough to keep ahead of us and not leave her calf, so she turns to the left—out through the tall grass—hides her calf—keeps on running, circles on around back of us and back to her calf, then stopped. This was a highlight in our day. Last night the hyena were the worst they have ever been—their howl and hideous high-pitched laugh—there must have been a hundred of them.

JUNE 15th:

Today is Tuesday—we are moving camp today—there just doesn't seem to be lion in here—at least not enough, so we're packing up and moving on to better grounds.

JUNE 16th:

Most of the 15th was spent moving camp. We are in another beautiful location on the Tarlec River—oh, it is a wonderful place—game everywhere. It is about 20 miles from our other camp. In moving, we passed thousands of head of game. The hyena and lion kept us awake some last night. There are no monkeys or baboon here. One of the drivers and I are leaving for Nairobi this morning—the rest are out after lion—they are here, we could hear them all night. Nick, the young Hunter, and I take off over the African plains for Nairobi—it is 180 miles—there is no road—nothing—just tall grass and thorn trees. Again, we pass countless thousands of head of game—all kinds. We pass through a boggy, muddy place—get stuck in the mud and for three hours we work trying to get out of the hole we're in. In another hour we get stuck again—it takes 30 minutes this time to get out. Then, at 2:30 p.m. we bog down in a place that doesn't look bad at all, but nevertheless, we're again stuck in the mud. We were trying to make Nairobi tonight but it looks doubtful—for two hours we work—Harry, the B.O.A.C. Photographer, the driver, myself and one native that we have with us—but to no avail—we're in and can't get out. As a last resort, we send the native on foot to an Indian outpost where a truck is kept—the native says he knows where it is, but doesn't know how far (it was learned later to be 15 miles). This native walked and ran—during this time we three men worked until dark trying to get out—our wheels are down clear to the hubs—we're in hopelessly! When darkness came, we sat in the cab of the truck. The moon was high over head—there was a brisk breeze, rather uncomfortably cold. The sounds of the odd birds and animals of the plains came to us, the mournful howl of the hyena—they came to within 50 yards of our truck—you could see them in the moonlight. So this is the Great Leota Plains of Africa—a weird feeling comes over one when you realize how far from home and how far from any sort of civilization you are.

At 9:00 p.m. we saw a light some 10 miles ahead—we knew it was help—we rejoiced, for we then knew we would not have to spend the night there—remembering we did not have any bedding, no coats, no food, NOTHING—there was absolutely no wood for a fire of any kind. For well over an hour, we watched that light come closer; finally, after waiting almost an eternity, it arrived with our native boy Mohaman (we call him) who made the distance, barefooted, as they all are—along with him was the Indian (now that's an India Indian) and five Masai natives; they had a large dual wheel General Motors Army truck with all equipment. They worked with us until midnight before we were out. We had to keep on, we couldn't stop, but they were then stuck—this mighty five-ton vehicle. When we hit dry ground we waited nearly an hour. We knew we could be of no help to them as we had no equipment, so we drove on, but only for about 45 minutes—we were down in the mud again; for over an hour we worked. We realized that sooner or later the big truck would be along and help us. Harry and I sat in the truck cab—the driver and Mohaman lay down in the truck bed. We stayed there until daylight. Oh, what a night, in deepest Africa! We'll never forget it.

When daylight came, we worked diligently for an hour, then freed the truck, but by this time we were running low on gas—NEVER, NEVER let yourself be caught on the plains of Africa without food and equipment—I can assure you we won't ever again.

Two, three—maybe five—miles an hour is the time we made, but we were out about 8:00 a.m. We came to the trail—not road—that leads to Norok. We have 10 miles yet to go—we get four gallons of gas at the

Indian's place—15 miles from where we were stranded. As we were waiting there, along came a safari car with New York license plates. I stopped them and here it was Mr. Gilbert—one of the men in the party of Sandy McNab's, who with Lou Coulter just drove from Cape Town. Jack Holliday will meet them here in August to join their big game hunt. They are camped just a mile from where we met them.

We drove on to Norok where Col. Sandy McNab and Sidney Downey were trying to put a call through to Nairobi—only a hundred miles away—this was where Gilbert said they would be. Norok is a Masai native village. Had a nice visit with Sandy McNab and Downey—nice fellows—picked up the mail, the letters from home— one has little idea of how much mail from home means when one is so far away. We filled up with gas, bought a can of pineapple at the native store—this native store is something one can hardly believe—remember now, we haven't had a bite to eat since early yesterday morning; the pineapple was wonderful.

Soon we were on our way to Nairobi, the road is now a little better but not much, and arrived there at 3:00 p.m. Now, we've been two days and a night traveling 180 miles—that's Africa!

More letters from home at Nairobi. Immediately we arrange for another truck as the one we have is pretty well shot. No room available at the Norfolk Hotel and after much effort on the part of the Hotel, they arranged a room at the Torres Hotel—a rather nice place but like the others, all native help who speak Swahili only—wear long white gowns and barefooted.

Dinner at 8:00 p.m.—wonderful and how welcome!

Tonight I'm tired and sleepy—tomorrow noon we start back over the same unforeseen hazardous terrain, but I love it—it's Africa in the raw—a country unpopulated and uncivilized. As I have said before, it just cannot be imagined by one who has not been here!

JUNE 18th:

7:00 a.m. at the Torres Hotel in Nairobi—good night's rest. I needed that after night before last spent on the Great Leota Plains. Purchased some blankets today for the new native we are taking back with us. We are taking back two more skinners and two more native men to work about camp. I have arranged for another truck from the Government Locust Control—it is a new one, built just for safari. It was only through a lot of drag that we were able to get this truck—John Dubell of Mitchell Cotts arranged it all for me. By 1:30 I had told Harry Hensser of B.O.A.C. good-bye—he has been lots of company. He has his pictures and his story—he is going to call it "Two Moon Safari." Well, it was hard to say good-bye to such a swell fellow. The truck pulled up at the hotel and we were again on our way to camp. It took us nearly six hours to go to Norok, a mere 87 miles—that will give you an idea of the road. We left Nairobi at 2:00 p.m. and arrived in Norok at 8:00 p.m. We filled up with gas, drove up to the District Commissioner's house and stayed with him and his wife all night. They put me up in their guest house—a house built of small limbs covered with grass and mud, just like the native huts—it was very cool, almost cold.

JUNE 19th:

6:00 a.m. came all too soon—we were on our last lap back to camp, took all day—until 3:00 p.m. to travel 70 miles, no roads, just African plains and small trails. There is no use going into detail about the game we saw for no one would believe me—zebra, Grant's and Thompson's gazelle, wildebeest, topi, hartebeest, hyena, bat eared fox, giraffe, ostrich and on and on. At no time of day can you look out over the plains without seeing hundreds and hundreds of game.

I was very glad to get back to camp and felt very fortunate that we didn't again get stuck in the Leota Plains. When we arrived at camp, we found that Merrill Porter shot a beautiful lion— he got it the morning we left for Nairobi.

The lion was with his mate and they report they had a very difficult time driving her away. After the kill they discovered that the lion had pulled a zebra back into the bush. He shot this lion with the 150-grain bullet in his .300 W.M.

Porter also shot his buffalo yesterday, with his .300 W. Magnum, but from what he tells me, a buffalo takes a lot of killing. He shot it twice with his .300 Magnum and the White Hunter shot it once with his .470 and his .375—they take a lot of killing. I wasn't there, of course, but I'll be there to report first handed from now on.

This afternoon I saw a sight I'll never forget—four lion under a tree—we drove very close to them, then drove on a few hundred yards and shot a topi—dragged it back to where the lion were and dropped it off. No sooner had we driven off until the lion walked over and started in on the animal, but these weren't trophies so we just took pictures. We drove back to within 50 feet of them, sat there in the Lorry and took pictures of them tearing the topi apart. They paid absolutely no attention to us—they look so tame—but the big male lions do not come out like that. Later on, we saw four more in the tall grass. We looked for buffalo. The boys saw an elephant yesterday. Tomorrow, I start in hunting again.

JUNE 20th:

Today is Sunday—it is just getting daylight. I feel better after a good night's sleep. It is almost cold this morning, I slept with three blankets over me last night, besides my woolen underwear, but the days warm up to about 80 degrees. For breakfast, we had tea served to us in bed, as usual. The first thing we do each morning is to get out in the bush at daybreak and check our lion bait—then we come back about 9:30 or 10:00 and have breakfast. We usually have steak or liver for breakfast. Last night we had lesser bustard—this is a bird about the size of a small wild goose—a little on the tough side, but very good.

Nick, the young White Hunter, and I went out together this morning. We didn't see any lion, but I did shoot a nice black-and-white zebra—most of the zebra are dark brown and white. This zebra was 350 yards distant—I shot him with my .270 Magnum, 150-grain Peters bullet—shot him in the chest. He almost stood on his rear feet and went around in a circle, then ran a few feet and fell. When I got over to him he was as dead as a doornail—he was a beauty, too. This brings my total zebra to two—I'll get a few more then they will cover our den furniture. We skinned him out and before we were through there were about 150 buzzards and vultures waiting for us to move off— this is a sight one never forgets.

We came back to camp, ate breakfast—steak, potatoes, cornflakes and coffee. We cleaned guns, sighted in rifles, wrote letters until about 4:00 p.m., then out again with Nick—we looked for lion and buffalo— no luck! On the way back, we shot an almost record Tommy, 16-inch horns—shot him at 100 yards. Just about ruined his neck, the exit hole was so large. Then I shot a topi at 250 yards, with the same .270 Magnum, 150-grain bullet—it took two shots to down him—they are hard animals to kill. On our way in, I shot another hyena—this one was nice, as nice a hyena as I have seen here—his hide was good. Boy, they are mean looking animals! I'm going to have this one mounted for my den—don't know as yet just where I'll put him—guess I'll have him crouching in the corner so he'll scare the daylights out of anyone who comes to see me.

When I say I shot one zebra today, that's because the skinners can't keep up with us—you could easily shoot 1,000 a day—I do mean that—it's true!

JUNE 21st:

I awoke this morning at 5:00 a.m.—the moon was just setting—really, I thought it was the sun coming up—never have I seen it so bright. Tea in bed, as usual and by daylight, we were out after lion and buffalo.

It is now 6:30 p.m.—the day is ending, the sky is beautiful, there is a brisk, cool breeze—the sunset looks like a painting. The Cook is preparing dinner. One of the boys is cleaning my rifles—they have been shot plenty today, both my .270 and .375 Magnums. Late this afternoon I came upon a very nice little Tommy—I'm having him skinned out so that I may have the complete animal mounted. They are the cutest little animal I ever saw—there are millions of them and I do mean millions— every place you look you see them. The smallest rifle I had with me was my .270—it shot an awful hole in his side.

Later in the day we shot a wildebeest for lion bait, but before we shot this, I shot a zebra at some 350 yards with my .375 Magnum—it was so far I really couldn't tell whether I hit him or not—at any rate, he ran away—so then we shot the wildebeest, that was much closer. Nick shot him with my .270 Magnum—he was about 200 yards, but didn't go down for 100 yards. I shot him with the .375 Magnum, then a finishing shot with my .270—if you don't hit these animals in the right spot and if the distance is so great that the bullet loses its dynamic shocking power, they just don't die—we've learned that—I'll go into more about that later. At any rate, we were dragging the wildebeest to a tree to hang him for lion bait and came upon a zebra lying down, but alive. We learned that his two front legs were broken—how that fellow ever ran at all, is more than I can understand. As I approached, he tried to run—I placed a shot in his heart to finish him off. He was another beautiful black-and-white and even though it was growing late, we skinned him out, and that is the third zebra that will go on our den furniture, (this was the zebra that ran away from us earlier).

Of course, during the day there were the usual amount of shots fired at the hideous hyena. We had a time with our natives over the hyena I brought in last night for the boys to skin out so that I may have a trophy to remember them by—they wouldn't load him on the truck. They told my Hunter in their native tongue (the only language they know) that they couldn't touch a hyena as they eat men. The Hunter asked them, "What about lion"—but it didn't matter, they wouldn't touch the animal until I motioned them to load it and took hold of its head, then they helped. When we reached camp, then came trouble getting one of the skinners to touch it—but a few shillings turned the trick. So, some day, people will see an African hyena in the window of my store, after it has served its purpose of scaring some of my friends half to death in my den.

Back to the question of lightweight, high velocity bullets—which is the whole reason of this expedition. Not enough knowledge has been gained as yet to give a report. I have used all of my rifles now and so have the other men, but not under identical conditions for comparison. One thing is sure and that is— the bullet must be traveling at a certain velocity when it hits the animal in order to kill by shock, no matter where it hits. I must find out at what distance or the velocity the bullet must hit the animal so that the shock kills instantly. The .270 Magnum with the 150-grain Corelokt is not it—at least it has not proven to be so far. I am convinced at this point that the 130-grain .270 bullet is superior at almost any point. The 87-grain bullet in the mag seems to have more killing power at 100 yards than does the 100-grain bullet. You remember the buffalo that carried away one of my .375 Magnum 300-grain Silvertips, two of my 220-grain Silvertips from my .300 Magnum and one shot from the .470 double? You must hit them right unless the bullet has sufficient velocity to disintegrate. Now, I am going to try the 87-grain, .25 caliber on them—this may have the shock we are after. If this is true, it will revolutionize firearms in the future. On small animals like the Tommy, it just tears hell out of them. By the way, Merrill Porter shot his first leopard today— a beauty, too—he is really a proud man.

I must mention that we are in the heart of the tsetse fly area. As you enter this area you are told that you enter at your own risk. Well, you can't get by without being bitten by them—we all have, many times; however, the people over here claim that seldom do you get the disease (sleeping sickness) attributed to them. At any rate, I am careful, but they just do get on you and bite. They are about twice the size of an ordinary fly, but have longer wings. There are no Masai natives in here at all, due to the fly. Well, sir, it worries us, nevertheless.

JUNE 22nd:

We were up before the sun this morning—very cool as usual—almost too cool. We were on our way long before the sun came up. As we drove East out over the tolling plains studded with flattop thorn trees, the clouds began to tint up a crimson color. Soon the sun poked his face above the far horizon. We were nearing the wildebeest that we had hung in the tree the night before— we could see the buzzards—some still asleep on the ground and in the trees. They sit on the ground much like a chicken—that's the way they sleep. There's the hyena now—it's just getting bedtime for those boys—they've had full control of that wildebeest all night. Whether they or the lion pulled it from the high tree (and we had it hung so securely, too), we will never know—but we did not see any lion near the kill. We counted 15 hyena, 4 jackal, and some of the hyena were scurrying away carrying a leg bone or a rib—they didn't pay a great deal of attention to us and we drove to within 50 yards of them. The main part of the carcass was about 300 yards from where we had hung it—now whether a lion carried it to the bush (as only a lion can), then ate what he wanted and left the balance for the hyena and jackal, as I say, we will never know, but that is what we surmised happened.

We go on and on, looking on the sunny side of the hills at the edge of the scrub timber, looking for a lion who might be sunning himself as they so often do. No—no lion, not even one. We intend to be back at camp about 11:00 a.m. Before I go, I intend to shoot another topi—I want his hide. This time I am going to sneak up in the timber until I get real close to him, then with the 87-grain bullet in my .257 Magnum, I am going to see what the shock of a bullet traveling 4,000 feet M.V. will do when striking a non-vital spot.

I must find out during this hunting trip just what has the greatest killing effect on game.

Well, sir, I get out of the Lorry, walk to the edge of the timber and get myself to within 40 yards of a topi—he is standing facing me—I aim the .257 Magnum equipped with a Stith 2 1/2X scope and Buehler mount, at his chest, hitting him low and on the right side. He lunged forward, ran like hell, swinging his right front leg as he ran, for 50 yards. I let him have another as he passed—this one struck his rear ham—the animal fell, but was not dead. You remember that's the 87-grain bullet, traveling at 4,000 M.V., at 40 yards—there should be 3,900 feet left. This is supposed to kill anything in its tracks—I've seen it done and I've done it—but, listen, it didn't do it this morning. This afternoon, I'll shoot one in the same place at the same distance I hope, with my .375 Magnum, 300-grain-Silvertip bullet and see what happens. Now if this heavy bullet knocks him down and he stays down, then I'll begin to believe that one needs weight. However, we have shot them with the 180-grain bullet in the 30-06 and also our .300 Magnum and they have kept right on for a long way. Only time will tell. I have another month to spend here in Africa—will probably shoot 50 more head of game, maybe more. We will shoot lots more hyena and jackal.

I might mention that even before we started to skin out the topi there were hundreds of buzzards circling overhead. This .257 caliber, 87-grain bullet, entered his body and never came out. It completely shattered his shoulder, went on into his lung and heart area—and how anything could have torn him up more inside, short of a stick of dynamite, is beyond me. The inside of that animal was a mass of blood and destroyed tissue, but still he was alive two minutes after I shot him. He would have died very, very soon—but he did not die with shock and without reflex action—not this one anyway, but many have.

Later on this morning we came upon a Grant's gazelle with a very nice head. I shot him with the 100-grain Corelokt bullet from my .257 Magnum, in the rear ham, as he was running almost directly away from me. The bullet passed completely through the animal and made its exit hole just behind the shoulder—the exit hole being about the size of a nickel. The gazelle was about 125 yards from me when I shot, he stood there momentarily, then collapsed. A Grant's gazelle is about the size of one of our small California deer—it is a very beautiful animal, resembling a Tommy very much. This will be another trophy to decorate my home with some day.

I suppose many times during the recording of my experiences here, I will contradict myself regarding the killing power of rifles, but I hope by the time my trip has ended, I will have something really concrete on which to form a new theory.

It's afternoon now—I'm out with Doctor and Merrill and Brown— we're looking for buffalo and lion. Hour after hour we looked—we

Roy and son, Ed, with a pair of lions they shot while on safari in Mozambique in 1970

stopped to look at ant hills that we thought were lion. There they were. I spotted a lion and lioness, walking slowly up the hill on the other side. I stopped, jumped out of the car, but when we got over across the ravine, we only spotted the lioness. While we were looking for the lion, what did we run onto but a large buffalo. I shot the buffalo—he was only 100 yards away standing under a tree—the brush was rather heavy—my White Hunter followed up with his .470. I'm shooting my .375 Magnum, 300-grain Silvertip bullet. I shot again as the buffalo appeared again—he fell. I followed with a shot in the spine behind the head, he was dead—my first buffalo—spread 36 inches, very full, with large boss—this day is complete! It took the men a couple of hours to skin him out. On our way home we stopped to shoot a topi. The White Hunter shot him with my .375 Magnum, about 300 yards, but it wasn't a square hit as the animal fell, got up and never stopped running. It goes to show without any question, that an animal must be hit in some vital spot, even with large heavy caliber bullets. We have learned a lot so far. It doesn't seem to matter what caliber rifle I shoot, the game seems to drop just the same, but won't drop if you do not hit him squarely, unless they are within 200 yards—then almost 100 percent of the time, they die instantly.

149

JUNE 23rd:

We're on our way again after a good long night's sleep—the moon is as beautiful as ever—it's about 7:00 a.m. and we're on our way back to the buffalo kill—the lion should be there. Not 15 minutes from camp, I see 11 large buffalo walking off across the plain. As we came closer, to about 300 yards or so, we stopped—jumped out of the truck, ran for a distance and started shooting—three shots from my .375 Magnum and one bull hit in the leg and crippled—he started falling out of the line and headed for the bush. We went to the bush and there he was in the middle. I let him have another shot from my .375—the animal was through. This one had a 42-inch spread—that's a large buffalo— I'm happy now. This animal went down with the third shot from my .375 Magnum, using solid or full patch bullets. These buffalo some-times carry off 12 to 15 shots from large heavy rifles.

I'm convinced now that my .375 Magnum is large enough for any animal in Africa—or at least as good or better than any of the doubles. We skin him out, the skin is more than a half inch thick— we investigate to see where the bullets went and what they did and they did plenty— one in the foot—two in the body. However, I shot him once after he was dead with the 87-grain bullet from my .257 Magnum at 3,950 M.V.—then we cut into him to see what had happened. Some say the bullet will not go through the thick hide without blowing up—this has long been a controversy with the hunters. Let me tell you what it will do—it not only penetrated the hide, but it made a very nasty hole in the meat of the ham and clear on through the bone, shattering the hipbone into many pieces and right on through to the innards—now that's it, that's firsthanded. I am still a believer of high velocity and will be until proven wrong.

We drove on to yesterday's kill—hyena by the dozen, but no lion. We were walking upwind—the hyena neither saw us nor heard us. They were walking toward us—how I wished for my camera at that moment. They came to within 25 feet of us before seeing us—they stopped, looked up, and changed their course without much concern.

It was 4:30 p.m. before we started back out to hunt—we all went together—set out some more bait. A reedbuck jumped out of the grass—I jumped out and let him have an 87-grain bullet from the .257 Magnum—I hit him in front of the rear ham, it passed through the ham on the other side, tore the ham completely off—the inside was in bad shape, but still that little devil kept on going for 200 yards before he went down.

Well, sir, this shooting business is really something. I'm disproving all my own theories and everyone else's, but by the time I shoot another 50 head of game I'll know something worth repeating.

Soon after we picked up the reedbuck, we came onto four lion but they were small, about 300 pounds each. They looked at us, then sauntered off into the bush. One can hardly believe these are wild animals.

Later on, Merrill shot a zebra but didn't kill him—two 180-grain 30 caliber slugs, at 400 yards. Then Doctor shot a wildebeest but didn't stop him either—he was some 350 yards. The game here on the plains is generally about 250 to 300 yards from you, but as soon as you leave the truck, away they go.

Merrill and I shot a topi then, the .375 put him down. We hauled that topi about a mile, dragging him behind the truck to a tree so we could hang him up and by golly, we saw 11 lion—they came out of the bush and followed the truck waiting for us to drop the animal. By the time the animal was in the tree it was dark— we had to get to camp fast. For our dinner we had buffalo steak—very good, just like beef.

JUNE 24th:

With great anticipation we left early this morning to examine our bait. Only one lioness there—her face was bloody from jumping and grabbing a piece of the topi we had hung high in the tree. We left there and Merrill shot a zebra, at 300 yards, with his .300 W. Magnum, using a 150-grain Bronze Point expanding bullet—one shot. We saved the beautiful hide, then dragged him to the lion, waited a few hundred yards away, but the lion didn't show up—they were there, we know because whenever the buzzards won't go down, we know there are lion. We waited two hours, then left. We decided that we could find better lion country—we're like a bunch of Nomads—we're on the move again this p.m. for another camp some 25 miles from here.

Last night, as we were having dinner, one of the skinners came up to the table and conversed briefly, but rather excitedly, with our White Hunter, in Swahili, of course. Afterward, we asked our Hunter what the conversation was all about. He related to us that the native had told him he had seen a strange animal across the river that looked like a rock and that it retracted. We thought that was a wonderful explanation of a turtle. The men yesterday afternoon brought in an African turtle, about 12 inches in diameter, to show the other fellows in camp. We just let him go— he had slowly crossed the river and the natives had seen him. A turtle is rare over here and these boys had never seen one before.

When I return home, I believe I will be able to write a book on killing power—each day, I learn something new. Today, one zebra shot with a 150-grain Bronze Point expanding bullet died in its tracks—another shot with a 180-grain Corelokt bullet got away, while one shot the same day with the 180-grain 30 caliber Corelokt died instantly. The average hunter would then swear that the 180-grain 30 caliber Corelokt was the reason for the death, regardless of whether fired from a .30-06 or a .300 W. Magnum. To me, it goes to further prove that it depends upon what part of the body is hit and the remaining velocity of the bullet. A few days ago, I killed a zebra at 335 yards with a 150-grain Peters belted bullet in my .270 Magnum—dead with one shot—still I shot a topi at 100 yards with the 300-grain Silvertip in my .375 Magnum—he fell down, got up, and never stopped running. So— where are we? One point more important than any other—the animal must be hit in a vital spot unless it is close to you. Of course, velocity means greater killing energy at greater distances—it also means more shock and greater destruction, but there is no substitute for the right spot.

We moved camp today about 25 miles North of where we were—a beautiful spot. As soon as we stopped, we spotted two lion not over 200 yards from where we were going to make camp. Very soon we started out to shoot a zebra for lion bait—this looks like wonderful country. Our White Hunter shot the zebra with the .300 Magnum, using the 150-grain Bronze Point expanding bullet, at 335 measured yards—one shot and the animal died instantly. Now there it is again—335 yards— maybe next time at 100 yards the animal will not die. He was hit high in the shoulder, a little back. We tied him on the Lorry and started dragging him to where we were going to hang him for lion bait, when we saw another strange Lorry driving out across the plain toward us. This is the first people we've seen since we left Nairobi—it turned out to be Sidney Downey and his clients from the States— Sandy McNab, Mr. Gilbert from Atlanta, Georgia, and Dr. Laizlo from Connecticut. These are the men who, with Lou Coulter, drove from Cape Town.

Juan Naude Cordova, of Mexico, with Weaherby and the jaguar he took on a 1972 Mexican hunt.

They say the trip from Cape Town was rather uninteresting in comparison to Tanganyika and Kenya. They are camped just a mile from us and now we must move as that is just a gentleman's agreement, that when one hunter has camped in one area, no one else comes in until after they have moved. They told us of a most interesting experience; yesterday they shot a buffalo and this morning as they made their rounds, they saw three lion on the kill. A huge buffalo came out of the bush in a rage, to drive the lion from its dead companion—it chased one, then another. The lion ran its utmost and finally took refuge in a tree, and it's not the easiest thing for a lion to jump into a tree—sometimes young ones can, but seldom do the old males ever take to a tree.

We spent several hours last night at their camp enjoying the break in a long safari—swapping experiences. As we returned to our camp, we discussed going out to look at the zebra just to see how many lion were there, but thought better of it when we remembered that Downey told us there was a lioness with several young cubs, and we all know that in such a case it might have meant trouble, even though we were in the Lorry.

The night is beautiful—the moon is up—it is almost like daylight. The moon is much brighter here than in the States.

Before we went to sleep, we could hear the lion not over 200 yards from camp, with their low growl, and the hyena as we hear him every night; could hear the funny little bark of the zebra; now and then, you could hear a startled monkey or baboon. Before daybreak the noises are more than thrilling—birds and animals—it's almost like the sound of a well-stocked farm in the U.S.—it's wonderful! It was very cool last night.

JUNE 25th:

It is 7:00 a.m.—we have had breakfast and are moving out again, to a new camp—where, I don't know. I hate to leave here—it is so beautiful! Twenty-one miles later; we're at our new camp—a very nice looking place, nestled down here in sort of a valley, surrounded by yellow fever trees—at least, that is what the people call them. They resemble a very large thorn tree, flattopped. There are a few palms—monkeys and baboons in the trees—but as for game, it doesn't look so hot. We're looking for lion and where you do not find large herds of game, you can rest assured there isn't going to be many lion, but it should be great leopard country—some hills and lots of rock ledges, just where the big spotted cat hangs out. It's also good rhino and buffalo country, our Hunter claims—a few days will tell the story. As soon as we unpacked our gear, we took off to look the situation over.

Merrill shot a zebra for lion bait—the zebra was 390 yards away. Now when I refer to this distance, don't call me a liar—we don't have to guess over here—all you do is step it off, it's all level ground or thereabout. The error of stepping off one's yardage is very small—at any rate, he shot the zebra at the rear and high on the right shoulder, with a 150-grain Bronze Point expanding bullet from his .300 W. Magnum—one shot, that's all—the zebra kicked a bit and was dead before we arrived. Now, 390 yards is a hell of a long way to shoot any animal.

This afternoon Nick and I went out all over these hills, valleys and plains—shot a Tommy at 150 yards with the 87-grain bullet from the

.257 Magnum. He dropped dead as he should have done, but did do a bit of kicking—he was shot through the forepart of the ribs. A little later, I shot a hartebeest with my .375 Magnum—first bullet I fired was the 270 grain. I shot low—it hit the ground about three feet my side of him—the bullet ricocheted and struck his two front legs, just below the knee and broke both of them. The poor fellow tried to run—another shot with the 300-grain Silvertip bullet at 200 yards, across the back, made a nasty hole about six inches in diameter, tearing his hide for an eight inch radius across the back, but still he didn't die—he couldn't go any place but he wasn't dead—a shot through the heart finished him. Again, that goes to show they must be hit in the right spot with these big bullets that don't blow up or else they don't die immediately.

A little later, I shot a warthog at 150 yards with the 100-grain Soft Nose bullet—hit him in the shoulder—he went down but he didn't die—he was still kicking when I got there. Another close range shot in the head and his reflex action didn't stop for three minutes. So, again I'm convinced that shock does not hold true for all animals, or for most animals 100 percent of the time, unless shot in a vital spot.

Now there is no doubt in my mind and should not be in anyone's mind, but that velocity gives greater killing power, and that velocity gives a shock even though it doesn't kill instantaneously sometimes, but much greater than that of slower velocity rifles. With rifles of slower velocity, killing at long range is next to impossible unless the animal is hit in a very vital spot.

The day is coming to a close now—I'm waiting for the other men to come back to camp, wondering what they have seen and what they have shot. At this point, I want to say this about the African White Hunter—at least, this is my impression of the ones we have in camp. If they ever had to come to America to hunt, I'm afraid they would have to start out all over again. Hunting is so simple for them here—they drive their car or truck right up to where they expect to find game. They pay little attention to wind direction unless hunting elephant—for here they know sooner or later they will just stumble on the game they are after—there is so much of it—whereas, in America we've had to learn to really scientifically hunt our game.

JUNE 26th:

This is Saturday and we're on the move again since this spot is just no good. Nothing much of importance happened today—we just traveled over plains, hills and valleys—grass is very dry—not much game, only saw a few hundred head today. One generally sees thousands upon thousands—the animals migrate, so do the lion— they migrate, too. We go on and on and find ourselves just where we were three days ago—after all, it is the best spot.

As we drive over the plains near our camp, we find that in our three days absence, most of the zebra have moved on. As we near our camp, we see a truck or safari car—who could it be? To see anyone out here is very unusual. We find it is Donald Kerr, of Kerr and Downey. He has with him a lady from New York—she and her sister are here on a photographic safari. We talked for a while, but we had to get out and get up our kills as we have little lion time left—we must go to elephant country the 2nd of July and it is now June 26th.

Off we go as soon as we unload our trucks. Nick and I go out and shoot a wildebeest—I had Nick shoot him with my .257 Magnum—his shot was a bit far back and did not kill instantly but stopped him—a shot from my .375 Magnum finished him off—he was 220 yards away. We tied him to a tree so the lion could not carry him away. It was getting dark, we had to hurry but we took time to stop and shoot a Tommy at 75 yards with the .257 W.M., using an 87-grain Weatherby bullet—one shot, he never moved—shot him through the ribs—an awful hole, passed through to the opposite side. We ate him for dinner, or part of him. The other boys shot a topi and brought him in so we had topi liver for our dinner, too, plus guinea fowl that Merrill shot today. By the time we got back to camp, it was raining like hell— we didn't have the dining tent up so we ate in the rain after everyone was wet. Oh, what a life on an African safari—it's cold tonight, too!

JUNE 27th:

This is another new day—Sunday, June 27th—what a night, I slept like a log, after I once got to sleep. It was really a night that I will long remember—all the night sounds were drowned out by the roar of the lion. I don't believe he is over 200 yards from us—about every five minutes he lets go—but soon, in spite of his roar, I dropped off to sleep. To our great surprise, he came right into camp and carried off our topi. This topi was about 10 feet from where our native boys were sleeping and not over 50 feet from us. We didn't figure when we brought him in that we were setting out lion bait right in camp.

By daylight we're off. The wildebeest we tied to a tree is gone—all gone—not even a bone left. Where, Oh where, has our wildebeest gone? The twine is still tied to the tree—blood all around but no animal. So, on and on we go—we see wart hogs, hyena, jackal, topi, wildebeest, hartebeest, Tommy, giraffe—but no lion.

Then we see a lion. As we get closer, we see it is a young male, just starting his mane. We go off a hundred yards and shoot a topi—I shot it with the .257 Magnum, 87-grain bullet—put him down but only the rear end was paralyzed. I had to make another shot. We tied him to a rope and pulled him down to the lion. We had no sooner let him off the rope until the young male lion got up from his crouch in the grass and started toward our kill. We drove off about a hundred yards and watched—he picked the topi up and started carrying him toward the trees. Now a topi weighs upward of 300 pounds, it is larger by far than any North American buck deer. He dragged that animal over a hundred yards to a tree and sat there eating his kill, while dozens of buzzards and vultures sat near by with anticipation of what the lion might leave. No, don't worry, nothing bothers a lion while he has control of a kill—a lion can take control very easily of any kill, too.

We drove on and were within 30 or 40 yards from him— he paid very little attention to us—just kept right on eating. They start on the intestines first—we took movies and still pictures of this.

We went on and not very far away, we came upon three buffalo running across the plains—out we jumped and started shooting. Whether or not I hit one, I'll never know, but we followed them into a bush some 500 yards distant—the bush was about 300 yards long and 200 yards wide—plenty of room for three buffalo to hide. We thought we had wounded one but weren't sure. We circled the bush several times, with extreme caution, for the White Hunters tell us there is nothing worse than a wounded buffalo. My young guide, Nick, was scared to death. Perhaps it's because I never had experience with them but I have never feared a wild animal even though he is wounded. About the third time around, getting closer to the edge of the bush, we heard a pounding of hooves—a lot of them—where were they? Which way were they coming or going? Are they charging us? What should I do?

All those things came to my mind at the same time! Now is the stamping of feet that I hear, buffalo or is it my heart beating? I back up toward a tree nearby—my guide is running toward another—the native with us has taken heel for the truck. Well, sir, this is really a moment in my life—I'm really scared—but to our surprise and disappointment, they were going out the other side. We ran to the other end of the bush and there they were running across the plains. I shot once with my .375 Magnum—I knew I hit one of them but didn't know where—only one logical place, however, and that was in the rear end for that's all I could see of them. He is 300 yards from me—I take out on his trail—the buffalo faltered and fell out of line—here's blood on the grass, I know he's hit now, but into another large bush his track leads. Now here is where we stop—my young guide just wouldn't go in.

"No, I want to go back to camp for more help, I won't enter that bush without more rifles and men." So back we go to camp—it's eight miles—that's over an hour. On the way back, I shot a zebra for lion bait—300 yards with the .257 Magnum, 87-grain Soft Point bullet—one shot in the chest and down he went, and Oh, what a mess it made of that zebra! We hung him in a nearby tree as we had just seen two lion there.

We arrived back in camp—it's 2:30 now and we haven't even had breakfast, so I'm hungry. We eat and take off for the buffalo with the chief White Hunter, Merrill Porter, Dr. Nickelsen and a bunch of natives. We take up the trail and in the bush we go—we see blood on the trail—everyone with their rifles loaded and ready to fire—a great tense moment—looking each way and paying attention to each little sound we hear. Not over a hundred yards, we see it. We all cock our rifles, ready to fire—it is down—we throw a rock, it doesn't move—we draw closer, it's dead. There it is, a huge 2,000 pound animal with a 46-inch spread—a beautiful head—it's all mine!

It only has one of my shots in it and now listen, carefully— can you imagine where it is? Two inches to the right of the anus—right in his rear end—a 300-grain Silvertip bullet at 300 yards. I knew he was injured because he fell out of the pack—the bullet went deep into his body and caused death very fast. Now, again I say, it's where you hit them—but don't ever say that velocity doesn't add a lot to killing power. That buffalo died from one shot out of my .375 W. Magnum. Now seldom does a buffalo die with one shot from anything, but this one did. Now this is my third buffalo—none of them took over two shots from the .375 W. Magnum to put them down.

I'm happy now. I'm beginning to realize more than ever that velocity does make a great difference.

On our way in tonight we stopped to let Merrill shoot a couple of zebra. The first one he shot through the neck at 200 yards with the 100-grain bullet from his .257 W. Magnum—he dropped and never moved. The other zebra was 243 yards—one shot through the ribs and he stood there, stunned, soon he fell to the ground. Now remember, that's the 100-grain bullet at 3,700 M.V.—there is velocity again. We shot a topi yesterday—three times—with a 30-06 at not over 200 yards and I guess he's still going.

It is getting dark now—it's going to rain, and soon. No sooner did we get the zebra skinned out and hung up, than it started to rain. It's 9:00 p.m. now and it's still raining. I hear the old lion roaring now and then—he's very close by. Well, this day is closing—it's dark—dinner is over; we had Tommy steaks and liver, potatoes, rice and pineapple—very good. But now it is bedtime—we have to be up early in the morning—we're after lion—three days to go. Good night!

JUNE 28th:

It rained a lot last night but it's beautiful this morning, even though it is a little cloudy. We're off again—lion has our bait, it's gone again—that was a zebra. I shot another zebra this morning with my .300 Magnum, using a 150-grain Bronze Point expanding bullet, at 160 yards—shot in the high ribs—dead now, hardly moved. This is the last hide I'm allowed. Well, it's 2:15 now—we'll be going out again shortly. There are lion in this area, however, they are wild and scare easily—that is, the big lion—so they need careful hunting. The native hunters have just never learned to do that. In another decade or two they will have to learn to hunt or else not get their game for it won't be like it was yesterday.

The day is over—it's raining again—the rainy season is lasting a little too long this year. We went back to see what happened to the zebra that we covered with thorn bushes—the buzzards were there this afternoon by the thousands but as we drove closer we note only a few. The zebra is gone—bones, skin and all—that means only one thing, that a lion got it and carried it away. Well, I got a topi—skinned him out as the skins are wonderful—then we hung this animal high in a thorn tree. Old Boy Simba won't get him—I don't think. By the way, I shot the topi with my .300, using a 180-grain Bronze Point expanding bullet, at 148 yards—shot him in the front part of the shoulders—the bullet still had sufficient velocity to blow up—the damage was terrible. His shoulder was shattered—he went down with one shot. After we hung this topi (between rain spells), we started back to camp. It's getting late—the sky is dark, but we came onto a beauty of a Tommy— nice, better than average horns and this is the one I'll have completely mounted. It sometimes seems shameful to shoot these cute little animals, and the .300 Magnum is just too much rifle.

Well, I'm learning about killing power fast. Today Doctor shot a zebra with a 30-06—it didn't die—for a long time it ran and ran with the herd—soon it toppled over dead. He was hit in the lungs at about 275 yards. The rifles with high velocity are making many more instant kills. My only disappointment is that shock doesn't kill them without reflex action. Many of them die instantly—far more than with the standard rifles—but much is to be learned about high velocity. I haven't reached the point yet of killing with shock 100 percent of the time.

It is 8:00 p.m. now and raining hard—a safari can be made very uncomfortable by rain—but I've seen it worse!

JUNE 29th:

Everything is pretty wet this morning—rained a lot during the night—chains are needed on our Lorry this morning. Tea in bed as usual—off for lion as usual. Doctor has missed three chances at lion now—well, today is the day for sure. About an hour and a half after we left, as we were driving along one of the side hills dotted with bush—(a "bush" is what they call a spot of trees and brush and undergrowth, thorn trees and heavy brush, sometimes a few hundred feet in diameter, sometimes two to five hundred yards long and maybe a hundred yards wide, sometimes miles wide and miles long, but the "bush" I am going to tell you about was a small thin bush).

Merrill, with his ever eagle eyes, spots two lion behind the bush, some 500 yards to our left. We stop the Lorry and the two White Hunters and Doctor start up toward the bush—they almost arrived when old Leo and his mate took off for another, larger bush some 600 yards to the right. I grabbed my .300 Magnum and shot at the running monster three times—Merrill fired three times—Doctor fired twice—both our White Hunters fired twice with their .470's—but the lion kept right on—never a hit. How all of us could have missed, I don't know, but we did. We went into the bush but not far. I took to the south side, Merrill to the north—both of us get high in a tree in a good lookout. Four of the men went on through the bush, but one fierce growl from the lion sent them all out very quickly. Yes sir, no one wants to face an angry or wounded lion. Well, I can't understand it— but we didn't get him. This was our great chance but I guess we were all over enthusiastic!

No more luck today. Later in the afternoon, I shot two wildebeest—both with my .300 Magnum, one at 275 yards and one at 470 yards. It's raining again—it's 4:30 p.m., the sky is dark but really, I hate to leave this place—it's so cool, so green, so beautiful. We are going to elephant country now—it's only 900 feet elevation and they say it is very hot there, so our pleasant life in Africa has about ended.

JUNE 30th:

We are off again this a.m. for lion, but it's raining—not good. I shot two wildebeest this morning, one at 225 yards and the other at 450 yards—no, I'm not lying, it's true.

12:30 p.m.—we're leaving a grand place. It's overcast today, our trucks are loaded heavily with our trophies and hides and all our gear—we're off to civilization again. Tonight we will stay in Narok—that is, if we get there, it's 70 miles, and 70 miles out here is a long way when there are no roads. At last I saw a leopard, but none of us got a chance at him.

Later in the afternoon as we wearily rode bumpety-bump along, Merrill spotted a cheetah—he was stalking some Grant's gazelles—he heard our truck and took off across the plains very fast. Doctor and I both fired two shots at him—both missed. Try shooting at a cheetah sometime at 400 yards, when they have opened up all their speed, some 70 miles per hour of it—the fastest animal in the world.

We pass thousands upon thousands of head of game on our way—the day is ending—we near Norok. We stop at the game warden's place—his name is Temple Borhm—a wonderful fellow—met his wife—they live way out here with nature. Oh, what one wouldn't give for such a setting for his home in the city—a paradise, I tell you—a paradise. They serve us tea and cakes and cookies and small sandwiches. We haven't eaten since 11:00 a.m. and we're starved, so we really go to town on the tidbits. An hour, a very pleasant one, spent with the Borhms. Oh, so nice and so glad to see people. They are so far away from anyone—it is 10 miles to Norok. Now Norok has six white families; the road is bad, too, and when we arrive there it is dark. We go to the District Commissioner's house—he tells us how to get the key for the guest house where we are to stay tonight.

The night is very cool—the stars are bright—it's beautiful. Our "Wogs" (as they call the natives) are unloading our gear. A car pulls up, the only car in Norok—we remember that it belongs to the doctor here. He has five other people in the car—he stops and asks us to go up to his house and have a drink. We can't refuse— no, not by a long shot. We accept his invitation and are we glad we did! The doctor and his wife and two other white couples who live here (all of the people here are with the Government), make us very welcome—drinks are served, the table is set, food is brought on fit for a King—everything— ham, gazelle, bacon, cabbage, eggs, cheese, yes—everything. We're half-starved but soon we're content, very content. These people are as happy as we are for they get lonesome out here and love to meet people from the outside. They are wonderful folks and every hospitality imaginable is extended to the people they meet. Well, we go back to our guest house. Oh, what a glorious night, I'll never forget it—to bed at 2:00 a.m.—imagine, this is the first night since we have been out on safari that we haven't been in bed by 9:00 p.m.—but, of course, this is an occasion!

JULY 1st:

Yes, this is July 1st—the morning is beautiful, as they all are—it's very cool, about 60 degrees. We all got together this morning; the resident doctor gave me a native knife; I bargained with a native Masai and traded him out of his spear; also got one of their bow and arrow outfits. These Masai people! I could go on endlessly—a very interesting people, one could write a book about them. Cattle is their main livelihood—a man's wealth is judged by the number of cattle he owns. They do not eat meat—they drink the blood and milk from their cows. They wear very few clothes, just a skin hung over them. They are very tall, their ear lobes are torn and disfigured, generally they have a dozen rings, safety pins, or whatever they have been able to pick up from visitors, stuck through them. The women have bands around their legs that can't be removed—they do most of the work. A man has several wives—if he is rich with a lot of cattle, he has more wives—they trade cattle for their women. It is a custom of theirs that whenever a visitor comes to see them, they ask them which wife they would prefer and if the visitor stays all night, he selects the wife he wants and sleeps with her. I asked the doctor what they did about the children—his reply was that they seem to pay little attention to who the father of the child may be. Again I say—this is Africa! I told the doctor that if this was a custom in the U.S. there surely would be a powerful lot of visiting.

We're off now for Nairobi—100 miles—it should only take us about five hours as there seems to be sort of a road now.

JULY 2nd:

We're at the Norfolk Hotel in Nairobi this morning. Let's start the day with tea, as it comes to you every morning, the boy gently tapping on your bedroom door. They call it "Chai"—it is a wonderful way to be awakened in the morning. The sun isn't up yet—it is cloudy but you hear the birds outside your bedroom window just the same. Few people in the world realize what a wonderful place Africa, East Africa, really is. I suppose it is because it is so far away from the rest of the world—even the European continent—it is so far away from the average man's means—if it were close, it would no longer be the wonderland it is today. I have been wondering how many years it will take for civilization to spoil the Africa of today—I should like to see it remain always as it is now, but it won't always be this way, for the English people have now perfected an inoculation for their cattle to guard against the disease of the tsetse fly. This is one of the main reasons why East Africa has not been settled before. Now people are coming to East Africa and buying up property from this English protectorate and homesteading, much like the people did as they

163

moved west in the United States. Lever Brothers has purchased a million acres of land in Tanganyika. Planted peanuts—peanuts for oil—oil for soap. Now we know what happened to the game on a million acres of ground. This is only an example of what is taking place in East Africa, and in another decade or two, I'm afraid this paradise will be ended. The climate, as I have said before, is just like California except that it isn't damp, neither is it foggy. Everything is green, flowers bloom all the year round—tropical birds, a world of wilderness just outside the city limits. Today I am making arrangements for our trip into elephant country. We have to buy more provisions and will be leaving day after tomorrow, on the 4th. This will be new country for us, it will be down on the edge of a desert many hundreds of miles from here and this is where it is really hot, also disagreeable, but then people don't live there so it doesn't matter—there are only the wild animals and crocodiles of Africa.

What I am going to shoot the elephant with, I don't know. I am trying to decide whether to use the .300 Magnum or the .375 Magnum, but I will let you know regardless of what happens. Believe me, I have learned a lot about killing power between the three of us in our camp. We have shot over a hundred head of game, ranging from the small Thompson's gazelle, weighing 40 to 50 pounds, on up through the larger gazelle, the topi, the wildebeest, the eland, which is the largest of the antelope family, to the mighty Cape buffalo weighing a ton or more.

The Cape buffalo is hailed as being the most dangerous animal and he has taken many a life. I was rather abashed at my young guide the time he did not want to go into the bush after a wounded buffalo that I had shot. He has killed about two hundred buffalo in his short life and the last one he killed, just a few months ago, got him. He had fired two shots from his .470 double barrel—as the last shot was fired the buffalo was not over 10 yards away—he kept on coming and mauled my guide very seriously, knocking him unconscious, and when he came to, the buffalo lay there dead. The guide was badly wounded and had to spend several weeks in the hospital. That was a very close call, and when one has had that sort of an experience, one can hardly be blamed for being cautious about going into the bush after a wounded buffalo.

As I sit here in this really tropical wonderland I can't help but think what an odd race of people are the Masai! I have lots of memories of them—the spear, the bow and arrows, and what trophies—an interesting experience indeed!

I wanted to get some of those metal bands that the women wear around their legs—I thought they would make wonderful trophies, so in my feeble way, I was trying to bargain with a group of natives, pointing to the bands on their women's legs—they are large coils of rings, very shiny. I had a ten shilling note and, holding it up, offered it for the bands. The natives made an awful fuss about it—some of them were looking very puzzled, others were laughing. One native indicated that he wanted more money—so I asked the Doctor in the area, who understands their language, what it was all about. He told me that the bands are not removable, that they grow there from childhood, and that the natives thought I was trying to buy their women—that ten shillings was not enough, they wanted fifteen shillings. (That's about seventy-five cents in our money).

You look at the Masai and wonder how they live—dirty, filthy, they live in mud huts, they live just like animals only worse. Their ear lobes torn badly and hanging, their faces disfigured, which is a sign of beauty, their heads painted a tomato red with some sort of a smear, a skin thrown over them for clothing, not protecting their body at all, and the children run around without anything, except on a very cool morning. So ends the Masai tribe for me now—I'd like to write more about them but time will not permit.

Now we go to the Mohammedan tribe. They are meat eaters and unlike the Masai tribe as they never eat meat—you remember I mentioned that the Masai people only drink the blood and milk from their cows. Now the Mohammedan must kill his game alive, they will not eat any meat unless they cut the throat while the animal is still alive. I will give you more details about them when I get into their country.

Don't let anyone say that all of Africa is a hot, sweltering tropical zone, for it isn't. As you look over the great plains you can well imagine that the tall waving grass is a large wheat field somewhere in the midwestern part of the States—anything can be grown here that is grown in our own country, only this place is not populated—no one lives here—there aren't over 20,000 white people in the whole of Kenya Colony. Tomorrow will be another day -

JULY 4th, Sunday:

I am eating my breakfast now at a small village by the name of Nanyuki, about 130 miles north of Nairobi. I'm sitting in the northern hemisphere—Dr. Nickelsen is just across the table from me—in the Southern Hemisphere, and Merrill Porter is at my side and is enjoying his breakfast directly on the equator! Now this is something to be long remembered. We are at 6,400 feet elevation, the temperature is about 50 degrees, the name of the Hotel is "The Silverbeck"—sitting back from the road and beautifully covered with bougainvillea—a restful place. We left Nairobi this morning at 4:00 a.m.; it took us about five hours to go 130 miles—that's African highways! We leave this place and we will again be in the Northern Hemisphere.

It's 7:30 p.m. and it's dark, and we're setting up camp. What a day: 280 Miles from 4:00 a.m. to 7:30 p.m. The country we have been traveling through this afternoon is not at all like the wonderland we have just left. We have dropped down now to an elevation of 1000 feet. We are on the edge of the desert—the temperature is up—the country is full of inactive volcanoes, sort of a lava belt, scrub bush, dry grass. We passed a few ostrich, many camels, some Peter's gazelles, gerenuk and dik-dik, but not in numbers we have been accustomed to. I cannot imagine why these animals inhabit this area while only a few hundred miles away it is so wonderful. We finally arrive at a native village called Jarbatulla. It's a strange place, grass and mud huts, but more livable than those of the Masai, even though it is a pretty low standard of living. These people look much more intelligent than the Masai—their faces show it but whether they are or not, I do not know. There is a row of four or five mud and grass huts and about 20 feet across is another row. The six foot stick and limb fence that surrounds the place has an open gate. They rather enjoy having their pictures taken and act very proud. The small children wear no clothing and the grown-ups not much more—this is a strange world.

We are getting deeper and deeper in the wilds of Africa—the scenery is changing again—now we are in palm trees, sandy ground—very tropical. This is what I thought Africa was going to look like. Our camp lies in the valley at the edge of the Kenya River. Baboons in the trees—lion roar—another day.

July 5th:

What a glorious night's rest! The sound of the breeze through the palm leaves, the bark of the baboon, the lion's growl, the howl of the hyena, and the yip of the jackal. A perfect tropical summer's night! We have our elephant trackers out and we are on the hunt for elephant. Temperature is about 90 degrees. Dr. Nickelsen shot a 25-inch Peter's gazelle today— that should be near a world's record. The Peter's gazelle is a duplicate of the Grant's gazelle but with longer horns and a little larger. They are both of the same family as the Tommy. One of our trackers reports an elephant nine miles distant. Says it is a nice one, so we're off—but upon arriving there we found only one, the tusks were about 90 pounds, but the tracker had failed to make close examination and one of the tusks had about 18 inches broken off, so we would not take that trophy.

Tonight we had ham and beans for dinner with the delicious white meat of the greater bustard. This is a large bird—has about an eight foot wing spread and long legs. They run into the wind, flapping their wings until they are airborne. When they alight, they alight into the wind and run along with their wings outspread like an aeroplane.

July 6th:

No elephant—not here anyway—we came to this conclusion after traveling all morning through high grass over hill and dale. We met two natives looking for honey—they follow the honey-bird. Their belief (and it is true) is that the honey-bird leads them to the tree where there is wild honey. They also believe that they must leave some honey in the trees for the birds and if they don't, the next time the honey-bird will lead them to a lion. We crossed one beautiful stream, just a few feet wide—Africa has very few of them.

We are moving now and just as we are packing up, a native comes to our White Hunter, telling him that 20 miles yonder there are not only three elephants, but three thousand elephants! Our White Hunter does not know whether to believe him or not, but we will find out when we arrive. There is some water there and we find huge elephant tracks everywhere.

On the way to the new camp, I shot a Grevey zebra with my .300 Magnum, using the 180-grain Silvertip bullet. This is Western's new bullet. Well, sir, it does the job it is intended for. It does its expanding and will penetrate deeper, but does not blow up. I shot him through the ribs at 100 yards. It did not stop him—I had to trail him for 500 yards. I hit him in the rear, this time stopping him, but he stood there in a stupor, then started out again. I put another one in his lung area but still he stood there. Before I had gone ten steps, he fell but was not dead. Upon closer examination, I found each bullet had gone on through the body, therefore, the animal did not receive the full shocking power. The 150-grain Bronze Point expanding bullet blows up inside and causes much faster death. However, this new Silvertip bullet should be very good for game such as buffalo, where deeper penetration is needed. The Grevey zebra is a considerably larger animal than the common zebra—the stripes are more narrow—the ears much larger. I presume the animal weighs around 700 pounds or so. It was getting late, we did not have time to skin him before dark so we loaded him on the truck. We have ten natives with us and if you don't think it's a big chore for ten men to lift a dead zebra, then think again, for they almost failed to do the job, however, it is in camp tonight. I will have this beauty mounted and in my store next year.

We had a wonderful dinner tonight—gazelle steaks, cabbage, potatoes and fruit salad. I hope the hyena let us sleep tonight. This morning about 4:00 a.m. they awakened us with the darndest howls and laughter one ever heard—I do not think they were over a hundred yards from where we were sleeping. One must hear these to realize just what it is like.

JULY 7th:

Even when on an African safari, days sometimes pass without too much interest. However, today was not one of those days. There is something to tell you—our tracker was here at our new campsite when we arrived about 11:30 a.m., waiting to tell us that he had already been out and that he had spotted three large elephant with good tusks, only about three miles from camp. Well, sir, that is what we were waiting for. Off we go, loaded for elephant and not for bear. According to arrangement, it is Doc's first shot so he takes the .375 W. Magnum with 300-grain full patch bullet. One hour—two hours, and now we are here. The elephant—there he is! Only one, but he's a beauty! Brown, our White Hunter, goes closer to see if everything is OK. The elephant hears us, his trunk is in the air trying to catch our wind. Brown shakes his head, but I think surely those tusks will go 85 pounds and that is a good elephant any time—but he is coming back. The elephant has either seen or smelled us for his ears are out and he is on his way. My heart is broken to see that beauty go—but Brown says, "Sorry fellows, but you don't want him—another broken tusk." Just no trophy, so we'll get a better one. Well, that's the way it goes out here. Back we go through the tall thick grass, pass thorn bushes and trees deluxe. It is not exactly what you would call a cool day either—we are all wet with perspiration. Nick, my young White Hunter, and I take the Lorry and go back to another camp for the rest of our gear. Well, anyway, I am looking for a good giraffe, another waterbuck, Peter's gazelle, gerenuk and a few more dik-dik, so maybe I'll see one of these as we go along.

About three miles short of our other camp, we spot some good Peter's gazelle through the rather thick bush and trees about a quarter mile away. We thought we would walk over and see if there was a good head among them, so I take my .300 Magnum and Boy, is this grass tall and are these thorn bushes hell! We see some gerenuk, too, and a little further, a herd of zebra. You know I have to shoot another Grevey zebra—the skinners spoiled my last head—they did not know I wanted a shoulder mount and they cut it down the under part of the neck. To my surprise, there are two very good waterbuck ahead of me, so now what am I going to shoot—Peter's gazelle, zebra, or should I shoot a waterbuck? There aren't any of them just in position yet but a few more yards and I will shoot for something.

Now I see two beautifully marked giraffe—that settles it—I'll get my giraffe today! One of them almost looks like he is black-and-white, his brown markings are so dark. Now this is something—to shoot a giraffe—few people do unless they can use one. Well, I can—I want one mounted for my sporting goods store—mounted from his front feet to the top of his head just back of the shoulders—it will look as though he is just coming through the wall. I have always wanted this and now is my chance. He has spotted us. Both of them start off in their usual slow motion gallop. They only go about a hundred yards and stop to look back at us. The zebra has something to do with them being frightened for every time this herd of zebra starts a stampede, the giraffe does, too. About 200 yards the smaller of the two stops broadside. The smaller is by far the prettier. He is really one of the most remarkable specimens I have seen so far on this trip. This is the articulated variety of giraffe. Well, I aim—I fire—nothing happens except that both of them run. Could I have missed an animal of that proportion? I fire again as he runs—he just keeps on running and never falters. I start off in pursuit so that when they do stop, I will get another shot. Just a short distance and they stop again, broadside.

I take careful aim and shoot again—they are not over 250 yards. Well, this time at least he knows he has been hit with something. I am using the 220-grain Silvertip. His hind leg is out of order, he is limping some now, but he is going on strong. I change ammunition fast, to the 150-grain Bronze Point expanding bullet that I have loaded to a velocity of 3,600 feet per second and plant one in his shoulder at about 250 yards, and this time, he is down. Again I say, there is no substitute for velocity and one thing sure, it isn't bullet weight. Give me a fast bullet that blows up the whole inside of the animal—this has happened many times on this hunt. The other giraffe slowly runs off through the brush and palms. We walk over to inspect our kill. Well, sir, let me tell you I had the surprise of my life—the size of a giraffe is unbelievable. He is the largest animal I have ever shot so far. He dwarfs our North American moose and the African Cape buffalo. There is only one larger animal over here and that is the elephant and that is in weight only, not in height. This fellow measured 18 feet from the bottom of his feet to the top of his head, and remember he was the smaller of the two. Just step off 18 feet and see if that is not a tall one! From the ground to the bottom of his belly in front, he measured 5 1/2 feet. Now think of a 5 1/2 foot person who could stand under a giraffe. When lying on the ground, his side protruded 5 feet in the air. These animals weigh 3,000 pounds and maybe over. Well, some day you will see him walking through the wall of my store and I will have to have a pretty tall ceiling. Their hide is extremely thick—we left three skinners out there and they have been working on him almost all day. We had to go get the local natives to help turn the animal over for the skinners, promising them the meat for their labor. Later on, we had giraffe tongue for dinner—not bad. We have eaten almost everything but hyena meat so far on this safari. Believe me, I will never forget my first giraffe—and probably my last one— I really do not know where I would put another.

On the way back to camp this evening a couple of natives came running out to the Lorry from the bush—they apparently had heard our motor. I do not know how far they had been running, but they were pretty well out of breath by the time they reached us. They shook hands with both my guide and myself, and then carried on a native conversation with my Hunter. My Hunter relates to me that the men told him that one of their tribe had just died and they wanted us to lend them a shovel so they could dig a grave. It was unfortunate that we did not have a shovel with us. These people seldom see whites and are really a simple people—so meek.

Tonight we are again eating greater bustard, the delicacy of the African plains, all white meat.

JULY 8th:

It was not so warm today—I was up at 4:00 a.m. and on my way after lion. The hartebeest we killed for bait last night is about 20 miles from here so we have to get started early. We load up with natives, and are off for the day. Soon daylight comes as I mentioned before, there are only 12 hours of it over here and that is the year round. Daylight at 6:30 a.m. and it is dark at 6:30 p.m.

No sooner did dawn break than I ran onto some gerenuk—I ran like the devil until I could get a good view. The buck had stopped and was standing looking in my direction. One shot from my .300 Magnum, 150-grain bullet, and that is it—shot through the shoulder and dead.

We stopped about a mile from our lion bait and started walking slowly, working our way up behind thorn bushes and trees. We could see a few hyena and jackal at the kill. Soon we got into full view and there it was—old Leo himself—still at the bait—eight hyena and two jackal standing off at a goodly distance, waiting like buzzards for the lion to leave. This was a beauty and now is my chance. He is about 250 yards—I could shoot him at that distance but I don't want to take any chances, so I am going to try to get a little closer. Silently we creep until we are within 150 yards—I take my time—I aim—the lion is sitting on his haunches—periodically, he grabs at the bait and maybe snares off a little meat, but he cannot get it out of the tree. I put the Lee Dot scope on the lion's shoulder—bang—and the lion falls over and never moves. That is all there is to it. A beauty—500 pounds of savage beast—the king of them all! But how much time, how much patience it takes to get that one shot. How many you pass up because they are not trophy material, until the right moment comes along and when that moment arises you must take advantage of every ounce of wit and knowledge you possess, for outwitting the lion is a great feat. One mis-move, one

171

poor shot, so many things could have made it just another day with no lion. For weeks I have hunted for this fellow and now I have been repaid for my labor.

To my surprise, even after the shot of the rifle, I see oryx ahead of us. I do not have an oryx yet. We leave the skinners to take care of the lion and we go on after oryx. They run like scared rabbits. They are a beautiful animal. I slowly creep up behind a tree and fire at one, 375 yards. I hit him in the paunch—he stumbled around a bit and soon went down. I shot him with my .300 Magnum, using a 150-grain B.P.E. Now I have the gerenuk, an oryx and a lion today.

This afternoon we are in the rhino country. Hunting rhino is a hard job. It is sort of like hunting elephant—our trackers track them down. After hours of much discomfort we see no rhino, however, we had heard the tick bird—this is a warning sign for the rhino to get out. The tick bird is a nuisance—he rides the rhino's back, eating the ticks and lice from his body. At any rate, I have had a successful day.

When I return to camp that night, I learn that Dr. Nickelsen has shot his elephant. The camp was in an air of excitement—everyone was happy—the natives chanted and danced around our table for a quarter of an hour. They picked up Doc, carried him about on their shoulders and put him back on his chair. Such excitement, I have never seen!

JULY 9th:

Today we go to Doc's elephant—all of us. We take the natives along to cut off the feet and tusks—this is a day's job. Pictures are taken of the huge animal—four tons or so. One cannot imagine the size of these huge animals until you are next to one of them. I will go into more detail about the elephant when I shoot mine. Merrill Porter is next—then comes my turn.

At noon I go out with my White Hunter for another zebra or eland or whatever comes along. We start off down through the African bush against a strong southerly wind. This is a wonderful way to hunt as the game cannot hear or smell you. Not 30 minutes had passed until we came face-to-face with a beautiful Grevey zebra. There is one of them in view but we can hear others stamping about. He is facing us and not over 100 feet. I may have mentioned before, but in case I haven't— every day I wear the Army camouflage suit and it definitely is a help in stalking game as you blend in so perfectly with the foliage.

He does not see us—up with my .300 Magnum—I aim at the front part of his shoulder and fire and before the animal ever heard the shot, he was dead. He just did not know what happened. The others stampede out of there in a hurry. He is a beauty—we skin him out. While our men were skinning the zebra, we heard a crash several hundred yards to the east of us as though an elephant had just pushed over a tree, as they so often do. Startled for the moment, we grabbed our rifles and silently stalked through the dense bush country. We never did find signs of that elephant but it had to be one. We carried the zebra hide to the Lorry and went down into lower country.

I shot a Peter's gazelle at 175 yards. Not wanting to spoil the front part of the animal, I fired at the back of the shoulder—hit him a little far back in the ribs, knowing that my .300 would kill him instantly no matter where he was hit. Well, sir, I am in for another lesson in killing power. As I fired, he went down as I had expected. However, as I walked toward him and was within 20 yards, he jumped up and ran as though he had never been hit. He ran 50 yards before I placed another shot to finish him off. I don't know which animals are subject to shock and which ones are not? My next kill was a waterbuck at 225 yards with the .300 Magnum, using a 150-grain bullet—the same load I used on the Peter's gazelle—shot him through the neck—stone-dead. We skinned him out and hung his carcass in a tree for lion bait as we have a permit for two lion in this area. By the time we had him hung in the tree it was dark and we had 20 miles to go through the bush back to camp and, to my surprise and happiness, I find that Porter today shot his elephant. The same excitement in camp—the same chant and native dances—one would have to see and hear this to realize it. Tomorrow it is my turn at elephant!

JULY 10th:

This is the day! Yes, the day I am supposed to find my elephant. The trackers have gone to try and find him—we have driven them in the Lorry about five miles from camp and they have taken off on foot. Brown and I wait for their return—hours pass—such long ones. A native girl comes by—we learn that her husband is one of our trackers. I took many pictures of her and gave her some of the ten cent store jewelry that I brought with me for the natives. She was only about 20 years old, rather a cute little thing for an African native. I learned later from the tracker that he paid two cows, three goats and six pieces of cloth for her. Of course, I learned this through the interpretation of my White Hunter. In these parts, when a native wants a wife, he goes to her father and if the father agrees, they then bargain. A man can have more than one wife if he can afford to buy them. If he grows tired of one wife, he cannot get rid of her, but generally makes life rather difficult for her and she sometimes leaves him. In this instance, he generally goes back to her father and demands the goods that he gave for her.

JULY 11th:

We leave the camp rather early to go to Porter's elephant that he shot two days ago. The men who went after him yesterday failed to find him, so we are taking a tracker with us today so that there will be no doubt about finding the dead elephant. We must cut a path so as to get the truck to where it is—so slow—so very slow going. Our natives are out front cutting down trees and clearing away the bush. We must cut off the elephant's feet, tusks and ears. The feet will be used for wastebaskets, his tusks, of course, are the great prize, and his ears will be skinned out and made into purses, bags, etc. Those ears are five feet across. After hours of hard labor, we arrive and much to our surprise the natives in these parts have found him, too.

Now this is interesting—there is an old man and a little boy about eight years old, and a little girl about twelve, and three skinny cur dogs. They are cooking some of the meat in a pot. They have cut the hide from the elephant's back and cut away pieces of meat and have them hanging on trees, drying these strips into jerky. The smell about the place has to be experienced to be appreciated! The meat is absolutely rotting now—but it matters little to these natives. I cannot tell whether the elephant smells more putrid than the jerky which they have hanging on the bushes all about us. As one of the natives was pulling the tusks from the elephant—now mind you, this tusk has been worked on for more than two hours before it could be pulled out—little pieces of decayed meat were hanging on the sides of the tusks and little native boys would reach over and grab a piece just like wild animals and eat it raw. Soon we were on our way with the trophies back to camp. However, we were now to experience a piece of bad luck: one of our white hunters was down with malaria.

JULY 12th:

Our White Hunter is better today, but not up. Our elephant trackers are out looking for the big bull. While waiting for them, I walked about 30 minutes from camp this morning and saw, within shooting distance, four dik-dik, five giraffe, three gerenuk, three zebra, two monkeys and lots of grouse.

Our skinners in camp are very busy caring for the elephant feet. What a job to remove the meat and bones from an elephant's foot. It is warm today—about 90 degrees, but there is always a breeze which keeps it somewhat cooler. This area is semidesert, very dry, thorn trees, palm trees and fig trees quite plentiful, however. The buzzards are on the trees all over the camp—they have the patience of Jobe. The skinners took the carcasses about 50 yards from the camp and the vultures and buzzards clean them up in nothing flat.

There are elephant here—we have two of them down and one left to go. We walk four miles through hot sun and thorn bush. Soon we come close to where our trackers tell us we will find the elephant. We crawl noiselessly—not a broken branch—not a sound—silence! This is one major consideration—one false move and off the elephant go. Our trackers have told us there are three of them—one large one with tusks about 90 pounds. We are within 50 yards of where they are supposed to be. We move foot by foot, always upwind from them. Soon we can see the movement of one ear. Now we can see the whole elephant and as he moves around we can see two, and the second one is "it." He is facing us head on, but we cannot shoot him and make sure of an instant kill. We must wait for the huge beast to turn sideways, so we must maneuver around. It is risky for us to move. We stand motionless—10 minutes—45 minutes pass! He has his great trunk upwards, pushing and rubbing against the tree, but old Jumbo won't move. Now who is going to make the first move—the elephant or us? The trees wave back and forth and you look for them to be up-rooted any moment. Four to five tons of animal there you know—twice as high as you stand. We are within a hundred feet of him—there are trees between us—we must make the kill on the first shot.

I have the .300 Magnum, specially loaded with 220-grain full patch bullets—two of them—one in the chamber, one in the magazine, followed by two more Silvertip 220 grain. However, the first shot must do it for if it doesn't one never knows what might happen! If the elephant screams, all hell will break loose. The elephant may charge us—also, the one shot, if not wounded badly enough, he may charge! Thoughts run through my mind rapidly. Should I not have my .375 Magnum? Should I use Brown's .470? No, we killed one fellow with a .375 Magnum and Porter's kill was with the .300. I am sold on velocity— I must shoot him in the brain. Once you look at the size of one of these animals, you realize that without question there is no bullet fired from any shoulder rifle, whether it be my .300 or the great .600 double barrel, that will kill an elephant unless hit in a very vital spot—there is just too much animal there. Even a heart shot will not stop him—he will keep on going, sometimes for miles. Soon the old boy turns sideways—up with my rifle—and I aim where his brain should be— and remember that there is a lot of bone and meat that the bullet must penetrate before it reaches that fatal spot—a foot and a half of it. I squeeze the trigger and the animal falls—never a sound.

One elephant bounds off into the bush, then the other. The second elephant turns and comes back—tries to pick up his fallen comrade with his trunk—gets behind him and pushes—makes a terrible fuss. It is time for us to move and move fast before he gets our wind, so away we go. We sneak back in about 15 minutes—he has gone—only the dead elephant remains. A shot through the head—I suppose the brain—but anyway he is dead. The elephant is more than the largest animal in the world—he is huge—massive, and you must see one in the bush to have any idea of the size of this Leviathan.

We are moving camp again—this time to the rhino Country. There are a few rhino here but not enough. The day is ending. The weaver birds have three nests in the trees just above my table. They have retired for the night. Their nests are most interesting. They hang from some small branch, like apples—they are about the size of a small grapefruit and have their entrance at the bottom of the nest. More interesting birds I have never seen.

JULY 13th:

There's game in Africa—there's lots of it, but the elephant, the buffalo, the lion—these are the big three. They are the ones you just don't say, "I am going out to shoot one of these animals and come back with one"—you hunt them, especially the lion and leopard.

We came back to camp quite early today. While strolling about the camp, one of the natives in that vicinity opened his mouth and showed us one of his molars was loose and indicated that it was aching. We rather pitied the old boy, but he thought white men could do anything. Dr. Nickelsen, in our camp, is a surgeon—not a dentist. I took a pair of long handled pliers out of my tool kit and, believe me, right there Doc pulled that man's tooth while I took movies of the episode. The old boy appeared quite grateful. We gave him aspirin to ease his pain and the next day he was all right. The local natives, as soon as they learned that there was a Doctor in camp, came from far and near— whether it was a toothache, an earache, or a pain they just imagined they had.

JULY 14th:

I have lots to do in Nairobi before going back to the States. I have all the game I really want, so I am going back. The new camp is quite interesting—mountains and volcanoes with a reasonably large river, with the banks studded with palm trees and the sand banks covered with crocodile. This is the Euaso Nyiro River.

I would like to stay here and shoot crocodile but I am going to have them drive me into Nanyuki where I will take a train to Nairobi. It is uphill all the way from where we are to Nanyuki—slow traveling.

I don't know what these backward people would ever do if they came to America. They don't know what the word "efficiency" means over here. Now it is a funny thing—I am supposed to sleep on the train tonight—they charge me two shillings for my bedding and I have a compartment. The compartment is about 5 X 8. If you want to go to any other part of the train or to the dining car, you have to wait until the train stops at one of the dozen stops they make—then you get out and walk to the next car. However, I am tired and sleepy and anything looks good to me now.

JULY 15th:

The train moves at 5:30—it awakens me but soon I go back to sleep. At 6:00 a.m. we have stopped at a village—a knock at the outside door, with the usual East African greeting "Chai"—that's tea—it's always served whether you want it or not. Oh well, it's beginning to get daylight now so I'll drink my tea and dress for the day. The train moves on slowly on its narrow track. Now bacon and eggs for breakfast. Soon we stop again. We walk back to our compartment and someone else takes our place in the dining car.

We are about half way to Nairobi—the country here is beautiful—the weather cool. The valleys are green with banana trees, palms, grass, dotted with native huts here and there. As we stop at these small villages, the natives are all out to see the train pass, some bringing corn, some bringing bananas to sell the passengers. They stand outside holding their wares up for you to see. They have learned the value of money. Some stand outside and beg for money.

Remember, it is only 150 miles from Nanyuki to Nairobi and it takes from 5:30 in the morning to 3:30 in the afternoon—this is 20th Century speed! Soon we arrive in the great metropolis. It does seem as though it is a big city after one has been in the "bush" so long. A taxi takes me to the hotel. Oh, it is a great feeling to be back in civilization again—a hot bath, a shave, and a good night's rest.

It is grand to be out in the wilds of Africa and a glorious feeling to stalk the wild game. To see the simple savage lives of the natives, to hear the roar and growl of the lion, the hideous howl and laugh of the hyena, the bark of the monkeys and the baboons, the song of countless tropical birds—but one can hear enough of this, and a month and a half is enough for me at one time. But it will not be long before I will be ready to go back—I love it—the memory will live with me forever.

My experiences and the education I have gained is priceless and forevermore I will hear the thunder of the zebra hooves, their doglike bark. I will see the hyena sneaking away from our kill, the thousands of buzzards that come down like flies as soon as you have made a kill—the old marabou stork—the lion and the cheetah dashing off like greased lightening—the millions of wildebeest, congoni and topi in great herds on the plains of Africa.

However, after returning home from my African safari, the entire picture has changed. There seems to be something instilled deeper in my mind than the beautiful experience of seeing game in countless thousands and in fulfilling a lifetime dream. Well—just about the only way I can explain it to you, is the modern world we live in today and the contrast of nations. Seems as though you look at the whole world differently. You remember I started my diary with "I can't help reminiscing over the past two weeks"—now I can't help reminiscing over the past three months—I can't help but remember a Thursday noon as we left the middle of Africa. As we flew over Nairobi to Kisumu on the shores of Lake Victoria, boarding the South African Airways plane and starting north, soon the green and fertile part of Africa disappeared, and again I looked down upon this great desolate desert that covers the north half of Africa, and in the middle of this desert you could see where the Blue and the White Nile meet, and at the mouth of these two rivers lies Khartoum. We landed, refueled, and were on our way again. Our next stop was only a few hours later, but 1 a.m. on Friday morning. This time it was Tripoli, the last town in Northern Africa.

As we took off from Tripoli, I looked out the window of the plane as we roared from the field—I shall never forget the plane's shadow cast on the white sands below, and watching it disappear as we hit the blue waters of the Mediterranean. I thought of all my wonderful experiences—the great thrill of hunting in Africa—the things that were now behind me, and will remain my fondest memories. In just a scant few hours came daylight—and I looked down on Sicily, Corsica and the shores of Southern France—this remember, was still Friday morning. Then over the majestic Alps—soon Geneva, Switzerland—Paris, France and then looking down on Dieppe. There you could see the runways where the Germans launched the V-2s for bombing London—this, only yesterday, a war-torn country and today, peaceful as the white fleecy clouds above the white cliffs of Dover, so visible as we crossed the English Channel. Early Friday morning we landed in London. We spent the day shopping about that great city. That evening we flew to Prestwick, Scotland—there we had dinner. It was 11 o'clock when we left Prestwick for the United States.

Ten o'clock the next morning we reached New York—a couple of hours to clear Customs, and again boarding a plane, this time for Los Angeles. It was 8:30 Saturday night when we landed at the West Coast Airport. The first thing I could think to say when my family met me was—"Do you realize that it was only yesterday morning that I flew from Africa, across the Mediterranean, Corsica, France, Switzerland, the English Channel, spending the day in London yesterday, dinner in Scotland, this morning in New York, while tonight I am in Los Angeles?" Half way around the world in only a few hours. This modern mode of travel is almost unbelievable.

But it has been the contrast of nations that was really impressive—the conditions in all the countries that I have traveled through—the lack of food and clothing in London— the rationing that still exists—the black market centers of Paris—the poverty—the slums. The same applies to Tripoli with Cairo a thousand times worse. As I looked about me in all of these countries—the automobiles, airplanes, tractors, farm equipment although we have only a small portion of the world's surface and population, just before the war we produced 90 percent of the world's automobiles and airplanes, and today we have two-thirds of the world's telephones—we have 70 percent of the world's educational institutions. One could go on endlessly of the richness of the United States, and then you ask yourself "why?" Could it be because we live in a democracy—could it be because we live in a free country? We ask ourselves, "Is the price we pay too much?" We may be able to get this same democracy for less, and it behooves us to strive to improve our government, but at any price let's keep it a democracy, so that we may have the things which other nations cannot enjoy. Without question we are the richest nation in all the world, and all it will take to prove this to yourself, without any question of doubt, is a trip around the world. It doesn't matter whether it be England, France, Japan, China or Russia—it's all the same the world over. America has the highest standard of living of any nation on the face of the globe. Let's always keep it that way.—*Roy E. Weatherby.*

6

Weatherby Magnum Cartridges

It may be difficult for hunters who have come on the scene in the last two decades to understand why Roy Weatherby's ideas on cartridge design were controversial. Most hunters now accept the idea that high velocity cartridges not only kill better, but that they are easier to hit with (a result of less drop at longer ranges). Forty years ago, that wasn't the case. Those Weatherby magnum cartridges were responsible for a lot of arguments.

In the late 1940's and the 1950's, many hunters believed that large bullets traveling at relatively slow speeds were best. The .30-30, .45-70 and a host of other cartridges were put forth as the models of this theory. Now, there were some high-speed rifle cartridges out there, the .270 Winchester, the .220 Swift, the .300 H&H Magnum, to name just a few. Although there were some advocates of high velocity before Weatherby, no one had really pushed the concept, nor made the claims for it, the way Roy did. Where others said, in effect, that high velocity was nice, Roy said high velocity was best—period. He backed that up with a line of new high-velocity cartridges.

At times, some of the followers of the high-velocity theory made outrageous claims, but Roy kept talking about hydrostatic shock— shock waves in fluid caused by a fast moving projectile. Also, he relied on his own field experience. His powerful cartridges simply killed game animals better. As more hunters tried the Weatherby cartridges (as well as other high velocity cartridges), more successes in the game fields

Weatherby magnum calibers include (l to r) the .224 W.M., .240 W.M.,.257 W.M., 7mm W.M., .300 W.M., .340 W.M., .378 W.M. and the impressive .460 W.M., most powerful factory big game cartridge in the world. Not shown is the latest addition, the .416 Weatherby Magnum.

began to be reported. The result was that many hunters came to accept what Roy had been saying all along.

Just as the Weatherby rifles have been copied, the line-up of the more popular hunting cartridges shows that the public eventually came around to understand and accept the role of high velocity cartridges. No doubt Roy Weatherby was influential, at least in part, in the introduction of such popular cartridges as the .25-06 Remington, the 7mm Remington Magnum, and the .300 Winchester Magnum.

The first Weatherby cartridges were based on other cartridge cases. The series consisting of the .257, .270, 7mm, and .300 Weatherby Magnum cartridges were based on the .300 H&H Magnum case, albeit much modified. The cases were blown out to reduce the drastic taper of the venerable British cartridge (which increased the room for powder); then the shoulder was given a unique double radius, an identifying characteristic of the Weatherby cartridges. With the huge .378 Weatherby Magnum, Roy was breaking ground with a completely new cartridge case. The case held so much powder that Federal Cartridge company developed a new, powerful primer to ensure reliable ignition.

When looking at the impact of Weatherby cartridges on the firearms industry, it's important to remember the time frame of the introductions. To the armchair ballistician, it might not seem that the Weatherby rifle cartridges are that much faster than the competition. That's simply a testament to how the industry followed Roy's lead. Consider that when the .300 Weatherby Magnum was introduced in the mid 1940's, it pushed a 180-grain bullet more than 300 feet per second (fps) faster than the .300 H&H Magnum. Winchester's .300 Magnum wouldn't be introduced until 1963. The .257 Weatherby Magnum had a muzzle velocity an incredible 600 feet per second faster than the .257 Roberts. The Remington .25-06 wasn't introduced until 1969, and it still wasn't as fast as the Weatherby.

The Weatherby line covers the entire range of centerfire rifle cartridges, starting with a .22 caliber—appropriate for groundhogs, prairie dogs and coyotes—all the way to the mammoth .460, the most powerful sporting cartridge in the world.

.220 Weatherby Rocket. This varmint cartridge was based on the .220 Swift case, and was never available as a factory load. Shooters had to load their own. As a result, it never proved terribly popular.

.224 Weatherby Magnum. Although this cartridge isn't the fastest in its category, it is unusual in that the case is of the belted design—a design usually reserved for larger cartridges. It was introduced in 1963.

.240 Weatherby Magnum. This 1968 addition to the line is the fastest factory cartridge in its class. It propels a 100-grain bullet almost 400 feet per second faster than the popular .243 Winchester. The difference means more striking energy for the Weatherby, as well as less drop from the point of aim at long ranges.

.257 Weatherby Magnum. Since 1948, when factory ammunition was first available for this cartridge, the .257 WM has been one of the best long range varmint/big game cartridges ever created. At the time of its introduction, it so far outstripped other 25-caliber cartridges in both power and flat trajectory that it left shooters open-mouthed. Perfect for animals from deer to black bear, it has been used successfully on much larger (and more dangerous) game. Varmint hunters who had been accustomed to holding over their targets at long ranges could hold right on with the factory load, which has an 87-grain bullet at 3,825 fps. Hunters of mule deer, sheep and goats found the same thing. So successful was the .257 Weatherby Magnum cartridge that custom gun makers soon began chambering rifles for it.

.270 Weatherby Magnum. Since 1925, shooters have afforded the Winchester .270 a well-deserved reputation as a long-range big game cartridge. Roy Weatherby took the .300 H&H Magnum case, blew out the body, necked it down to take the .270 bullet, and offered hunters a flatter shooting, harder hitting .270. This cartridge was introduced when Roy started his commercial business in 1945. With 100-grain bullets, it serves well as a varmint cartridge, but it is at its best with the 130 and 150-grain bullets as a big game round.

7mm Weatherby Magnum. One of the original Weatherby cartridges designed in 1944-45, at its introduction the 7mm Weatherby Magnum was compared with the 7mm Mauser, a good, if underloaded, cartridge. The Weatherby gave hunters a full 400 fps increase in velocity. This cartridge has been used successfully for just about every species of big game imaginable. It is well suited for any North American game as well as the thin-skinned African species. No greater compliment has been given the 7mm Weatherby Magnum than Remington's own 7mm magnum, introduced in 1962. The popularity of the Remington round (a belted cartridges which almost duplicates the ballistics of the Weatherby) simply validates Roy's innovation.

.300 Weatherby Magnum. Certainly the most popular Weatherby cartridge, the .300 was used by many well-known sportsmen in hunts all over the world. As these hunts were publicized in outdoor magazines, the advantages of the high-velocity .30-caliber cartridge became known and accepted. As one of the original Weatherby cartridges, the .300 was based on the .300 H&H Magnum, which was also the cartridge with which it was directly compared. The Weatherby version bested its older, British cousin by more than 300 feet per second—an impressive margin. The .300 Weatherby has been described as a perfect choice for the one-gun hunter who travels the world. It certainly is a fine choice for most big game animals anywhere in the world.

.340 Weatherby Magnum. Unlike most other Weatherby cartridges, the .340 (which uses a .338-caliber bullet) was introduced in reaction to a competitor's magnum cartridge — in this case, the Winchester .338 Magnum. In typical Weatherby fashion, however, Roy took advantage of the longer case to pack in more powder, and got more velocity out of his version. The .340 WM shoots heavy bullets at high velocity—a decidedly powerful combination. Although it is at its best on game animals the size of elk or larger, the .340 has found favor with many deer hunters. With well-constructed bullets, it will handle any big game, including Africa's most dangerous. Local game regulations in

Africa, however, sometimes require rifles of .375 caliber or larger for some species.

.375 Weatherby Magnum. No longer in production, this cartridge was a result of the "Weatherby treatment" given to the .375 H&H. By blowing out the case so that it would hold more powder, Roy was able to get 200 fps more muzzle velocity from his improved version. Anything the respected Holland and Holland version can do, the Weatherby .375 can do a bit better. The .378 Weatherby Magnum, introduced in 1953, rendered the .375 WM unnecessary.

.378 Weatherby Magnum. A unique design, the massive cartridge case for the .378 WM is a wonder to behold. The cavernous interior holds so much powder that Federal developed the super-hot Federal 215 primer to ignite it. Deep penetration and bone smashing power are the calling cards of the .378 WM. Compared with the .375 H&H, a powerful cartridge in its own right, Roy Weatherby's creation develops an incredible 34 percent more energy — about 6,000 foot pounds at the muzzle. With 270-grain, pointed bullets, it also is a flat-shooting cartridge. Just as the performance of the 378 is impressive, so is the recoil.

.416 Weatherby Magnum. The most recent addition to the Weatherby line of proprietary cartridges, the .416 WM was the idea of Roy's son, Ed, who is now president of Weatherby, Inc. By necking up the .378 case to take a .416-caliber bullet, Weatherby not only eclipsed the .416 Rigby (introduced in 1911), but stole a bit of the thunder from the Remington .416 Magnum, announced at about the same time as the Weatherby version. Many African hunters looking for more penetration than could be had with the .458 Winchester, but who didn't want to go all the way to the .460 Weatherby, had asked for a .416 Magnum cartridge. Weatherby's version provides penetration, energy, and flat trajectory. Most hunters of dangerous game would be well satisfied with the newest offering from Weatherby.

.460 Weatherby Magnum. Of course, there are those who need (or just enjoy) the biggest, the most powerful. For them, the .460 Weatherby Magnum is the answer. Its claim as the world's most powerful commercial hunting cartridge has never been questioned. Professional hunters in Africa who have found lesser cartridges wanting often adopt the .460 WM as a trusted friend. Most hunters would rightly put the Winchester .458 into the super-powerful category, but the .460 develops at least 50 percent more energy! Naturally, Newton's laws of motion dictate that recoil will be substantial. Those who have success-fully stopped charging elephants, buffalo, lions and other dangerous game with the cartridge, however, seldom mention recoil. Not every-one needs four tons of smashing power, but for those who do, there's only one choice — the .460 Weatherby Magnum.

Testing the Effect of High Velocity

Because the theory of high velocity was not widely accepted and remained a controversial issue during Roy's early days in business, he conceived various means of dramatically testing the effects of high velocity. In conducting one of these tests, Roy set up five-gallon drums of water for targets, shooting at them with a standard .30-06 caliber rifle and with his .300 Weatherby Magnum caliber, both using 180 grain soft point bullets.

The .30-06 split the seams of the drum but it remained pretty much intact. The bullet didn't penetrate the back side of the drum.

When shot with the .300 Weatherby Magnum and the same bullet, traveling some 500 fps faster, water sprayed into the air like a geyser. It was impossible to tell whether the bullet passed through the other side, for the drum was blown apart.

Another test he performed was on a eucalyptus tree with a trunk measuring about six inches in diameter. The .30-06 caliber rifle made a small hole through the trunk, but the .300 Weatherby Magnum completely severed the trunk, with the top half of the tree plunging to the ground.

At one point Pete Kuhlhoff, gun editor of *Argosy* Magazine, tested the .300 Weatherby Magnum cartridge and the .300 H & H Magnum against a piece of 1/2-inch special armor plate. The U.S. government's armor-piercing load had not been able to penetrate the plate. The .300 H & H Magnum merely made a mark on it. "But the .300 Weatherby cleanly penetrated the armor plate at 100 yards," Kuhlhoff wrote.

7

Building the Rifle

For years Weatherby produced his deluxe rifles on any action available, such as the Model 70 Winchester, Remington Model 700, and the Springfield. He was buying rifle barrels from Ackley and Buhmiller, chambering them and fitting them to whatever action he could obtain.

From the very beginning, a feature of the Weatherby rifle was the highly polished and blued barrel, with a streamlined taper. At that time Weatherby was still selling his rifles only to individual customers. Gun dealers were reluctant to carry them because they were still in the "wildcat" class and ammunition was not available. Depending upon the action that was used, his deluxe rifle was priced at $150 to $165 retail.

Investigating European Manufacturing Sources

Although the volume of his rifle business was continuing to increase each year, Weatherby was faced with tremendous overhead costs. Some of them stemmed from his belief in advertising nationally on a large scale. By 1954 he had hired an advertising agency, but he still played a major role in the actual composition of his ads.

Building the rifles in the U.S., in California, was very expensive. Many workers were required to assemble all the rifle parts in South Gate, and this labor cost was a big financial drain. The imported F.N.

action from Belgium was reasonably priced, but the U.S. costs for barrel steel and stock wood kept rising because of postwar inflation.

Skilled workmen at high wages were also required to produce the rifle barrels in his shop, to operate the stock carving equipment, and to completely finish the rifle stocks. Checkering, inletting, bedding and range firing added to the final cost. As a result, although it was to be several years before it would come to pass, Weatherby was already thinking of the benefits to be derived from having all of these manufacturing steps performed in a European country where labor rates were so much cheaper.

He believed it would be much more profitable if he could get out of the manufacturing phase entirely, having the finished product made by someone else. Then, Weatherby could function in the US solely as a sales and distribution organization, with only the custom rifle work continuing as a local operation.

Looking for a manufacturer, Roy had been corresponding with Husqvarna in Sweden, Birmingham Small Arms (BSA) in England, Schultz & Larsen in Denmark and Sako in Finland. In the fall of 1954 Roy visited each of these European plants to discuss details. Maynard Buehler, a good friend and president of the Buehler Scope Mount Company in Orinda, California, agreed to accompany him on that European jaunt.

One of Roy's pleasures was the collection and restoration of antique automobiles. He had acquired by this time a '31 Marmon, a '39 Graham, and a Franklin, and was in the process of restoring each of them. Maynard Buehler shared this affinity for classic automobiles, but Weatherby was also pleased to have Maynard along because of his wealth of knowledge about guns and shooting, and his years of experience as a machinist, toolmaker and tool engineer.

Weatherby was very impressed with the BSA organization and their very large, well equipped factory. They seemed receptive to the idea of working with Weatherby, and he left there convinced that their standard rifle was one of the finest on the market. He especially admired another newly designed rifle of BSA's, despite it not having a recessed bolt face.

They discussed the possibility of Weatherby importing their standard rifle under the BSA name and distributing it in the United States. BSA seemed willing to build their rifle under the Weatherby name, but with the Weatherby design features, at a slightly higher price. No firm decision would be made until Weatherby visited several other firms.

In London, Weatherby and Buehler toured the Rolls Royce Company. This was of appeal to Buehler since his interest in and acquisition of old cars had centered around Rolls Royces. Later on, in the '70s, Weatherby himself purchased a Silver Cloud RR which required very little restoration before he resold it. This tour through the Rolls Royce plant was a highlight of the trip for both men.

Weatherby and Buehler then flew to Copenhagen, where they were met by Mr. Larsen of the Schultz & Larsen Company. The Schultz & Larsen Company is located in the town of Otterup, about 100 miles from Copenhagen. Prior to his visit, Weatherby had provided them with the drawings necessary for them to build up a rifle chambered for his new .378 case, since he felt that even the new F.N. Magnum Mauser action was not strong enough to handle it. They had the rifle completed, ready for him to test, and he was extremely pleased with the results. Since he had already received a number of orders for this rifle, a result of the publicity of its introduction on his 1953 African safari, he asked S&L to build a quantity of these rifles as quickly as possible and ship them to South Gate.

One thing Roy did not like was the potbellied appearance of the Schultz & Larsen stock in the area of the receiver. It was due to the fact that the action did not have a staggered magazine. Instead, the three cartridges held in the magazine fit one on top of the other. Roy even discussed the possibility that they build a receiver to accommodate staggering the cartridges in the magazine, but he wasn't prepared to pay the cost of additional tooling. Later, Schultz & Larsen did introduce an improved version of their action incorporating Roy's suggestion of a staggered magazine.

Roy's first visit to the Sako plant in Riihimaki, Finland, about 50 miles north of Helsinki, was next on the agenda. It was an old factory. Once owned by the Finnish Home Guard, when Russia took over Finland in the early days of World War I they intended to dismantle the factory. But the Finns finally promoted a deal with Russia for the factory to be taken over by the Red Cross. Following the war, they went back into rifle production with rifles being made only for civilian use.

The Sako plant equipment was relatively obsolete, but there were also other problems. At the time the Sako action was small, accommodating only the .222 caliber and smaller. Also, any arrangements made with Sako would have to be handled through Jan Winter at Firearms International in Washington, D.C., who had the exclusive US distribution rights for Sako (as well as F.N.) all tied up.

Before his visit Roy had asked Firearms International to send some Mauser actions to Sako with the request that they build sample rifles duplicating his Weatherby Deluxe rifle. When Roy arrived those samples were finished. He learned that, even paying a middleman profit to Firearms International, he could still have the Weatherby rifle built by Sako and shipped to him as a completely finished product for less than it cost to produce it in South Gate. Right then, on the spot, Roy formalized arrangements for the next 1,000 F.N./Weatherby actions to be shipped direct to Sako from Belgium for these rifles.

On his 1953 visit to Husqvarna Vapenfabriks in Sweden Roy was enthusiastic about their new HVA action. Tradewinds, Inc., in Tacoma, Washington had exclusive distribution rights in the U.S. for the Husqvarna rifle action, so early in 1954 he asked Irv Walentiny, president of Tradewinds, to send him two of the new HVA actions.

Weatherby Deluxe rifles were built on them by the South Gate craftsmen, and Roy sent one of them to Husqvarna by the middle of 1954. He asked that they bid not only on production of the rifle, but on altering their receiver somewhat as F.N. had done, with the name Weatherby to be engraved on the side. As it turned out, Husqvarna could not take on any added production for 1955. They were literally swamped with orders for their own rifle with this new action, and declined to even quote prices on building rifles and actions for Weatherby. Weatherby canceled his planned visit to Husqvarna on this 1954 trip.

From Copenhagen Weatherby and Buehler flew to Berlin where they were met by Mr. Kohler, a representative of Heym, a firearms firm located in Bad Neustadt, a small town in the very rural section of Germany. Here Weatherby learned that Heym had been a very large firearms firm prior to the war, located in East Germany. But the owners escaped to West Germany, and opened up a new factory with practically nothing. Whereas they formerly had about 700 employees, now it was about 200.

Although their building was new the machinery was quite obsolete. They were building double barreled shotguns and drillings the old way, with many hand operations, so their price was high. Although Heym had the capacity and facilities for building an action and a complete rifle to Weatherby specifications, they wanted Roy to pay for all of the tooling. That didn't interest him at all.

In Vienna they visited the Springer Company, makers of fine rifles and shotguns for many generations. It was interested in working with Weatherby, and provided him with samples of some of their engraving. The factory had very poor, obsolete equipment and was dark and cold, but the engraving was the finest Roy had ever seen. He thought it would be practical to send floorplates and trigger guards, and even actions, to them for engraving, and have them returned to South Gate.

In Zurich, Weatherby changed roles, going from a buyer to a salesman. He called on the firm of Glaser, the largest gun dealer in Switzerland, and was greatly surprised to find the name "Weatherby" as well known in Europe as in the United States. The firm of Glaser had already been handling some Weatherby rifles on a per order basis. As a result of Weatherby's visit, they agreed to handle not only Weatherby rifles and ammunition, but would order the Weatherby Imperial scope direct from Hertel & Reuss, and stock it in their inventory as well. It was Weatherby's first venture into the European retail market.

1956 European Trip

In 1956 Weatherby made another trip to Europe, this time a very hurried one lasting only two weeks. He took with him a sample of his own, new Mark V action.

Steyr-Daimler-Puch in Steyr, Austria, which was then manufacturing the Mannlicher rifle, appeared very eager to work with him on the production of this action once they saw the prototype. The sample Roy had with him was still not the final one, however, as each time one was completed he would find other changes he wished to make.

When he told Steyr about some of some of the changes he had in mind, they agreed to make a new prototype for him at a cost of $2,000. They made it clear, however, that any changes they made in the new prototype would come under their production rights and they would not allow Weatherby to have these built into his action if Steyr were not the manufacturer. They also quoted an initial tooling charge for this action of approximately $200,000. Weatherby was certain this was more money than he would be able to invest and, knowing that he planned to visit other firearms firms on this trip, he made no commitment to Steyr.

When Roy arrived at Schultz & Larsen they were completing the first 125 .378 rifles that Weatherby had ordered the year before, but gave him the bad news that higher labor costs would mean an increase in price for additional guns. That reinforced Weatherby's conviction that he must find somebody to manufacture his own action. He knew there would be no problem in building the .378 cartridge on this Mark V action.

Sako was interested, but were so swamped with work they couldn't get to Weatherby's action for another 18 months. And there had been delay in the production of the thousand rifles Weatherby had ordered from them on his last visit, largely because they still hadn't received from Belgium the initial shipment of the Weatherby-identified F.N. Mauser actions. Roy noticed that wages were up in Finland, and he still felt that Austria was the best bet from a labor cost standpoint.

In Birmingham, England, at the BSA factory, Roy made his last pitch with his new action. BSA was impressed with his sample action, and were especially enthusiastic about the safety features he had incorporated. At one point they even suggested they redesign their new action they were developing to incorporate the best features of both actions, and asked his opinion of whether to call it the "BSA-Weatherby" or the "Weatherby-BSA." If this could be agreed to, they advised there would be no tooling charge. If they were to tool up specifically for the Weatherby action, the fee for tooling would be about $20,000.

Although he didn't tell them, Weatherby felt that even this relatively small sum was not a realistic quotation, but he acted as if it were a very normal fee.

BSA seemed a bit disturbed at the price of $53 FOB Austria that had been quoted by Steyr to produce a complete rifle on the Weatherby action. But their director, Mr. Gaydon, kept overriding all objections put forth by his staff, and commented, "We'll come close to it anyway, let's go ahead."

With the wages in England being about double of those in Austria, Weatherby didn't hold out much hope for a final quotation to be this low. But the difference in the tooling estimates was so vast he decided to leave his prototype action with BSA. It was agreed that they would write him immediately with a bid for the tooling of his action and the time involved to start production of his rifles. They would also quote on a rifle built on their own action after modifying the tooling to incorporate features from both actions. In turn, Weatherby was to provide them with the price of barrel steel from the U.S., and stock wood to be shipped to them.

Later in the spring Roy's optimistic bubble was quickly burst when the BSA sales manager returned the prototype. Their engineers had decided that Roy's principle of having nine locking lugs instead of the conventional two, plus having them be the same diameter as the bolt body, was not feasible and just could not be done. He was unable to convince them otherwise, and all negotiations with BSA came to an end. Roy later noted, however, that when BSA put their new action on the market, a number of his innovative safety features had been incorporated.

A Multiplicity Of Projects

By mid-1956 Roy had so many irons in the fire it's a wonder he had any time left to see to the day to day business. He was producing rifles in his own shop, using the F.N./Weatherby Magnum Mauser actions. He was having his cartridge case brass produced at Norma in Sweden, and was loading all of the ammunition in his own shop. He had designed a brand new cartridge case—the .378 Weatherby Magnum— that Norma was adding to their production. Schultz & Larsen in Denmark was building 125 of these .378 caliber rifles for him on their action. Sako in Finland was tooling up to produce 1,000 complete Weatherby rifles on the F.N./Weatherby action.

Roy hoped that this Sako arrangement would eventually replace his South Gate production entirely, except for Custom rifles. By this time Roy was also buying the left hand action produced by Mathieu Arms in Oakland, California, and was providing the southpaw shooter with a version of his Weatherby Deluxe rifle. He had also built three of the five prototypes it took to finalize the Mark V action design, and was continually in search of somebody to build a complete rifle for him on this revolutionary new action.

Constantly seeking ways to improve quality and cut costs, in 1956 Roy decided the chrome lining of his rifle barrels could be discontinued. Henry Timken of Timken Roller Bearing Company in Canton, Ohio was another Weatherby rifle customer who had become a good friend. Roy learned that Timken was producing barrel steel with a higher chrome content than the Carpenter steel he had been using. Not only was the cost of this new steel 40 percent less than what he had been paying, but the steel itself was much more stable, required almost no straightening, which resulted in improved and more efficient production. It also meant much less time and money spent in range firing the rifles because of the inherent accuracy of this barrel steel.

The .460 Weatherby Magnum Cartridge

The .460 Weatherby Magnum caliber, the biggie, was developed by Roy early in 1957, and resulted from changes made in hunting regulations in Africa. They prohibited hunters from taking the larger thick skinned animals, such as elephant, rhino and Cape buffalo, with anything smaller than a 40 caliber.

For several years Weatherby had become aware of some resistance on the part of most of the African professional white hunters to the Weatherby cartridges. Many of these guides were from the old school favoring big bore calibers with heavier, slow-moving bullets, and they were reluctant to change.

Although no direct reference was made to Weatherby when these new caliber restrictions were put into effect in Africa, he nevertheless felt this was done at least partially to limit, if not reduce, the ever increasing number of Weatherby calibers being used by hunters on their safaris. Roy believed that his big .378, moving a 300-grain bullet at 3,000 feet per second with 6,000 foot-pounds of muzzle energy, was enough for any animal. He deemed it essential, however, that Weatherby believers and followers should be provided a cartridge with which they would be allowed to take even the largest of game. So, spurred on by these new African regulations, he proceeded to neck up his .378 case to take the .458 caliber bullet.

He called it the .460 Weatherby Magnum. That was early in 1957, and it would become known as the world's most powerful caliber, shooting the 500-grain bullet at 2,700 feet per second, and giving almost 8,100 foot-pounds of muzzle energy.

Weatherby used the Brevex Magnum Mauser action when he made up his first .460 caliber rifle, and it was on this action that all of his production rifles in this caliber were built until the advent of the Mark V action.

He took the first model .460 with him on his Alaskan hunt for Kodiak bear in May, 1957. Although he didn't use it to shoot his bear, he did do some field testing and was extremely pleased with the results.

Early Development Of The Mark V Action

In all of his discussions and negotiations with the European firearms firms, Weatherby was discouraged by the length of time it took to consummate any kind of an arrangement. Also, over the years as he looked at the various bolt actions available, Roy became more and more convinced he could develop a better, safer action. He was particularly interested in strength. Too many handloaders were overloading, resulting in blown primers and ruptured caseheads, allowing the gasses to come back through the bolt mechanism and into the shooter's face and eyes.

Roy found the Mauser-type action okay, but felt that it left the head of the case sort of hung out in the open. He knew that most actions on the market at that time would withstand about 70,000 c.u.p. (copper units of pressure), but he wanted one to handle 200,000. He wanted a bolt which provided a countersunk bolt face to enclose the cartridge casehead, with the bolt fitting into a counterbored barrel breech, making it almost impossible for the casehead to rupture. He also wanted three vent holes in the bolt body to relieve gases in case of a blown primer. He also wanted a solid enclosed, or shrouded, bolt sleeve, making it impossible for gascs to come back into the shooter's face.

His design featured nine lugs, like an artillery breechblock. Along with these multilugs, he was determined that they would not stand out beyond the periphery of the bolt itself. He wanted them the same diameter as the bolt body, and the bolt body to be the same diameter as the inside diameter of the receiver so that when the bolt was worked back and forth, it would have a smooth, fluid movement instead of the sloppy fit typical of some other actions.

Weatherby took the first rough, handmade sample of his new action with him when he went to Washington D.C. in the spring of 1955 for the NRA annual meetings. He contacted Burt Munhall, his friend at the H. P. White Ballistics Laboratory in Bel Air, Maryland, to get his opinion of this new action. He showed it to Gen. Hatcher and Col. Harrison at the NRA, as well as other experts in that organization, seeking their opinions. They were all very impressed and encouraged Roy to develop and get this action on the market as quickly as possible.

Weatherby asked Gen. Hatcher if he could suggest anyone to work on the design, since Roy did not feel he had the capacity of putting on paper all of the technical specifications. Hatcher suggested John Garand, the inventor of the Garand automatic. When Weatherby contacted him in Springfield, Massachusetts, he learned that John was definitely retired and was not interested in taking on any new job. Walter Howe, the editor of the *American Rifleman* Magazine, then called a friend of his at Marlin Firearms in New Haven, Connecticut, and was told of a development and engineering firm by the name of Mathewson Tool Company there in New Haven, who had done a great deal of work with Remington, Winchester, High Standard and the Government. This firm did nothing but design and build prototypes.

Weatherby traveled to New Haven to meet with Dave Mathewson, who greeted him with great enthusiasm. He was very impressed with Weatherby's rough sample, and told him he would do the designing, draw up the blueprints, make a prototype and have it ready within two weeks. His estimate for this work was about half what Weatherby had already spent in his own shop on this action. He left the sample with Mathewson, told him it needed some streamlining, and asked that he work out a couple of the manufacturing problems that Weatherby had not been able to solve.

The two weeks stretched into several months, however, and it was not until late in the fall that Weatherby received Dave Mathewson's prototype. He was a little disappointed with this first working model as it did not include all of the changes he had asked Mathewson to incorporate, and, in fact, he felt not too much had been accomplished over the original model left with him in the spring.

Naming The New Action "Mark V"

Little did Weatherby realize at that time the number of design changes and sample actions that would be required before he was to get into production more than two years later. In 1957, when the first complete rifle was finally made up as a working sample, he showed it to Elgin Gates. It was the fifth and final working model, as during the past two years they had designed and abandoned four other prototypes before finally settling on this one.

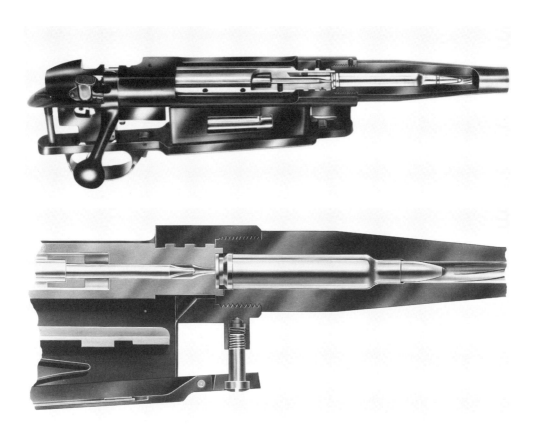

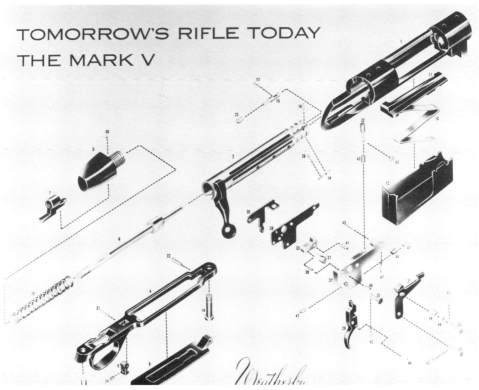

TOMORROW'S RIFLE TODAY
THE MARK V

The Mark V action developed by Weatherby is extremely strong, necessary to handle the powerful magnum calibers that bear the Weatherby Magnum name.

"We're stumped as to what to call this new Weatherby", Roy told Elgin. "Shall we call it the Model Five, or should we give it some fancy name like the Californian. What do you think?"

Gates, who was the west coast representative for Mercury Outboard Motors, a company that dubbed its various models as Mark this or Mark that, thought a moment and said, "Call it the Mark V." Weatherby replied, "We'll do just that! It will be the Mark V." And so it is.

Testing the Mark V Action

This fifth and final prototype action had been built with the help of a newly-hired engineer, Fred Jennie. It was even more streamlined, and also incorporated a new simplified trigger and safety mechanism to reduce tooling and manufacturing costs.

Was this the safest action ever produced, as Weatherby claimed? Roy thought that, finally, it was time to subject his new action to vigorous performance tests. Built on the prototype action, a rifle in .300 Weatherby Magnum caliber was used for the tests. Prior to any firing, careful measurements were taken of the diameter of the bolt face housing, head space measurements were recorded, and all other pertinent dimensions.

The first test firing was with a cartridge that had been loaded with 82 grains of 4350 DuPont powder, using the 180-gr. bullet. This load gave an average breech pressure of 65,000 psi. After firing, there was no sign of pressure and extraction was easy. The same 82-gr. load was fired in the Mauser action and a slight sticking of the cartridge case resulted. Four more loads with the powder charge being increased in two-grain increments were prepared, each one using 4350 powder and the 180-gr. bullet. After firing the 84-gr. load, there was still no sign of pressure and no sticking of the cartridge case, even though the breech pressure had been increased to almost 75,000 psi. When firing this 84-gr load in the Mauser action, it caused a blown primer and it was almost an impossibility to extract the cartridge case.

When the load was increased to 86 grains in the Mark V, the cartridge case began to show signs of pressure, but it still did not stick and extracted easily. Breech pressures were 85,000 to 95,000 psi. A measurement of this fired cartridge case showed that it had stretched at the belt by .0005 inches. When the 88-gr. load was fired in the Mark V with pressures in the neighborhood of 100,000 psi, there was a slight sticking of the cartridge case making the bolt slightly difficult to open, but the cartridge case could still be easily extracted. In measuring the belt again, it had now swelled .002 of an inch, from .533 to .535.

For the final test the cartridge case was filled with powder, leveling it off at the top. This was 90 grains of powder. After firing, the bolt was difficult to open, but without exerting too much pressure it could be opened and the case extracted. There were now extreme signs of pressure on the case, but no gas had escaped back into the magazine and the primers showed very slight signs of leaking. The belt of the cartridge case still measured .535 inches. After this firing, a difference between the outside diameter of the head of the bolt and the inside diameter of the barrel of .004 inches (or .002 a side) was noted. Even with this terrific overload, there was still no swelling or damage to any part of the bolt, receiver or barrel. The head space was checked between each test firing and at no time was there any change noted in the head space.

Weatherby was extremely excited after these tests, and felt certain that the Mark V would be the safest action of all time!

Some time later, after additional working models of this prototype had been produced, one last experiment was made. A 180-gr. .30 caliber bullet was lodged in the throat of the barrel. A standard load of 78 grains of 4350 and the 180-gr. bullet was chambered and fired, with the following results: both bullets traveled out the barrel, pressures were tremendously high, the primer was pierced letting gases enter the interior of the bolt, hitting the firing pin sleeve which acted as a piston, loosening the bolt sleeve cap somewhat. The bolt was opened by hand. The cartridge case remained in the chamber, but no problem was involved in tapping it out with a steel rod. The case appeared to be in very good condition with the exception of the primer being pierced.

In checking the dimensions of the barrel and action, it was found that the barrel in front of the receiver ring expanded from 1.147 inches to 1.1496 inches. The diameter of the bolt head expanded from .7178 to .7190. Head space increased from .2163 to .2174. All other dimensions remained the same as prior to the test.

This experiment was repeated 15 additional times. The severest test was when a 220-gr. bullet was placed in the bore, and a standard 180-gr. round fired in back of it. On this particular firing, the head diameter of the cartridge increased to .545 inches. It was also noted after these additional 15 firings that the head space was set back a mere .001. This was truly the ultimate in tests for the strength and safety of this remarkable new action.

Production of the Mark V Action and Rifle

After receiving bids from several companies for production of the complete action, as well as other bids for production of various parts of the action, a decision was finally made to go with a firm in San Leandro, California called Precision Founders, Inc. It agreed to manufacture all of the main parts of the action, nine castings, using the "lost wax" or investment cast process. This process necessitated a final machining of these nine castings, which was accomplished by yet another firm, Gardner Machine Co. in Hollywood, California. Picco Industries in Sierra Madre, California, produced the powdered metal parts: the magazine floorplate catch, trigger sear, and the thumb button safety. Several other local firms were involved in producing the various springs, small screws and other miscellaneous small parts. All products were delivered to Weatherby's South Gate plant, where the final polishing and bluing and assembly of the complete action took place.

The total cost of this U.S.-produced action, including the final assembly, was about $40. The total tooling costs required by all of the companies involved were just under $20,000. Added to the cost of the complete action was the barrel and stock assembly. Both were produced in Weatherby's shop on his barrel making equipment and the stock pantograph machine. The cost of these material and labor charges, plus the assembled action cost, brought the complete Mark V rifle cost up to considerably more than that of the FN/Weatherby rifle.

In November of 1957 (almost three years after Weatherby had built his first prototype of this action), all negotiations with Precision Founders, Inc. (PFI) had been made, and a purchase order calling for 10,000 action assemblies was issued to them. A like number of the miscellaneous parts required were ordered from the other suppliers as well. The tooling at PFI was to be completed within four weeks to four months, but it was nine months before any castings were received for approval. It was another two months before acceptable shipments started arriving. The rejection rate was extremely high, because when they polished the action to a high lustre, it was discovered that small shrinkage cracks and pinhole pits frequently could not be removed.

Although Weatherby found the investment cast action to be just as strong as a forged action, it kept running into the problem of being unable to entirely eliminate the porosity or tiny pinholes that appeared in the finish at the time of final polishing and bluing. This porosity would not have been noticeable if a matte finish had been used as on most rifles of other makes, but with the high lustre bluing that had become synonymous with Weatherby rifles, this was a definite problem.

Delivery of the nine component parts by PFI was so unbalanced that it made final assembly of a completed action, in the quantities required to keep up with the orders, erratic and unsatisfactory. Quality was unreliable, and the rejection rate continually ran about 50 percent. Weatherby kept insisting on improved quality or he would be forced to cancel his contract for the remainder of the 10,000 actions. PFI argued that they were producing the cast parts according to generally accepted commercial quality. To meet Weatherby's final finish requirements, PFI insisted, new production techniques would have to be developed at increased costs. Thus, the originally estimated cost of $40 for a completed action ended up being closer to $65.

These escalating manufacturing costs reduced Weatherby's profit and hurt sales. When he introduced this revolutionary new action at the National Sporting Goods Dealers Show in February of 1958, and launched a national advertising campaign in consumer publications, the response was overwhelming. Roy soon had such a backlog of orders that he knew it would take years to ship them all at the rate PFI was producing. He still had a supply of rifles built on the F.N. action, but they were difficult to sell. Almost everyone wanted to wait for delivery of the new Mark V.

Mark V Production At J.P. Sauer In Germany

In June of 1957 Weatherby had made another trip to Europe, his second in less than six months. He had learned of a firm, J.P. Sauer & Sohn, located in Eckernfoerde, West Germany, that he had not investigated on his previous visits to Europe since it was primarily a shotgun manufacturer. This time he took the new action to Sauer and met with the same good impression as had been the case with all of the other arms companies he'd visited previously. Udo van Meeteren, the owner,

201

was eager to negotiate a contract for the manufacture of not only the action itself, but completed rifles as well.

Within two months after his June visit to Eckernfoerde all negotiations had been completed, and a contract was signed for production of 10,000 rifles at an FOB Germany cost of $66.30 for a complete rifle, or $29.30 for the action only. Upon signing the contract in August of 1957, Weatherby forwarded a check for $15,000 to cover one half of the $30,000 tooling costs, with the remaining $15,000 to be amortized on the first 2,000 completed rifles produced.

Although he had also contracted with PFI for US production of his Mark V action, Weatherby felt there were many advantages to having his rifles produced in Germany. At this point he knew there definitely was a European market for Weatherby products. Sauer already had a sales organization throughout Europe, and a subsidiary in Canada (Canadian Sauer Ltd.) to which they could make direct shipments for the Canadian market.

Weatherby was already encountering delays and procrastinations on the part of PFI for US production, and he felt that the arrangement with Sauer would give him double protection. If either source were to fail he could continue production.

In February of 1958, Fred Jennie, Weatherby's engineer, made the first of many trips to the J.P. Sauer plant in Eckernfoerde. His visit concentrated on discussion of the first hand-built prototypes that had been sent to Weatherby for approval. What he accomplished there in four days would have required months of correspondence. Jennie was impressed with the thoroughness of Sauer in everything it undertook, and left there very confident that it would do an excellent job for Weatherby.

He also learned that the investment cast process in Germany was far behind that in the United States, probably because there were no government funds available for research and development. Sauer was amazed at the quality of the investment cast parts from the PFI tooling. With Walter Spiegelburg, Sauer's Technical Director, unsure of the German investment cast process, it was agreed that the receiver and the bolt should be made of forgings, at least for the time being.

One area in which Jennie was able to give them immediate assistance was head spacing. Because the Weatherby cartridges were designed on a belted case with which they had no experience, they were not aware of how to head space properly. They were head spacing from the head of the cartridge to the shoulder, rather than from the head to the belt. Fred explained this thoroughly and agreed to send them a complete set of go, no-go and adjustable head space gauges.

Sauer had recently purchased a new machine utilizing a revolutionary technique for the production of rifle barrels. This is known as cold swaging or hammer forging, and the resulting uniformity of the bore from breech to muzzle assures greater accuracy and longer barrel life. Although widely used in the firearms industry now, the Weatherby Mark V rifle was the first to introduce a hammer forged rifle barrel in the United States.

It took more than a year for J.P. Sauer to begin producing the Mark V rifle. Many problems had to be resolved, along with educating their people in the techniques of metal polishing and bluing, proper application and buffing of the Weatherby stock finish and similar techniques. Early in 1959, however, monthly shipments of Weatherby rifles from Sauer were arriving in South Gate. In June of that year Weatherby introduced the *lefthand* Mark V action from German production.

The Ammunition

When Roy began building rifles in 1946 there were no bullets on the market for handloading, so Weatherby thought he wanted to get into the bullet business. Government surplus bullet machines were available for sale. Very expensive pieces of equipment originally, they were being offered at $1,000 or less, but Roy didn't have a spare $1,000.

Lacking such a machine, Roy started making bullets by hand out of copper tubing and lead wire, and actually put them on the market. Bub Martin, son of the fellow who had helped Roy before he went into full-time business, pressed out all the bullets on the bullet press in the afternoons after high school. Later on Bub headed up the loading department of Weatherby for years.

Weatherby-made Ammo

For customers who were not handloaders, Weatherby would furnish reloaded ammunition for his calibers at $.30 per round, or $6 a box. He bought .300 H & H brass from any source he could, eventually getting most of it direct from Winchester. When loading it he often mixed corn meal with the gunpowder to reduce the cost of fireforming cases in each customer's particular chamber. The fireformed cases would then be reloaded to the Weatherby velocities and furnished to the customer as loaded ammunition.

For the shorter magnums, this meant that the .300 cases had to be trimmed at the neck and run through the sizing die before they could be loaded and fireformed. All of this for $.30 a round!

In those first few years following World War II, when so many people in business were just struggling to keep their heads above water, it appears that the larger companies were much more compassionate and understanding than they are today. As an example, a letter dated December 22, 1946, from the Explosives Department of E.I. du Pont de Nemours & Co. reads as follows:

Dear Mr. Weatherby:

This will acknowledge your order of December 20th.

The Interstate Commerce Commission regulations do not permit the shipment of sporting powders C.O.D., so it is impossible for us to handle your order in this way. You state that if we issue our bill, you will send us payment by return mail. Your order amounts to $110.50. We are asking our factory to make prompt shipment to you and in the meantime ask that you send us your check for $110.50 in payment. We realize these small shipments are very slow in reaching you and that you probably would like to avoid tying up your money until the shipment is actually made. If you desire, we will not deposit your check until we receive the shipping papers and issue our invoice.

We trust that this meets with your approval.

Very truly yours,

S.M. Strohecker, Jr.

Manager

It would be highly unusual to receive such a thoughtful and considerate letter from a firm the size of du Pont today.

Weatherby Cartridge Case Brass Manufactured by Speer

In 1950 Jack O'Connor moved from Tucson, Arizona to Lewiston, Idaho, and Roy visited him several times. On one of those he also visited the Speer Bullet Company in Lewiston, which was run by Vernon

Speer. Richard Spear, Vernon's brother, not affiliated with the Spear Bullet Company, was reputed to be going into the business of making cartridge cases, so Roy talked with him.

Richard told Weatherby that he had developed an exclusive "forged from solid" process which would give a superior grain structure to the cartridge case, thus giving it greater strength. Speer added that he had a tentative order with a cartridge company to furnish him cartridge cases that were drawn and headed, but not tapered, head turned or neck annealed, operations he planned to complete in his own plant.

Since Speer planned to manufacture custom ammunition and un-primed cases in many other calibers besides the Weatherby calibers, it was decided that the name Speer would appear on the head stamp rather than Weatherby. In April of 1950 Weatherby placed an order with Richard Speer for 50,000 cartridge cases in four Weatherby calibers—.257, .270, .300 and .375, with total delivery promised by the first of July. The price FOB Lewiston was to be $79.60 per thousand for the .300 and .375 calibers, and $71.40 per thousand for the .257 and .270 calibers.

By the middle of June Weatherby was worried. He had produced literature announcing he would have cartridge cases and ammunition available, and had placed about $2,000 worth of ads in the July issues of several national publications announcing the debut of Weatherby Magnum ammunition. Yet, up to this time he had not even received any sample cases for testing.

When he complained of this to Richard Speer, he received a letter from him stating he expected to start shipping cases around the first of July, and that his entire order of 50,000 cases should be completed by July 20.

The first few sample cases were not received until August 10th. When these cases were tested it was found that the brass was not of uniform thickness, resulting in some cartridges having less powder capacity than others; the brass in the neck area was too thin and soft to hold the bullets when they were seated; some of the primer pockets were too large, and some had flash holes that were undersized; some of the shoulders were crushed; and the overall length of the case was not uniform. It was the beginning of a nightmare for Weatherby that was to last for 2-1/2 years.

Expecting to get cases from Speer, Weatherby had stopped ordering the .300 H&H brass from Winchester that he had been using to fire form and furnish reloaded ammunition to his customers. As a result, at the beginning of the busiest season of the year, with many customers waiting to go hunting, Roy was unable to furnish them with ammunition. On August 22, 1950, Richard Speer wrote Weatherby: "I have reached a limit financially and will have to do without the help I had hired. I have been operating in the red from the beginning. I am resigned to this fact, and am doing everything possible to make your cases, regardless of cost, and to struggle along until such time as this business of manufacturing cases is out of the embryo stage."

In a later letter Speer suggested that he hire additional help and place them on Weatherby's payroll in order to complete his order, but Weatherby would not agree to this added expense on his part. By the end of October, Speer had furnished Weatherby with approximately 5,000 cases, all in .300 Weatherby Magnum caliber. By carefully testing and reworking each one of these cases, Weatherby was able to partially fill some of the many orders.

Within a short time letters of complaint started to arrive telling of sticky cases, blown primers, split necks and other case problems.

Each month and each letter from Speer brought promises of improved quality and improved delivery. There was some improvement, but about 10 percent of the cases received by Weatherby from Speer were completely unusable. Despite that, in July of 1951 a written contract was signed for an additional 200,000 Weatherby cases to be produced by Speer for a price of $22,000. Along with the verbal order for 50,000 cases that had been placed in April of 1951, this meant a total of 250,000 cases had actually been ordered.

That total was never reached. From the time the first shipment was received in October of 1951 through January of 1953, only 174,280 cartridge cases was received. Weatherby paid Speer a total of $15,222.13. During this period Weatherby got more and more letters of complaint and had to refund more customers' money because of poor quality brass. On May 15, 1951 Richard Speer wrote: "It is extremely unfortunate for all concerned that some of the cases I made for you are unsatisfactory. I am sure this condition can be corrected and will not occur in the next run of your cases. The only thing to do now is to guarantee replacement of any case defective in material or workmanship. As mentioned in our telephone conversation, if you will send such cases to me along with the letter of complaint if possible, I will replace them without charge when the next run of your cases is made."

It wasn't just the refunding of the customer's money, or the replacement of defective brass by Speer, that Weatherby was concerned about. It was the damage being done to his reputation.

In 1952 the first personal injury suit in the history of Weatherby's was filed by Dr. Arthur Schoch of Dallas, Texas. His claim was for $35,000 to cover personal injury sustained as a result of his rifle exploding in his face when using a Speer cartridge. This suit was settled out of court early in 1953 for $9,000. On July 31, 1953, in a telephone conversation between Weatherby and Richard Speer, the contract was terminated and Weatherby advised Speer not to sell any more Weatherby cartridges.

In August of 1955 Weatherby filed a suit against Richard Speer seeking $100,000 for breach of contract and $50,000 for breach of warranty damages. The case never reached the courts since Weatherby knew that Richard Speer had no assets and couldn't make a settlement of this kind. In June 1957 he settled for $3,000 cash and an additional promissory note signed by Richard Speer for $1,000, which was paid in full in November of 1957. This amount was a mere pittance compared to Weatherby's cost of replacing defective Speer brass and the resulting damage to the reputation of his company.

The Continued Search For an Ammunition Source

By the end of 1951, Weatherby was no longer building rifles on a "per order" basis. With his own Weatherby-identified F.N. Magnum actions arriving on a regular basis from Belgium, plus his barrel making equipment and the stock carving machine, he was now building his Deluxe rifles on a production basis. Orders could immediately be filled from inventory, and the 1951 price of a Weatherby Deluxe rifle without sights was $230.

Weatherby continued to receive a great many rifles of other makes from customers who wanted them rechambered to a Weatherby caliber. The charge for this rechambering was $15, plus slight additional charges if the bolt face required altering or the magazine box lengthened.

Ammunition was still a problem. After the costly experience with Speer brass, Weatherby was more determined than ever to locate a reliable source to manufacture both cartridge case brass for the Weatherby calibers and loaded ammunition as well. The quantities he needed were too small to interest Remington, Winchester and Federal, so his contacts with them were fruitless.

He finally received a quotation in July 1952 from Fabrique Nationale in Belgium. For a minimum quantity of one million rounds, they quoted 15 cents per round for loaded ammunition, or 5 cents each for empty unprimed cartridge cases. He had been paying almost 18 cents each for .300 H&H brass from Winchester, and the cartridge cases he had received from Speer cost 11 cents each.

The bad news with F.N. was that they required a one-third down payment, about $50,000, before starting production. Also, their quotation was based on using the European Berdan primers, and Weatherby wanted to use American primers which required only one flash hole. As negotiations progressed, and Weatherby was preparing to send cartridge case drawings for the .257, .270, 7mm, .300 and .375 Weatherby magnum calibers to F.N., he was advised that the minimum quantity had been increased to 500,000 rounds for each caliber. Weatherby could not handle that large an investment, even with the help of his partner, Herb Klein, so his quest for an ammo source had hit another huge closed door. He abandoned that plan and began looking elsewhere.

Then Roy heard about Norma, an ammunition firm in Sweden— Norma Projektilfabrik. He called the president of Norma, Amund Enger, and explained his needs. The response he received was encouraging, and he visited Norma during an upcoming trip to Europe.

Weatherby also discussed with them the possibility of Norma loading his ammunition. They didn't have a loading machine that would handle Weatherby cartridge cases, but Roy suggested that he could ship them the two used Waterbury-Farrel loading machines that he had operating in South Gate. This idea appealed to them, but there were other stumbling blocks.

One was powder. There was no source in Europe for the proper powder for his cartridge cases, so Roy also offered to check into the possibility of having Dupont No. 4350 powder shipped to them from the United States. He spent two full days working out every detail of the Weatherby program with the plant superintendent, plant manager, engineers and other top brass.

Even before visiting Norma, however, many of the preliminary arrangements were transacted by mail. Finally, in the spring of 1953, Norma agreed to manufacture cartridge cases only in all of the

Weatherby calibers at a cost of about 5-1/2 cents each. Most importantly, however, they agreed to produce minimal quantities of 25,000 to 50,000 rounds per caliber, greatly reducing Weatherby's initial investment. Norma wanted to get into this project on a gradual basis and they did not want to produce ammunition at that time. It was agreed that the loading of the cartridge cases would continue to be done at the South Gate plant until such time when Norma felt they were ready to move into this phase of the operation.

Roy visited the Norma Company on several trips, one in 1956 when their initial run of the new .378 cartridge case had just been completed. By this time production of all of the cases was running smoothly. Norma was very anxious to begin loading Weatherby's ammunition for him, and again expressed interest in the two Waterbury-Farrel loading machines that Weatherby had been using in South Gate. He also learned that a firm in Sweden had now perfected a powder similar to the American DuPont No. 4350, which Norma felt would work satisfactorily in the Weatherby cartridges. He left Norma greatly encouraged, feeling that this could possibly be the last year they would have to load the ammunition in South Gate.

Federal No. 215 Primer

There is an interesting, little-known story about the development of the Federal No. 215 large rifle primer. When Weatherby was working up loads for his experimental .378 Weatherby cartridge, he experienced some difficulty with existing primers. He found they would not produce a hot enough ignition to set off the huge charges of powder in this enormous case. He went to his friend, Charlie Horn, who had established the Federal Cartridge Company, and told him of this problem.

"We'll make you a primer that, by God, will set your powder ablaze," Horn told him. And, thus, the hotter No. 215 primer was born, which has been used ever since by Weatherby, as well as by handloaders, on the larger capacity .378, .416 and .460 Weatherby Magnum cartridges.

The Weatherby Stock

Roy Weatherby strongly felt that most bolt-action sporting rifles of that era looked like clubs, ugly and clumsy. He wanted something

209

good-looking and with the kind of balance that everybody expected from a shotgun. He felt that a rifle should point as naturally as a shotgun, so that when it was shouldered the hunter could instinctively zero in on his target. He sat and doodled with stock shapes, changing a line here and an angle there. One thing he arrived at was the 45 degree forend tip that has been widely copied by other rifle makers.

Originally, the forend of Weatherby stocks retained the rounded "doorknob" ends that were then in common usage. Later, he developed the flattened, pear-shaped forend, then added a gracefully flared pistol grip with a rosewood cap that would match the contrasting rosewood forend tip. Ever one with an eye for distinctive detail, Weatherby added his traditional diamond inlay in the rosewood grip cap, another feature that has been widely copied.

Leonard Mews, Weatherby employee and famous stockmaker, marks a raw stock blank for inletting.

He designed a Monte Carlo comb that slanted upward toward the butt, to reduce the recoil effect upon the shooter's cheek. The Weatherby stock also featured a full recoil pad with the white line spacer.

Most of these features are commonplace on today's commercial rifles, but at the time Weatherby introduced them they were considered to be flashy and overly ornate. From the very early days Weatherby offered his customers the choice of a "deluxe" stock made of the usual walnut wood or a "custom" stock. The latter was available in a number of different, exotic woods such as tigertail and birdseye maple, myrtlewood and screwbean mesquite, a wood to be found only in the dry, arid deserts of the Southwest. The mesquite was a very dense, sturdy wood dramatically contrasted with dark and light grain. Eventually, however, mesquite became increasingly scarce and was discontinued.

Walt Beall operated the Salstrom 18-spindle stock pantograph machine in the Weatherby shop in the early 1950s. Here, he shows a rough-turned blank before shaping.

The Weatherby Scope Sight

In the early '50's, there were only a half dozen or so different brands of rifle scopes on the market, with the Weaver, Lyman, Stith and Bushnell being the major ones. Weatherby felt that a rifle alone was not enough to offer the public. He wanted to put a scope sight on the market, and felt he had some innovative ideas for the design of a completely new scope sight, superior to any available at that time.

Roy wanted a "brighter" scope, which meant a larger objective lens. He envisioned combining the windage and elevation adjustments under one cap and the focusing under another. He also wanted to put both the focusing and the windage and elevation adjustment knobs on top of the scope in one tandem turret arrangement. That would give a much more streamlined appearance than the conventional scopes, with windage and elevation adjustments being separate on the top and side of the scope. Focusing would be done at the ocular end of the tube.

All of these, of course, were just ideas or concepts. Roy was not an optical engineer and could not actually design a scope. What he did, instead, was to send a letter to some 20 scope manufacturers in Germany and Japan outlining some of his ideas.

From the replies he received he narrowed the group to four German firms to see, and visited them during his European trip in 1953. Of these four he was most impressed with Hertel & Reuss, which had an excellent reputation as one of the finest optical companies in Germany. They were impressed with Weatherby's design concepts, and were eager to work with him to develop the ideas he had incorporated in his plans.

Weatherby named this scope the Imperial, and decided to introduce it in five different models, three in fixed power—2 3/4X, 4X and 6X; and two variable powers—2X-7X and 2 3/4X-l0X. He also succeeded in eliminating the need for a large cash outlay for tooling costs by getting Hertel & Reuss to agree to amortize these tooling charges over the first 1,500 scopes to be produced.

All these details were finalized with a mere handshake, with neither party feeling the need for a formal contract.

In early 1954 Weatherby launched an extensive advertising campaign to introduce his Weatherby Imperial scope sights. Acceptance was widespread, and the scope proved to be very popular with the shooting public. In addition to his own advertising efforts, Weatherby also benefited greatly from those of Buehler, the mount manufacturer, who featured the Weatherby Imperial as the scope mounted on their rings and bases in their ads.

Although it was not included on the early Imperial scopes, Weatherby later introduced a soft neoprene ring fused to the ocular piece for protection against painful head cuts. Pioneered by Weatherby, this neoprene eyepiece is now found on many other brands.

During his 1956 European trip Roy went to Hertel & Reuss in Kassel, Germany, to discuss a problem with the variable scopes they were producing for him. Tightening the rear scope mount ring would prevent the power-change tube from turning. Weatherby had described this problem in correspondence, and on this visit he was delighted to learn that they had finally solved this scope mounting problem.

Later, Weatherby negotiated with an optical firm in Japan to produce a 4X scope specifically for use with his Mark XXII rifle. It was to have many innovative features, such as a 7/8-inch tube diameter in place of the customary 3/4-inch normally found on these .22 scopes, thus permitting the use of larger lenses for poor light conditions; and a dovetail mount that was to be an integral part of the scope, providing easy installation to the mated dovetail receiver of his rifle.

He had also worked with this same optical company on the production of a Weatherby spotting scope, and both of these new products were scheduled for introduction to the public in 1970.

In 1969 Roy and his engineer worked with Oriental Trading Company, an optics firm in Japan, to develop a 20X-45X Zoom spotting scope, which he introduced that year as the Weatherby Sightmaster Spotting Scope.

Exit the Imperial Scope—Enter the Premier.

Roy always felt that his Imperial rifle scope, made in Germany, was optically superior to any other rifle scope then on the market. In the late 1960s, however, the image moving principle was introduced in competitive model scopes. This feature allowed the reticle to remain centered throughout any movement of the windage and elevation adjustments, and in the variable models the reticle remained the same apparent width regardless of any increase or decrease in power.

Because of the location of the erector lenses in his Imperial scopes, however, it was not possible to incorporate this self-centering reticle design into the Imperial.

Weatherby next developed an entirely new line of rifle scopes which he called the Weatherby Premier, and arranged to have the Asia Optical Company in Japan produce them. The new line was introduced in 1972.

Following his tradition of continually improving existing products, in 1984 Roy replaced his Premier line of scopes with the Weatherby Supreme. These scopes were also produced for him by Asia Optical Company.

8

Rimfires and Shotguns

Introduction of Mark XXII .22 Rimfire Rifle

In December of 1960, Weatherby contacted the firm of Fabrica D'Armi P. Beretta in Italy requesting that they send him one of their .22 LR rifle actions. He explained that he was thinking of putting a .22 rifle on the market and would like to consider their action, incorporating some of his ideas. They immediately sent him one of their actions, along with complete blueprints, and advised him that any changes he made should be as slight as possible to keep retooling costs to a minimum.

By May of 1961, Weatherby and Fred Jennie had completed work on a prototype model .22 rimfire rifle which was to be called the Mark XXII, and they left for Europe taking the prototype with them. Their first visit was with the Beretta factory in Gardone, Italy. There they met with Dr. Pier Giuseppe Beretta, the president, and his right hand man, Mr. Sordelli. Weatherby was extremely impressed with the enormous size of their factory, which he estimated to be about five times the size of J. P. Sauer. They employed about 1500 people and had a typical Italian work schedule — from 8:00 A.M. until 12 noon, then two hours for lunch before returning to work from 2:00 until 6:00 P.M. The wage scale was about on a comparison with that in Germany.

Both Dr. Beretta and Mr. Sordelli were very hospitable and attentive. It was obvious they wanted very badly to build this rifle for Weatherby.

They were particularly interested in the mechanism and design changes Weatherby had made, especially his single shot selector feature. Almost immediately they wanted to know if Weatherby would let them build this rifle for European consumption. Weatherby replied that this would be agreeable to him, but it would have to be called a Weatherby or at least a Weatherby-Beretta rifle, with them paying a license fee the same as J. P. Sauer was doing on Mark V sales in Europe. They then showed even more enthusiasm for this product, and indicated that they felt they could sell the rifle in Europe for about $60, whereas their current Beretta .22 rifle was selling for about $40 there.

"They scared me to death," Weatherby later recalled, "when they told me the tooling cost would run about 150 million lira. I had to get out my pencil to convert this, and felt quite relieved to find it amounted to only $24,000!" Dr. Beretta then advised that if an agreement could be reached for them to produce these rifles for sale in Europe, they would absorb one half of the tooling charge, bringing Weatherby's cost down to $12,000. Not wanting to hold anything back or misrepresent himself in any way, Weatherby advised them he planned to present his prototype to other firms while he was on this trip for them to quote as well, namely Hammerli in Switzerland, Carl Walther in Germany, as well as J. P. Sauer in Germany.

They advised Weatherby not to show his rifle to too many concerns for fear that one of them would copy his ideas and designs. However, they felt that the three firms Weatherby had mentioned were all reputable enough not to do this. They finally quoted an FOB price of $28 each to duplicate and produce Weatherby's Mark XXII. Weatherby replied, "I would rather see it at $25 FOB Italy. If you can agree now to this price, I will look no further." They replied that they didn't think it would be possible for them to build it at that price.

When Weatherby left Beretta, taking his prototype with him, he was already of the opinion that he was just wasting his time for he felt sure none of the other companies he planned to visit would be able to come close to the quotation he had received from Beretta. And, he was right, as all of the other quotations he received were much higher.

Upon returning home, a great deal of lengthy correspondence with Beretta ensued, for Weatherby found that nothing moved swiftly when dealing with the Italian firm. The first working prototype model built by Beretta was not received at the Weatherby factory until late December of 1961, and it wasn't until April of 1962 that a formal contract was signed, calling for the payment of $5,000 cash toward the tooling charge of $12,000, with the remaining $7,000 to be amortized over the first 10,000 rifles at 70 cents per rifle. Weatherby also had succeeded in getting the FOB price reduced from $28 to $24.90, and, in addition, Beretta agreed to pay a royalty fee of $2 per rifle for the first 15,000 rifles they would sell in Europe, at which time the fee per rifle would be renegotiated. According to this contract, delivery of a minimum of 300 rifles per month was to begin in November of 1962.

The prototype rifle received in December of '61 was displayed at the National Sporting Goods Dealer Show the following month, resulting in orders being placed by dealers in excess of 800 units. This prototype was also displayed at the NRA Show in March, generating a great deal

The original "standard" model Weatherby Mark XXII .22 Rimfire rifle with no rosewood forend tip or grip cap, and metal butt plate instead of rubber butt pad.

of interest and public acceptance. By the end of 1962, Weatherby had more than 2,500 orders for this new rifle waiting to be filled, and was actually starting to receive cancellations from dealers whose customers were unhappy over the nondelivery. But, with each sample received from Beretta, there were either minor design changes required, stock shaping and finishing that needed improving, or malfunctioning problems that had to be corrected. Thus, in April of 1963, Weatherby made a second trip to the Beretta factory in Italy, and this time he was accompanied by two representatives from one of his new partners, J. P. Sauer, Mr. Walter Spiegelberg, their technical director, and Manfred Holzach, the managing director.

As a result of his many trips to the different factories in Europe, Weatherby had acquired some understanding of both the Italian and German languages, even though he could not converse fluently in either language. As a result, interpreters were always present at any of his meetings if the individuals he was dealing with were not fluent in English. He never let his inability to speak their language intimidate him, however, and, in fact, he usually found himself to be the party in control of these meetings no matter how technical the discussions became.

For example, at this April meeting in Italy, the discussion that took up most of the day centered around the revisions that Beretta would be required to make in order for the rifle to function properly, and the resulting cost increases they were attempting to pass on to Weatherby. Most of the conversation had been carried on in German, with considerable complaining being done by all parties. It was late in the afternoon when Weatherby rapped on the table and proclaimed in English, "There is too much confusion here with everyone talking at once. We are not getting any place, and I would appreciate it if everyone would speak one at a time. Let's list all these cost increases and see where we stand and what can be done. Concessions will have to be made by both parties, or we'll just have to cancel the contract. Our retail price was established based on the price agreed to in our contract signed last year, and I'm not going to put a rifle on the market and have to lose money on every rifle sold."

Eventually, all of the monetary and production problems were solved. However, the first delivery of 450 rifles was not received in South Gate until January of 1964—more than 2-1/2 years after negotiations with the Italian firm were started. By this time Weatherby had over 4,000 orders waiting to be filled in spite of hundreds of orders that had been canceled. A great deal of time and money was spent in answering letters, telegrams and telephone calls from irate customers, some of whom had already paid their dealer for the rifle they had on order.

Mark XXII Rifles Built by KGT and Nikko

Although Beretta was producing a high quality Mark XXII rimfire rifle, Roy was not pleased with the delivery schedule. He simply couldn't get enough units to fill his orders. Equally important, he felt that the cost from Beretta was too high, and it kept rising.

To cope with both problems, Roy again turned to Japan. He contacted a Japanese firm called KTG, and in 1967 it began delivery to Weatherby of the clip magazine version of the Mark XXII. The company produced some 17,000 rifles before that relationship ended in 1971, and the following year—1972—Roy began getting Mark XXIIs from another Japanese firm, Nikko Kodensha. Nikko built both the clip version and the tubular magazine version of the rifle until its contract was ended in 1980.

Weatherby Mark XXII Rifle Built By Mossberg

For years, Weatherby had argued with both Beretta in Italy and KTG and Nikko in Japan, when they were producing the Mark XXII rifle, that their costs were much too high for this .22 rimfire. Roy was not willing to sacrifice quality for price, however, so he had no choice but to go along with their cost figures, which kept rising through the years.

In the spring of 1978 Roy Weatherby and Alan Mossberg, president of O.F. Mossberg & Sons, briefly discussed Mossberg's contract manufacturing program that they were beginning, under which Mossberg could possibly produce the Mark XXII rifle at their Connecticut plant. Both thought Mossberg could build them for less than what Roy was paying, especially when U.S. Customs duty could be eliminated.

In January 1979 they signed a contract for the manufacture of 25,000 Mark XXII rifles, at a price about 30 percent less than Weatherby was paying for the Japanese produced rifle. Along with the signed contract, Weatherby sent Mossberg a check for $25,000 as an initial deposit for tooling, with an additional sum of $51,655 to be paid upon completion of the tooling and approval by Weatherby.

In February Mossberg's manager of their precision machining division, Ralph Saucier, advised Weatherby that they had completed a set of updated drawings, and would be invoicing Weatherby $8300 for this work. With the $76,655 tooling Weatherby had already committed for, this now brought the start-up costs to almost $85,000, over and above the unit cost of each rifle.

Throughout 1979 Roy Weatherby and his two engineers, Fred Jennie and Ron Peterson, made several trips to the Mossberg plant to work directly with their engineers. At one such meeting in January of 1980, Ralph Saucier told Weatherby the first sample rifles should be completed and ready for shipment within the next couple of weeks. He also said that the cost of tooling had amounted to $23,000 more than they had anticipated. Since the original total tooling amount had been agreed upon and included in the signed contract, they suggested that Weatherby and Mossberg split this additional amount 50/50, to which Roy agreed. However, as a follow-up to this verbal agreement made in January, in a letter of March 3, 1980, Ralph Saucier advised Roy that the additional tooling actually amounted to $46,000, and Weatherby's 50 percent would be $23,000. When Roy objected to this doubled amount, Mossberg very graciously agreed to invoice Weatherby only for the $12,500 as originally discussed. The manufacturing start-up costs had now reached nearly $98,000.

During this first months of working with Mossberg, Roy was still receiving completed Mark XXII rifles from Nikko in Japan in accordance with that contract. Because of this incoming production, Roy had told Mossberg their deliveries need not begin until 1981.

Not until June, 1980 did Weatherby receive from Mossberg the first eight pre-production samples, four clip and four tubular rifles, for evaluation. Not unusual, there were a number of problems relating to functioning, fitting of parts and appearance. Test results of these first samples, as well as all subsequent samples received, were provided in detail to Mossberg along with Weatherby's recommendations and instructions for correcting the problems.

In December five additional samples were received, but they were still unacceptable. In his letter of December 1980, to Alan Mossberg, Roy Weatherby stated, "Fred Jennie has been working almost constantly checking out these rifles since they arrived. I am enclosing a copy of his report. Honestly, it's beyond my comprehension why or how these five samples could have been sent to us for approval. I don't see how it is possible that any of your people could have fired these rifles for functioning or for accuracy before they were shipped. Every reason for the malfunctions and all of the problems we found with these five samples are in this report, and they all can be corrected."

Approval was finally given in May of 1981 for Mossberg to start actual production. By then the contract with Nikko in Japan had been completed, and all of those rifles had been received and sold. With no rifles on hand for delivery, Weatherby was unable to fill the thousands of orders that were piling up from his dealers. That created much ill will with customers, and resulted in cancellation of many orders. By the end of 1981 and throughout the early part of 1982, small quantities of salable rifles were received from Mossberg, taking care of some of this backlog of orders.

In 1983, nearly five years after negotiations had first begun, Weatherby and Mossberg together decided that there were too many difficulties that could not be resolved. By mutual consent the contract was terminated. It was a great disappointment to Roy.

Mark XXII Rifle Produced By Howa Machinery Ltd. in Japan

Weatherby lost no time in contacting Howa in Japan, which was already producing the Mark V and Vanguard rifles for him, and immediately entered into a contract with them to add the Mark XXII into their production schedule. By 1984, they were in full production, and Weatherby was receiving monthly shipments of a quality product.

Once again it took almost 18 months to fill the backlog of orders that had accumulated. And, instead of being able to decrease the price as he had hoped to do with an American made product, he had to increase it slightly. Howa continued to produce this rifle for four years, but in 1988 it was discontinued and dropped from the Weatherby line. Continual cost increases simply kept pushing the selling price much too high.

Shotguns

Adding shotguns to the line of Weatherby rifles had been considered periodically over the years, but in the middle 1960's Roy made the

221

decision to do it. He contracted with Zoli in Italy to produce an over/under, and began discussions with KTG in Japan about building both a pump and an automatic.

Over & Unders

Weatherby received the first production of the new Weatherby Regency over/under shotgun, made by Zoli in Italy, in late 1969, but the introductory announcement and the big advertising push took place in early 1970. He was pleased with the beauty and workmanship of the Regency, but experienced delivery problems with Zoli. Inflation and general economic conditions in Italy, just as in Germany, kept

Roy tests the new Centurion automatic shotgun with three Weatherby employees: (l to r) Jean Rockwell, Roy, Walt Ross, and Ed Weatherby.

increasing costs each year. The retail price, $500 when introduced to the public in 1970, rose to almost $1000 by 1977. Roy knew he could put a quality over/under shotgun on the market that would be more competitively priced. He again turned to Japan.

In 1977, after working more than a year with the firm of Nikko Kodensha, he introduced his Weatherby Olympian over/under shotgun in trap, skeet and field models, with a suggested retail of around $500. This was an addition to his shotgun line, since he continued production of his higher priced Regency.

A New Line Of Weatherby Shotguns: Athena & Orion

In 1980 two Japanese firms that had been producing shotguns for Weatherby filed for bankruptcy of a Chapter 11-type. One was KTG,

Roy and his engineer, Fred Jennie, display the first production models of the Weatherby Centurion automatic and Patrician pump shotguns.

223

which had produced the Patrician pump and Centurion auto shotguns, as well as the Mark XXII rimfire rifle, for Weatherby. The other was Nikko Kodensha, with whom Weatherby had contracted several years earlier to build the Olympian over and under shotgun. Nikko at one time had also produced the Mark XXII rimfire rifle for Weatherby. Both of these firms took immediate steps for reorganization but, uneasy with the situation, Roy began investigating other sources of manufacture.

He decided it was time to replace his Italian made Regency with another top-of-the-line, highly engraved model over and under, and also to bring out a less ornate model in the medium price range. He contacted New SKB, a reorganized version of the SKB company that had also declared bankruptcy several years earlier. Again, with the help of Fred Jennie, Roy designed what would become the Athena and Orion line.

New SKB built them. The Athena was as beautiful as his Regency had been. The forearm and buttstock were of super fancy grade walnut, the receiver and side plates were beautifully engraved with a floral pattern and finished with an attractive silver nitride finish, and the barrels featured ribbed ventilation between the barrels, as well as the matted ventilated top rib.

The lower priced Orion was identical in function, but cosmetically not as ornate. The receiver featured only a small amount of engraving and had a blued finish. The stock was of a lesser grade of walnut, and only the trap model Orion had a vent rib.

Pumps & Automatics

In 1971 Roy completed the drawings and specifications for his Patrician pump and Centurion automatic shotguns. He contracted for tooling for these two new products to be completed by KTG, the firm that was then producing the Mark XXII rifle. These two new shotguns were introduced in 1972. With them and the Regency over/under, Weatherby felt he was finally penetrating the shotgun market.

Although the Patrician pump and Centurion auto shotgun were doing well, Roy wanted an automatic that would shoot both magnum and standard shells. By the late '70s he had his engineer hard at work to design an automatic shotgun that would do just that, which was not possible with the Centurion. After six years of extensive design, research, and testing, Roy felt he was ready to make these changes. He decided to discontinue the Patrician pump and Centurion auto and introduce two completely new models.

During the eight or nine years that the Patrician and Centurion had been on the market, their manufacture had been shuttled back and forth between the firms of KTG and Nikko in Japan. Since New SKB, which was now to make his new over and under shotguns for him, was not experienced in the production of repeater shotguns, Weatherby decided to have KTG build the new pump and auto for him. By this time KTG had reorganized with new owners after its bankruptcy,

By now it was time to decide on a name for these two new models. In the past, ever since Elgin Gates had been responsible for coming up with the name of the Mark V action, Weatherby had called upon his employees for suggestions to names prior to the introduction of any new product. Then Roy and several of his aides would go through the list, and make the final selection. There had been no problem selecting "Athena" and "Orion" for the new O&U's just a few months earlier, but now they couldn't agree on a final selection for the pump and auto. It was Fred Jennie, Roy's engineer, who finally said, "Since it's going to be introduced in January of next year, why don't we name it the 82 auto?" Once this was agreed upon, the companion name of 92 was given to the pump.

This pair of shotguns came and went quickly. They were first carried in the catalog in 1982, but were absent from the 1989 catalog. The decision to abandon them and concentrate on the higher end over-and-under was a product of the economic downturn in the late 1980's that affected the entire firearms industry.

9

Weatherby Collectors Association

With millions of Weatherby owners worldwide, most of whom border on the fanatical in their dedication to the brand, it's somewhat curious that a Weatherby Collectors Association was not formed until 1989. In little more than two years, however, there are hundreds of members, and the first annual meeting and banquet was held in Chicago in March, 1991.

The first issue of the WCA Newsletter, in April 1989, gave a concise, clear statement as to how the group began and what the aims are: "Several months ago a couple of our members became acquainted over the telephone, while one was trying to purchase a Weatherby rifle from the other. After much correspondence, they got the 'bright' idea that it would be great if an association could be formed, where many Weatherby admirers could pool their knowledge and experience for the benefit of all.

"That became the primary purpose of forming the Weatherby Collectors Association: to compile a history of, and become more knowledgeable of Weatherby firearms. We are interested in both past and presently manufactured Weatherby products."

That first newsletter set the stage for what has actually taken place in the publication to make it valuable to members: a question and answer section where members can get answers to their questions about Weatherby products; a swap and shop section where members only

227

can advertise Weatherbys; and a forum for comments, discussion, complaints or suggestions.

Typical of the newsletter use is a question and its answer in the July 1989 issue: "I have a Weatherby Mark V, serial number 1901X, which I have a question about. In the stock, on the right hand side near the rear receiver ring, there appears to have been a notch which has been filled in. It looks as though someone cut the wood away to allow for the mounting of a receiver sight except that it's on the wrong side of the receiver. The work done is very professional-looking. Are any of our members aware of a receiver sight that was made for the right hand side of Mark V?"

And the answer: "The mysterious notch in the stock of your Mark V is probably the result of the rifle having been returned to the Weatherby factory to have a newer type safety installed. In 1960 Weatherby began a change from the original slide-type safety to what was termed the 'Improved Safety.' This safety is the common type found on most Mark V rifles and is mounted on the bolt shroud. With the previous slide-type safety, a notch was cut away in the stock, as you describe, to allow the safety lever to slide fore and aft. After Weatherby made the change to the newer safety, anyone owning a Mark V with the old type could return it to have the 'Improved Safety' installed, and the notch filled in. Apparently, this is the case with your gun."

In the short time that the Association has been active it has achieved a remarkable lot. In addition to providing members with a swap-buy-sell-trade forum in the newsletter, the WCA has offered its members commemorative Weatherby rifles (with another on the way), WCA jackets, and custom-made WCA knives. It has also, as described above, been a very active vehicle for the dissemination of information about Weatherby firearms.

For further information contact:
Weatherby Collectors Assoc., Inc.
P. O. Box 128
Moira, NY 12957

10

Ed Weatherby: The New Era

Roy Edward Weatherby, Jr.

In November of 1951 Roy Weatherby accomplished yet another of his goals (with a little help from his wife) when his first and only son was born. Realizing his new son might some day take over his prospering gun company, he named him Roy Edward, Jr., thus taking the first step in transitioning the company to the next generation of Weatherbys. Ed, as he is called by those close to him, is more reserved and less outgoing than his father, yet brings his own style to the leadership of the Weatherby company.

From early on Ed spent most of his summers and after school working at his father's firm. It was Roy's opinion that Ed should learn the business from the bottom up. "I remember the long and boring hours," said Ed, "making boxes, loading ammunition and sweeping floors. But now I look back on the experience with gratitude for the opportunity to learn in this way."

After Ed's graduation from high school in 1969, he and his Dad headed for Africa for Ed's first safari. Here father and son could test the guns and the relationship that Roy had been building throughout the years. They were joined by Roy's partner at the time, Leo Roethe, and his son, Lee. "It was certainly one of the highlights of my life," Ed explains. "Seeing it on TV is one thing, but to experience it with all the smells and sights is quite another. I can't wait to take my kids some day." Roy took him back again the following summer, where they could round out their African hunting experience.

After four years of college Ed was ready to settle down, with both a full time job at Weatherby and a wife and family of his own. In January of 1973 he married his high school sweetheart, Sherie McClung. Keeping with the practice of starting from the ground up, Roy began Ed's full time employment in various management positions, learning by helping others do their work. He worked in credit, service and sales many years before becoming sales manager in the late '70s.

In 1976 Ed's first son, Adam, was born and the possibility of carrying on the Weatherby name for another generation was now possible. This possibility was increased with the birth of Sherie and Ed's twins, Daniel and Jessica, in 1978.

With a growing family Ed felt maybe it was time to leave the big city and strike out on his own. In 1979 he moved his family to a ranch in southern Oregon. In describing his experience Ed explained, "At that time I felt it really didn't matter what I did for a living, as long as I was living where I wanted. What I soon learned was it didn't really matter where I lived as long as I was doing for a living what I really enjoyed."

Leo Rothe (left) and his son, Lee, with Ed Weatherby and his father, Roy. The boys took time out to enjoy some skiing on one of the trips Ed made with Roy to Fort Atkinson, Wisconsin to attend a Weatherby/Nasco board meeting.

Roy Weatherby, with his only son, Ed, whom he groomed from early years to take over the firearms building operation. Ed is now President of Weatherby, Inc.

With that in mind, two years later Ed returned to the Weatherby company, where he has been ever since.

Shortly after Ed's return he became Executive Vice President, and in 1983 was elected by the board of directors as President. Roy took on the title of Chairman of the Board. In that same year Ed and Sherie had their fourth and last child, Melissa.

Ed and Sherie and their four children presently reside on a ranch in central California. During a recent interview Ed shared some of his thoughts about the firearms industry and life in general.

So what is it like to be head of a gun company?

Ed: Well, like any other job I suppose, it has its good and bad. Many people think I spent most of my time hunting. The fact of the matter is, I spend most of my time behind my desk, planning and solving problems. I always hope some day it will be different, but it never seems to be. Now that my kids are old enough to hunt I have to make more of an effort to make the time.

Are you having fun?

Ed: It is fun. There may be things I would rather do, but one of the things that makes it fun is being head of a company where you can become involved in the sport of the activity. I would just be bored to death if I were president of a company making doorknobs or springs.

To be able to make a firearm and to be at the top and have the quality...that's what makes it exciting. And you can go out and actually use the product. I enjoy hunting and I like the hunting industry. Of all the things there are to do, I might not always put hunting at the top of that list, but I enjoy it, and if the opportunity is there, I go.

I am family oriented. Because this is my business and I'm with it all the time and it takes so much of my time away from my family, I feel when there is time to do something else I like it to be an experience that the whole family can do together. Whether it be snow skiing or sailing — things like that. I look forward to and enjoy taking my children hunting. But it's a bit difficult to do as a group — to take four kids and your wife and go on a hunting trip. And it's hard to take just one of them.

Tell me about your family.

Ed: Well, I've been married 18 years and, as I said, we have four kids. The oldest is Adam, 15. Then twins that are 12, Daniel and Jessica. And another little girl, Melissa, who is 8. They keep our hands full.

President George Bush, an avid shooter and bird hunter, accepted from Ed Weatherby a beautifully engraved Athena 20 gauge shotgun. The presentation took place in the Oval Office at the White House.

We recently moved to Paso Robles. So my wife, Sherie, really has her hands full with the four kids, nine horses, new schools, new friends, and church activities. And I am away a lot on business.

Sherie copes with that okay?

Ed: Sure. We both enjoy the outdoors. We both enjoy living on a ranch. She would much rather be cleaning out her horse stall than to be at a cocktail party somewhere. You know, that's just Sherie. And it fits right in with hunting and shooting.

But back to your original question. Yeah, I like being CEO of Weatherby. It's fun, it's challenging and frustrating. But you know, it's been good. It's continued to be good and I look forward to taking the company from where it is today to something bigger and better in the future. Trying to provide a quality product to our industry that people can enjoy and have pride in using.

Probably the most important thing to me in the business is providing service to the customer. I don't think it's good enough to provide a good product if you don't back it up. If the customer doesn't feel that he's important when he calls you, or if he gets four different answers and gets moved around within the company, those are the kinds of things that I'm trying to build out of our company. I want to give superior service. I feel that is our niche...not only providing the highest quality product, but providing the highest quality service. It'll make it easier for our dealers to do business with us. These are the kinds of things that I find it fun to do, to figure out ways of constantly improving.

Weatherby has a pretty good reputation in that respect.

Ed: Several years ago we conducted a survey among our dealers, asking them to rate our service. To paraphrase the summary it was, "Your service is not very good, but you are so much better than everybody else in the industry." Obviously, we need to improve and I feel we're well on our way. I can't believe the patience of some of our customers that put up with some of the things that happen. I'm speaking of isolated instances, but they do happen, and I intend to eliminate any such happenings if at all possible.

That happens in all walks of life with other products, but hunters don't expect their Weatherby to ever fail.

Ed: There's a lot of truth in what you're saying and that makes it harder for us...because we are Weatherby. If we were someone else we might get away with some of the things that happen, but the Weatherby owner who paid $1,000 plus expects his gun to be perfect forever. We'd like that, too.

What's your favorite Weatherby caliber?

Ed: I find that I use the .270 more than anything else. I think the reason is that it's adequate for a deer/elk size animal. And it's a pleasant caliber to shoot. On the range you can shoot as much as you want and it doesn't knock you around too much. Shooting a few five-shot groups with some of our bigger calibers from the bench and I'm kind of done for the day.

But I go back and forth between the .270 and the .300, depending upon the kind of hunting and the kind of animal. The .300 obviously has always been our most popular caliber. It's a great caliber because it's so versatile.

What are your thoughts on the firearms industry in general?

Ed: There have been a lot of shake-ups, a lot of consolidating, and that's not unusual. You see that in other industries, and I think we'll probably see more of it in ours. The strong will survive and the weak won't. I think as we look into the future ten years and beyond, we'll see fewer but stronger, more diversified gun companies, rather than a lot of little ones. You can't afford to make many mistakes. You've got to do a lot of things right, because the gun business is very competitive.

The number of hunters in California has dropped substantially in recent years.

Ed: Yes, as the cities expand hunting becomes less and less a part of our heritage. All we see and hear is what the local newspapers, radio and TV present, and all the media have bombarded both hunting and guns. We don't stand much chance in that kind of environment. We do much better outside California...out there in the mainstream of America, where people are still hunting, putting meat in their freezer. Where it's a way of life and always has been from generation to generation. But these people are becoming fewer and fewer, and the population of the cities is getting larger.

I'm pleased to see the emphasis in shotgun sports that is gaining in popularity...sporting clays and Star Shot and the like. If we can get people involved in shooting as a recreational activity, just as they play golf or tennis, we're a step in the right direction toward getting them to be pro gun.

11

37 Years with Weatherby

Betty Noonan probably knows more about Roy Weatherby and the Weatherby Firearms company than does any other person. She worked for Roy as his private secretary for many years before being moved back to oversee the inner operations of the sales office. She was gradually assigned more and more responsibility, and the last six years of her employment she served as Vice President of Sales.

She was Roy's confidant, critic, cheerleader, and sounding board. Through all of her years with Weatherby she earned the respect and admiration of the firearms industry.

Betty met Roy Weatherby through Marty, her husband, who was a long-time friend of Roy's. Marty and Roy were shooting and hunting buddies in California before Roy began building rifles, and shortly after the company began operation Roy enticed Marty into working for him. After serving in a number of capacities for the firm, Marty formed his own rep firm and represented Weatherby firearms in three western states.

Betty "retired" from Weatherby in 1989, but has been lured back on several occasions to "help out." She served as an officer of the Weatherby Foundation since its inception in 1988.

She and Marty, also retired, are avid golfers. By the time this book is in print they will probably have moved to their retirement home in St. George, Utah. It's a small city, but it boasts eight beautiful golf courses.

Betty is responsible for all of the detailed information in this book about the Weatherby company. In the past two years she has done a marvelous job of researching and recording the complicated history. She wrote much of this volume, and gun folks owe her a vote of thanks for insuring that this fascinating segment of firearms history and lore will endure.

This chapter is Betty's—her random thoughts about the man she worked for and admired, about the son who picked up the reins, and about the Weatherby Firearms Company.

In August of 1952, while Roy Weatherby was in Florida for the Annual NRA Meetings, his secretary in South Gate suffered a mild heart attack. As was his custom whenever he was away from the office on a trip, Roy returned Dictaphone tapes of his various notes and correspondence to his office almost daily for transcription and handling. As an interim measure I was asked to "fill in" for his ailing secretary until Roy returned and could find a replacement. Little did I know that this was to be the beginning of a 37-year tenure with the Weatherby firm.

Roy was a very complex person in many ways, but a very simple, down-to-earth individual in others. At times he was a slow, almost plodding thinker when trying to comprehend fully a given situation, yet at other times he was anticipatory and swift in the conclusions he would draw or decisions he would make.

He was a great one for putting his thoughts in writing in advance of a meeting, either with his employees, his suppliers or his children. He always wanted to be well prepared with any message he was trying to get across. During the seven years I served as his secretary his two oldest children were in school, and he frequently wrote letters to their teachers prior to a personal visit—always going to bat for them when problems occurred with their school work. In the same fashion, when his automobile needed servicing, he prepared a detailed list of the items that needed attention, leaving nothing to guesswork on the part of the repairman.

Having been raised in the midst of the greatest depression our country has ever known, Roy Weatherby was extremely cost conscious, and continually looked for ways to cut expenses. All of us employees were well aware of his penchant for going through the office turning off lights and air conditioning when not needed. And, in the early days he simply could not afford to make his necessary business trips across the country by air, so he drove by car, usually accompanied by his attorney friend, Bill Wittman, or by one of his employees.

In 1952 the NRA Annual Meetings were held at the Adolphus Hotel in Dallas. This time Roy, Camilla and I drove to Dallas. Never one to waste any available time, Roy had me bring along all of the material for the next edition of "Tomorrow's Rifles Today" on which we had been working. With Camilla doing the driving, Roy and I spent two days in the back seat of the car with art work and paste-ups of the pages spread out between us. Roy dictated to me new copy and revisions. This was done in order to meet the printing deadline upon our return.

Weatherby was always a very compassionate and generous person wherever anyone's family was involved. As an example, on this trip to Dallas, knowing that I had a sister in Oklahoma City who had lost her husband just a few months earlier, he suggested to me that perhaps she would like to come down to Dallas and share my bedroom in the suite, so the two of us could visit and spend some time together. This thoughtfulness on his part was greatly appreciated by both of us.

Another interesting incident took place on the trip while I was driving back through New Mexico, with Roy in the front seat and Camilla in the back. Roy was helping pass the time by reading "How to Increase Your Word Power" from the current issue of Reader's Digest, quizzing us on the meaning of the words, and I found myself cruising along on this wide open stretch of highway at about 80 miles per hour.

The "auto classroom quiz" was interrupted by a police siren and a flashing red light. Almost before I could bring the car to a stop, Roy had jumped out of the passenger side and met the highway patrolman before he reached my window. He appealed my case: "Officer, this is my secretary driving and I want you to know she is an excellent driver and would never have been going this fast if I hadn't disrupted her concentration by conducting a word quiz with her and my wife. If anything, it's really my fault, and I don't think she deserves to be cited. She just told me that in 20 years of driving she has never received a traffic citation of any kind."

By this time both of them were standing next to my window, and after checking my license the officer merely issued a warning about excessive speed, keeping my perfect driving record intact. Weatherby's persuasiveness had paid off again!

On yet another occasion, early in 1962, my husband, Marty and I traveled with Roy and Camilla to Las Vegas to make preliminary arrangements for the Big Game Trophy Award dinner, which was to be held there later that year. This time we were is separate cars.

Weatherby was always intrigued by gadgets of any kind, especially in electronic advancements. He was one of the first to own a television set when they were introduced, and the pattern was the same with sophisticated stereo equipment, and then VCR recording and camera units. At the time of that Las Vegas trip he had just acquired two high powered walkie talkies, and with a unit in each car the vocal communication made the five hour drive much more interesting. That was long before cellular phones, of course.

It was almost unbelievable to witness the amount of drive and energy Roy had in the early days of his business. He was aggressive almost to the point of being brash if he thought his company would benefit in any way. He was very much aware that he didn't appeal to a lot of people because of this "pushy" trait. But he simply believed he had to take advantage of every opportunity to exploit his name or product in order to become known and successful in the firearms industry.

As an example, during the '50s and '60s when he attended the NRA Annual Meetings he always had a suite in the hotel. And somehow or other he managed to have gatherings every evening with arms writers, executives of other companies, and any well known personality, whether he knew them personally or not prior to that evening. Thus he was able to widen his circle of friends and business acquaintances, which proved to be of benefit to him through the years.

Roy was very loyal when it came to his employees, but he was also very possessive of their time. Because he expected the same loyalty from them, he couldn't always understand why anyone who was called upon to do so wasn't eager to put in as many extra hours per day or week as he did for the company—even with the incentive of overtime pay.

In the very early days, as with most struggling businesses, Roy often had difficulty meeting the payroll. I can recall Marty bringing his paycheck home on a couple of occasions and remarking, "Roy doesn't want me to cash this for a couple of days." And I can relate to another instance several years later as evidence of his concern for his people and making sure his obligations were met. When he started hiring independent sales reps he made sure their commission checks always went out on time each month, no matter what other bills might not get paid. "If these men are going to work for us they've got to have their income so they can travel, and they've got to know they're working for a company that's reliable," he said.

He was a man of integrity, despite his willingness to do just about anything to succeed. For the first couple of decades he was constantly having to piecemeal payments to his creditors. But he was always up front with them and never tried to evade anyone. His retail sporting goods store was a successful enterprise, and actually carried the company during some of the leaner years. As a result, however, many of its suppliers were owed money to the extent that most of them refused to extend any further credit. Had it not been for one of these wholesale suppliers, American Wholesale Hardware in Long Beach, California, the future of the Weatherby Company would have been in jeopardy. The owner of this firm, Judge Anderson, actually kept the retail store in business. I think at one time we owed his firm around $90,000, which was a lot of money back in those days. Every month Roy made certain something was paid on the balance, even if it was just $5,000 or so, as he greatly appreciated Judge Anderson's support. Several times in later years I heard him tell Judge, "I wouldn't be in business today if it weren't for you!"

Roy used me as a sounding board through the years, when he was at his highest and his lowest, so I probably was as close to him and the operation as anyone else in the company. I worked with him when he was under unbelievable stress at various times, but he was a survivor, never giving up or giving in to defeat.

Roy was quite a showman and had a flair for putting things together, whether it be an advertising approach or showing his African films to various groups. During those days we had a black janitor, Art Reed, who was very devoted and dedicated to Roy. He was delighted to don a white jacket and dark pants and serve as bartender and butler at the Weatherby home for any large party. If Roy was showing his African films locally, Art would dress up as a native tribesman, wearing skins, carrying an African spear and beating a tom-tom drum in the lobby as the audience arrived. Art loved every minute of it. Roy always added that little bit of glitz and glamour to everything he did.

Through the years he had his share of problems with employee theft, from retail store clerks to office or shop personnel. But even when they were caught red handed, he never prosecuted one of them. To me this was wrong, because he certainly wasn't doing them a favor, but that's where his soft heartedness and compassion for people took over. He just couldn't make himself do it. He'd fire them and he'd lecture them and try to get them to repay him if they could. But he never once brought charges against any of these individuals.

I recall one such instance when the theft of a rather large quantity of our Imperial rifle scopes by two shop employees was uncovered. They had actually been advertising and selling them by mail and had really made quite a haul before they were apprehended. After they were dismissed and most of the scopes were recovered Roy got together with his advertising agency and produced a national ad about "the great scope robbery" and how people would even steal to get a Weatherby scope! I doubt that many readers knew how much truth there was to that ad.

I consider myself fortunate and thoroughly enjoyed having the opportunity to work with Roy Weatherby during the prime of his leadership of the company. Tantamount to this, however, was being around to observe and work just as closely with his son, Ed, when he took over the reins of the company early in the '80s.

Roy was a pretty wise ole codger and must have known when Ed left on his sojourn to Oregon that he would be back at some point in time. I'm sure that's why he said, "Ed, why don't you stay on the Board of Directors and come back for Board meetings? You know some day, no matter what you're doing, you'll have to have the final say in the direction of this company if something happens to me. You need to keep abreast of things." That was a very wise move, because Ed did stay in tune with the operation and was ready to take an active role when the time came.

Ed's contribution to the growth of the company started immediately on his return, with the changes he made in the Vanguard rifle. We'd sit in management meetings, go over the proposals, pick them to pieces and decide what we were going to do. Roy let the project proceed, but he also let us know his feelings. "You know the Weatherby stock design is part of what built this company—the high lustre finish and that flared pistol grip. These completely different stocks on the Vanguard will never sell. You're wasting your time—but go ahead," he said. Roy turned out to be wrong, and Ed is the one that pushed this project to success.

The same was true of the fiberglass stock rifle, the Fibermark. Roy called it the "ugly stock." Well, it isn't pretty, but at that time no gun

Betty Noonan knows more about the history of Weatherby firearms than does anyone else, and it was she who researched and documented the material in this book. She was Roy's confidant, critic, aide, secretary, sounding board and eventually Vice President of Sales for Weatherby. Now retired, she and her husband, Marty, one of Roy's best friends and a long-time field rep for Weatherby, live in St. George, Utah.

company had a production model like it on the market. Ed said, "Let's bc the first."

In this respect it was interesting to watch Roy change as he aged, from the aggressive, innovative and often frustrated personality ready to take whatever risks he deemed necessary, to a much more conservative individual, seemingly content with things as they were.

For the first 35 years he was in business, any ideas for new products or innovative designs stemmed from Roy's creative mind, even though he utilized the expertise of his technical employees to bring these ideas to fruition in the form of the actual product. However, early in 1978, Roy hired a progressive young sales manager named Steve Zieg.

It was Steve who first came up with the idea of offering laser carving instead of hand checkering on Weatherby stocks—a process whereby an intricate pattern of clean, sharp lines was cut into the forearm and pistol grip area by means of a beam of light. While Roy was not adverse to this idea, neither was he overly optimistic about its acceptance by the consumer. Part of his resistance undoubtedly was due to the fact that the idea was not his to begin with, which was something he had never had to contend with before. However, with Ed's solid support (he was president at the time, just before his move to Oregon), the Lazermark model Mark V rifle was introduced early in 1980, and immediately became a successful addition to the Mark V rifle line.

Soon after Ed returned from Oregon, he became the creative scion. He was once again President, and he developed a keen sense of the trends developing in the marketplace, with fiberglass stocks being one of these trends. He sent Weatherby barrelled actions to a number of independent producers of fiberglass stocks to have them installed, before finally deciding to have Gale McMillan in Phoenix, Arizona produce a mold to the Weatherby stock design.

Special techniques had to be developed to strengthen the fiberglass content so that it would withstand the recoil of the powerful Weatherby Magnum calibers. In spite of the fact that most fiberglass stocks in that day and age were of the camouflage variety, Ed felt that a plain black stock with a dull wrinkle finish would have more eye appeal, especially if it were mated to a barrelled action with a non-glare matte finish.

When the prototype was finished, however, his real job of selling came when he tried to convince his dad that this model, too, would become a good seller. "It's an ugly thing, son," Roy told Ed, "and it'll never sell. You must remember that Weatherby rifles were popularized because of the beauty of the stock wood and their finish. This fiberglass craze will pass, and I'm not sure we should invest in setting up production for a model that will just be a passing fancy."

Once again, Roy was reluctant to give his outright stamp of approval to an idea that had not originated with him. However, Ed was able to convince him, and early in 1983 another Mark V model was introduced—the Fibermark. Much to Ed's delight, his dad had to eat his words later on, for the popularity of this rifle, the first one in the industry to be commercially produced with the fiberglass stock, was overwhelming. For more than two years Weatherby couldn't manufacture them fast enough to fill all of the orders. It remains one of the top sellers today.

Buoyed by his success with the Fibermark, in 1983 Ed decided that the Vanguard line of rifles needed some overhauling. Lightweight rifles were becoming increasingly popular with shooters. When the Vanguard rifle was originally introduced, the stock design was identical to that of the Mark V. Both Roy and Ed, however, were aware that the amount of tedious handwork required during the finishing stages of production, especially in the area of the flared pistol grip, was very costly and responsible for keeping the selling price higher than most of the competiion.

Ed felt there was a certain segment of hunters who were not as concerned with beauty of design as they were with price. He therefore developed two new models, to be called the VGS and VGL, both with non-Weatherby style oil finish stocks that proved to be more economical to produce, thus reducing the ultimate selling price. Keeping the original Vanguard as the top model of the line by changing the checkering pattern to a more custom design, he renamed this model the VGX.

Roy's negative reaction to the VGS and VGL models was even stronger than that toward the Lazermark and Fibermark. "I won't stand in your way because you've proven me wrong on the Lazermark and Fibermark, but these rifles don't even look like a Weatherby. I guarantee you they won't sell with that stock design," he told Ed.

Roy was completely taken aback, however, when these three new models were introduced in early 1984. Total sales of all Vanguard models in that first year were quadruple what had been sold in the past. Consequently, the next year, in 1985, the Fiberguard, a fiberglass stocked Vanguard, was also introduced into the line with much success.

Ed's success with the revamped Vanguards and the Fibermark really reinforced Roy's confidence in his son's abilities, and he gradually transferred more and more authority to him. He let Ed take charge in our management meetings. When our Japanese suppliers came over to meet, Ed was the vocal one. Roy was still very much a part of the goings on, but with Ed there, he was no longer the head honcho.

Father and son were two distinctly different personalities. Of necessity, Roy probably had more drive in his younger days, and there is no doubt that he was much more outgoing than Ed is. Roy's aggressiveness and his ego in wanting to be recognized for what he had done set the two apart. Ed is much more reserved and prefers to be somewhat in the background rather than the focal point of attention.

In the early '80s Ed was an active member of a group called the Young President's Organization. He learned a great deal through the sharing of problems with which other businesses were faced and the solutions necessary to correct them. Frequently he was able to utilize this knowledge in his everyday problems of running the company. Although Roy undoubtedly learned a great deal from others also, he was not the kind to actively seek advice, for I'm sure he felt no one else had ever experienced his particular problems.

Ed is a polished, very articulate public speaker, with a subtle sense of humor. Whereas Roy, unless he had his prepared written notes, had a tendency to ramble as a speaker. However, he had an air about him that made audiences really listen—even though his delivery might not have been as smooth as Ed's.

Like his father, Ed is a great family man. Several years ago he took his oldest son, Adam, with him to fish for salmon in Alaska, where they camped out along the river bank. He has taken both of his sons, Adam and Daniel, hunting with him.

A few years ago he decided to use Adam in one of our ads, to illustrate how the sport of hunting should be passed on from generation to generation. This ad pictured the back of a father and son walking through a field, with the father carrying a firearm. Of course, neither individual in the photo was identified. It was an excellent ad and we received a great response and many positive comments from our readers.

This is one of the areas that the Weatherby Foundation has as its goal—to reach the youth groups and their mothers and fathers and acquaint them with the joys and pleasure to be derived from the sport.

We need to help them understand what hunting and the shooting sport is all about; to let them learn first hand that it can be a lot of fun as well as a very worthwhile and rewarding pastime.

In this manner we can perpetuate the memory of one of the greats in the industry—Roy Weatherby.

12

Weatherby Firearms

Commemorative Bicentennial Model Mark V Rifle

In July of 1976 our country celebrated its 200th birthday, and in honor of this occasion Roy produced his first commemorative model rifle—the Bicentennial Mark V. A limited quantity of 1000 were produced in the four most popular calibers, i.e., 200 each of the .257, .270 and 7mm Weatherby Magnums and 400 in .300 Weatherby Magnum caliber. In addition to having a fancier piece of wood than the production model Mark V, it also sported a fine line custom checkering pattern, a fully customized action which included a specially engraved floor plate reading "Weatherby Bicentennial" in script, and special serial numbers of B0001 through B1000. The serial number, the caliber, the engraving on the floor plate and the lettering on the receiver were all filled with a gold coloring for accent. The final touch was an oval brass plate inlaid in the butt stock. Each plate was engraved, "1976 Bicentennial" across the top, Roy Weatherby's signature in the center, and the rifle's individual serial number along the bottom curve of the oval plate. All thousand rifles were sold well in advance of their receipt in July of 1976.

Ducks Unlimited

In 1978 Roy was approached by the Special Projects Committee from the national headquarters of Ducks Unlimited in Illinois and asked to bid on furnishing them with their 1979-80 commemorative model pump shotgun. Similar bids went out to a number of other shotgun manufacturers by DU, with the request that each firm submit their own suggested artwork and designs, which were to include the DU shield, duck head logo, and game scenes. When all of the bids were received and had been reviewed by the Executive Committee of DU, the end result was that the contract for the 1979-80 commemorative model shotgun was awarded to Roy's firm.

Consequently, 1600 DU Patrician II shotguns with special serial numbers, 79DU0000 through 79DU1599, were produced and shipped to individual DU chapters throughout the United States and Canada, to be auctioned off at the time of their annual fund-raising dinners. The prices bid by the DU members or their guests for these guns was always well in excess of their cost to DU, with this revenue being used to further the conservation efforts of Ducks Unlimited. Thus indirectly, Weatherby was responsible for many, many thousands of dollars being contributed to this worthwhile effort.

In addition to receiving the DU contract for their commemorative model shotgun, Roy's firm was also given permission to produce 1600 trade model DU pump shotguns for him to sell directly to his dealers. These also carried special serial numbers, 79TM2002 through 79TM3603, thus differing slightly from the DU model. They also had to vary in appearance from the DU model, according to their terms. This was accomplished by reversing the finish of the receiver. The DU model guns had a black anodized receiver with all of the etching pattern in white, whereas the trade model had a polished aluminum receiver with black etching. Also, each commemorative model was packed in an individual gun case when shipped to the chapters, but the trade models were sold without a gun case. The benefit to DU on the trade model production was that a royalty for each gun sold by Weatherby was paid to DU after all 1600 trade models were sold.

In 1980 Weatherby was fortunate enough to once again be awarded the contract for the Ducks Unlimited commemorative model shotgun. This time they selected the Centurion II automatic, and 2000 were produced instead of 1600. These DU auto shotguns had special serial numbers of 80DU0001 through 80DU2000, and, as with the pump, were shipped in their individual gun cases. This time 1000 trade model auto shotguns were produced, once again with the reverse etching on the receiver to differentiate them from the commemorative model.

In l986 Weatherby was again awarded the Ducks Unlimited contract to produce the 1986-87 over and under DU Sponsor model shotgun, built on the Orion O/U frame. These guns carried special serial numbers, 86DU0001 through 86DU1100, and differed considerably from the pump and auto shotguns produced several years earlier. In these, the game scenes, the DU shield, the duck head logo and the serial numbers were all engraved on the Orion receiver and then gold filled with l8-karat gold. Each of these beautiful shotguns was packed in a special fitted gun case provided by Weatherby that was covered by a fabric featuring the DU emblem and trimmed with calfskin leather.

All three models of these specially produced Weatherby/DU shotguns became collectors items. It was most interesting to find that year after year the DU chapters, when placing their orders, requested serial numbers identical to those models purchased in earlier years. This afforded each chapter, when putting them up for auction, the opportunity for the ultimate purchaser to acquire the various commemorative models year after year with matching serial numbers.

Weatherby Silhouette Pistol

In the late 1970s widespread interest developed among handgun shooters for the competitive sport of metallic silhouette shooting. The popularity of this fun sport was due in a great part to the efforts of Roy's good friend, Elgin Gates, who was instrumental in the formation of the International Handgun Metallic Silhouette Association (IHMSA). Elgin also helped convince Weatherby that his firm should produce a silhouette pistol that would conform to the specifications required for competitive shooting.

Using his small Varmintmaster rifle action, Roy adapted it to conform to the special silhouette stock dimensions by moving the trigger mechanism forward on the receiver. He converted it to a single shot action, and equipped it with a maximum length 15-inch barrel. Weatherby produced only 200 of these special model handguns — 150 in .308 caliber and 50 in .22/250 caliber. The special Weatherby silhouette stock styling was his original design, and was widely acclaimed as one of the handsomest to hit the silhouette circuit.

The trigger modification, the stock making and final assembly were done at the Weatherby plant after receiving the barreled actions from the Weatherby factory in Japan. Shortly after the first 200 barreled actions were shipped to the U.S., however, the Japanese government advised Howa and Weatherby of their regulation that prohibited the export of any handguns from Japan. Even though a rifle action was being used, the barrel length made the end product a handgun. Accordingly, all production of the Weatherby silhouette pistol ceased.

Because only 200 of these were ever manufactured and sold, they immediately became collector's items, with their value increasing three to five times over the original purchase price.

Weatherby Commemorative Model Firearms

Having enjoyed tremendous success with Weatherby collectors when he produced his Bicentennial rifle in 1976, as well as the sales response to the trade model Ducks Unlimited Patrician pump and Centurion auto shotguns sold in 1979 and 1980, Roy came out with a 35th Anniversary model Mark V rifle in 1980. As with the Bicentennial model, this was once again a limited edition of 1000 rifles - 400 of them being in .300 Weatherby Magnum caliber, and 200 each in .257, .270 and 7mm Weatherby Magnum calibers. The multi-colored brass oval buttstock inlay featured the head of a ram against snowcapped mountains, and was inscribed:

Weatherby
35th Anniversary
1945 - 1980
1 of 1000

The floorplate featured beautiful scroll engraving, with the inscription "35th Year Commemorative" in gold. Many of the Weatherby collectors who had purchased the Bicentennial rifle just four years earlier, were soon clamoring to purchase the identical serial number in this latest commemorative model.

In 1981, Roy took a unique approach when he offered the Weatherby "Limited State Series" rifle. Only 100 rifles (two per state) were produced, and were sold to the highest bidder on a sealed bid basis. Each rifle featured a unique serial number for the individual state, using the year the gun was produced and postal prefixes. As an example, the Texas guns were serial numbered 81TX01 and 81TX02. Two each of 50 entirely different multi-colored ceramic oval emblems were handcrafted for installation as the buttstock inlay. Each of these emblems read "Weatherby Limited State Series", the name of the state, and 1 of 2, and also depicted an identifying symbol for each state. As an example, the Texas plate had an outline of the state of Texas with a Lone Star in the center of it. The stocks also featured an exclusive custom carving pattern on the forearm, the pistol grip area, and below the cheekpiece, which was accomplished by a sandblasting process rather than handcarving. The minimum bid for each of these rifles was $1800, which included a fitted gun case. Almost all of the 100 rifles were sold at a price higher than the minimum bid, with the top bid being $7501 for each of the two Texas rifles.

With Los Angeles being the site for the 1984 Summer Olympic Games, Roy felt it would be a "natural" to produce an Olympic Commemorative model rifle. Early in 1983, he approached the LAOOC (Los Angeles Olympic Organizing Committee) with this idea, outlining in detail the special features of his proposed rifle, and offering to allocate a significant portion of the sales revenue from each rifle as a contribution to the Olympic fund. However, a disappointing reply was received from the licensing and merchandising chairman, Patricia Morrow. In her letter of July 29, 1983, she stated, "We are limiting the number of licensed products for the 1984 Olympics to approximately 50, and our final marketing program does not call for the inclusion of your particular product category in our overall merchandising concept."

Undaunted by this initial rejection, Roy Weatherby contacted Dr. Sherman Kearl, who had been appointed the shooting commissioner of the LAOOC, and solicited his support in pursuing the project further. Through the efforts of Dr. Kearl, approval was ultimately received, and Weatherby was designated as the exclusive licensee for a commemorative rifle of the 1984 Olympic Games.

Every facet surrounding the production, advertising materials, promotion, and sale of these rifles by Weatherby was carefully controlled and subject to the approval of the LAOOC. A substantial royalty from the sale of each rifle was paid to the LAOOC on a quarterly basis as the rifles were sold. Additionally, as part of the contract, the first five rifles, with serial number OL0001 through OL0005 were donated to the LAOOC. These five rifles had special engraving on the floorplate which read "To honor your participation in the 1984 Los Angeles Olympic Games." Just prior to the opening of the Olympic Games that summer, the first three rifles were presented to President Ronald Reagan, who received No. 1, Juan Antonio Samaranch of Spain, the president of the IOC Executive Board, who received No. 2, and to Peter V. Ueberroth, the president of the LAOOC, who received No. 3.

As with previous Weatherby commemorative models, 400 of these rifles were produced in .300 Weatherby Magnum caliber, and 200 each in 7mm, .270, and .257 calibers. A burnished brass oval inlay, depicting the Olympic "Star in Motion" emblem in blue and red, and the five Olympic intertwining circles in blue, was installed in the buttstock of each rifle. The floorplate featured a delicate floral engraving with a curved banner in the center that read "XXIIIrd Olympiad—1984." All of the lettering on the rifle, as well as the engraving on the floorplate, was accented in gold color, and the trigger itself and the sling swivels were also gold plated. Each rifle was packed in its own custom fitted hard gun case.

Ironically, after working so hard to gain approval from the LAOOC to produce these 1000 Olympic Commemorative rifles, Roy discovered that the shooting public, and specifically Weatherby collectors, evidently didn't hold the Olympic Games as near and dear to their hearts as he thought they did. In the past, every commemorative model rifle or shotgun he had introduced had proven so popular that they were all presold prior to delivery. However, only about 700 of these Olympic rifles were sold during 1984, the year of the Games, and it took another year for him to dispose of the remaining 300, many of which were sold at a greatly reduced price.

In 1985, Roy decided to offer a special rifle commemmorating his 40 years in business. Having been burned by producing too many Olympic model rifles the year before, he decided to be conservative and produce this 40th Anniversary model with a limited number of only 200—95 in .300 Weatherby Magnum caliber, and 35 each in the 7mm, .270 and .257 calibers. A special laser carving pattern was designed for the forearm, pistol grip, and underneath the cheekpiece area of the beautiful walnut stock for these rifles, and once again, an oval satin finished brass plate engraved:

Weatherby
40th Anniversary
1945 - 1985
1 of 200

was installed in the buttstock. Intricate floral engraving adorned the floorplate with a banner that read "40th Year Commemorative."

As with past commemorative models, all of the lettering on the receiver, the caliber inscription on the barrel and the engraving on the floorplate was accented in gold color, and the trigger and swivels were gold plated. The special serial numbers assigned to these 200 rifles were 40-001 through 40-200.

Roy's decision to produce only 200 of this 40th Anniversary model proved to be a costly mistake, however, for within three weeks after Weatherby's announcement in late January that a 40th Anniversary model would be available for delivery by mid-year, all 200 rifles were sold, and there were many unhappy customers who were unable to add to their collection of Weatherby commemoratives.

Late in 1986, Weatherby was once again awarded a contract from Ducks Unlimited, Inc. to produce their 1987-1988 Ducks Unlimited Sponsor shotgun. The model selected was the Weatherby 20 gauge Orion, with a number of cosmetic modifications. The words "Ducks Unlimited" were spelled out in gold on top of the ventilated rib, waterfowl scenes were etched and filled with gold on both sides of the Orion receiver, and the Ducks Unlimited mallard head logo and shield were etched on the bottom of the receiver and filled with gold. Eight hundred of these sponsor shotguns were produced, and special serial numbers were assigned to them reading 87DU001 through 87DU800. These beautiful over and under shotguns were shipped to the various DU Chapters in a fitted luggage-type case, covered with Ducks Unlimited signature fabric, with a brass plate on top of each case engraved "Ducks Unlimited Sponsor Shotgun 1987-88."

Models and Manufacturers, Dates and Actions

Roy Weatherby's attempts to put together a rifle building business from scratch, to constantly search for better sources of parts, and to eventually begin his never-ending, world-wide quest for reliable firearms manufacturers who would build for him the kind and quality of product he demanded at prices hunters could afford, resulted in a convoluted tale of who built what and where. Here, we have tried to unravel the maze as best can be done, and that is quite good. Betty Noonan's search of the company records and archives, her personal knowledge of the meticulous records that she either kept or caused to be kept, and her personal friendship and relationships with long-time

Weatherby employees, enabled her to put these facts and figures together.

As the first and only such listing of all Weatherby firearms models, actions, manufacturers, dates of manufacture, places of manufacture, quantities of manufacture, and serial numbers ever published, to our knowledge, we believe and hope that it will be invaluable to hunters and the firearms owning community in general, and to Weatherby owners and collectors in particular, in the coming years. The list follows the section of photographs of Weatherby firearms and related products.

These four Weatherby Custom rifles on the F.N. action were built for (top to bottom) Herb Klein, a Weatherby partner and recipient of the first "Weatherby Award;" Warren Page, Arms Editor, Field & Stream; Gen. Nathan F. Twining, Chief of Staff, U.S.A.F.; and Gen. Curtis LeMay, head of the Strategic Air Command.

Some of the Weatherby Mark V Custom rifles are spectacular examples of the gun building craft. From the top: a .300 W.M. with myrtlewood stock, fully engraved silver plated action and Weatherby Imperial scope; .378 W.M., California mesquite stock, full metal engraving, and Imperial scope on Buehler mounts; .257 W.M., birdseye maple stock and full metal engraving; a Crown Custom Rifle (available in seven calibers, right hand only) that featured super fancy walnut stock, butt stock inlay, forearm inlays, gold mono inlay with initials, and stock carvings.

Other models on the Mark V action were (from top) the Euromark and "Europa," designed for overseas sales; a Mark V in .416 W.M., newest of the Weatherby calibers; and, at the bottom, the 1992 introduced Classicmark.

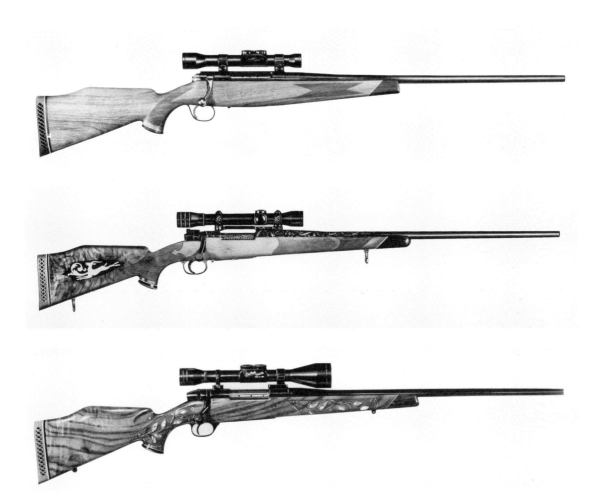

(Top) The "pot-bellied" look of this .378 W.M. Deluxe rifle, equipped with Weatherby Imperial scope, identifies it as being built on the Schultz & Larsen action. The other two rifles are more examples of the craftsmanship seen on Weatherby's Custom rifles. (Middle) A striking .270 W.M. on the F.N. action, adorned with hand made ivory animal stock inlay, engraved barrel, receiver and mount, and a custom stock. (Bottom) A 7mm W.M. with fancy grade walnut stock, laurel leaf carving pattern with abalone inlays, and Imperial scope on Redfield mount.

Opposite page) Weatherby built many variations on the Mark V action, including these (top to bottom): Lazermark, Ultramark, Fibermark, Alaskan, Safari Grade, and the Varmintmaster, which was chambered for the .224 W.M. and the standard .22-250 caliber.

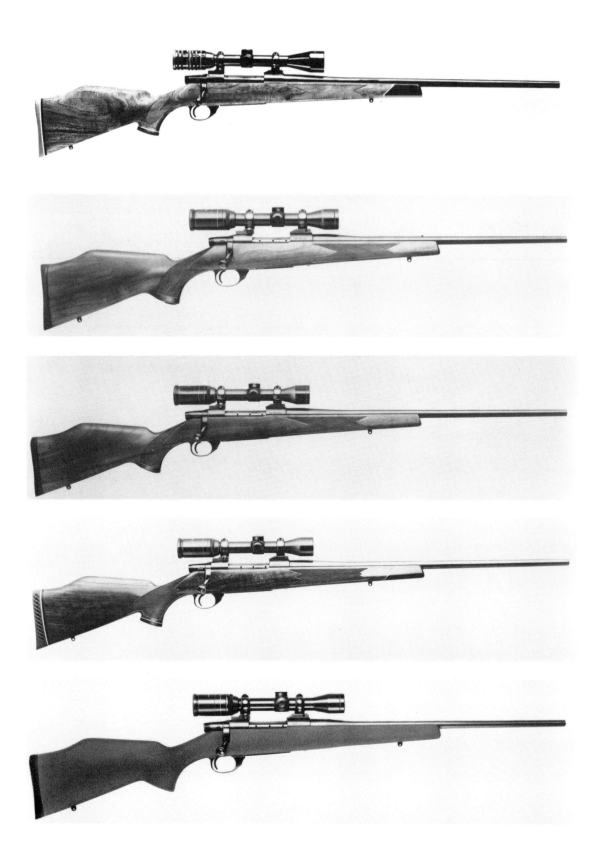

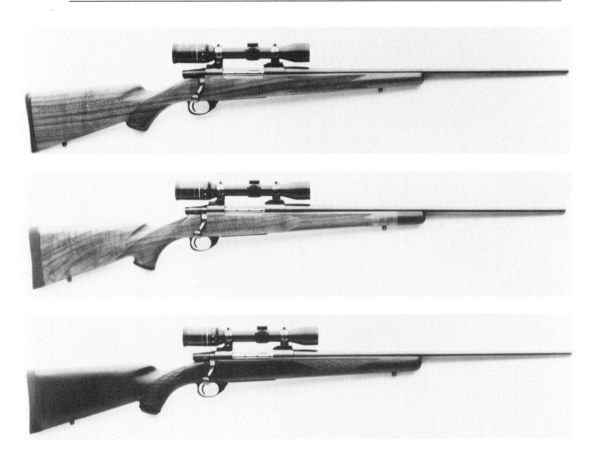

The Vanguard series has been a huge success for Weatherby, offering the Weatherby name, excellent performance and fine value in a less expensive rifle chambered for standard calibers. In addition to the VGX Deluxe, the current Vanguard lineup includes the above three models, top to bottom: the Weatherby/Vanguard Classic I, here shown with a Weatherby Supreme scope; the W/V Classic II, having a more traditional classic stock with rounded ebony forend, and grip cap with no white spacer; and the W/V Weatherguard, featuring synthetic stock impervious to weather.

(Opposite page) In 1970 Weatherby introduced a new rifle chambered for standard (non-Weatherby) calibers, the Weatherby Vanguard. On the Vanguard action made by Howa of Japan, it retained the traditional Weatherby look, a stock design identical to that of the Mark V, but 1984 saw the introduction of two Vanguard models with non-Weatherby style, less expensive stocks called the Vanguard VGL and Vanguard VGS. The original Vanguard was upgraded and retained as the top of that line, the VGX, and one year later the Weatherby Fiberguard made its debut. The Vanguards, top to bottom: the original Vanguard, VGL, VGS, VGX, and Fiberguard.

The Weatherby Silhouette Pistol (top) is the rarest Weatherby, with only 200 being made. Production ended shortly after those first 200 barreled actions were shipped to Weatherby from Howa, when the Japanese government informed both companies that export of any handguns from Japan was illegal. The Mark V Bicentennial rifle (center) issued in 1976 was the first of several Weatherby commemorative firearms. The Ducks Unlimited Centurion shotgun of 1980 was the second of three commemoratives for DU.

Weatherby first entered the shotgun market in 1967 with the Italian-made Regency O/U (top), and followed with the Nikko/Japan Olympian O/U in 1977. The initial production of the Regency had game scenes on the receiver, while the Deluxe Olympian (left) featured tasteful, diamond-shaped engraving.

The Athena is Weatherby's top grade over/under. Built by New SKB in Japan, it is available in several configurations. From top to bottom: the basic Athena, Athena Grade V, Athena Trap Single Barrel, and Athena Master Skeet Tube Set.

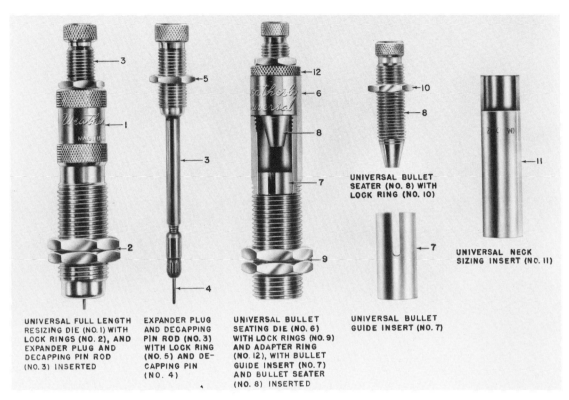

UNIVERSAL FULL LENGTH RESIZING DIE (NO. 1) WITH LOCK RINGS (NO. 2), AND EXPANDER PLUG AND DECAPPING PIN ROD (NO. 3) INSERTED

EXPANDER PLUG AND DECAPPING PIN ROD (NO. 3) WITH LOCK RING (NO. 5) AND DECAPPING PIN (NO. 4)

UNIVERSAL BULLET SEATING DIE (NO. 6) WITH LOCK RINGS (NO. 9) AND ADAPTER RING (NO. 12), WITH BULLET GUIDE INSERT (NO. 7) AND BULLET SEATER (NO. 8) INSERTED

UNIVERSAL BULLET SEATER (NO. 8) WITH LOCK RING (NO. 10)

UNIVERSAL BULLET GUIDE INSERT (NO. 7)

UNIVERSAL NECK SIZING INSERT (NO. 11)

In addition to firearms, Weatherby has produced and marketed other hunting products including rifle scopes, loading dies, spotting scopes and binoculars.

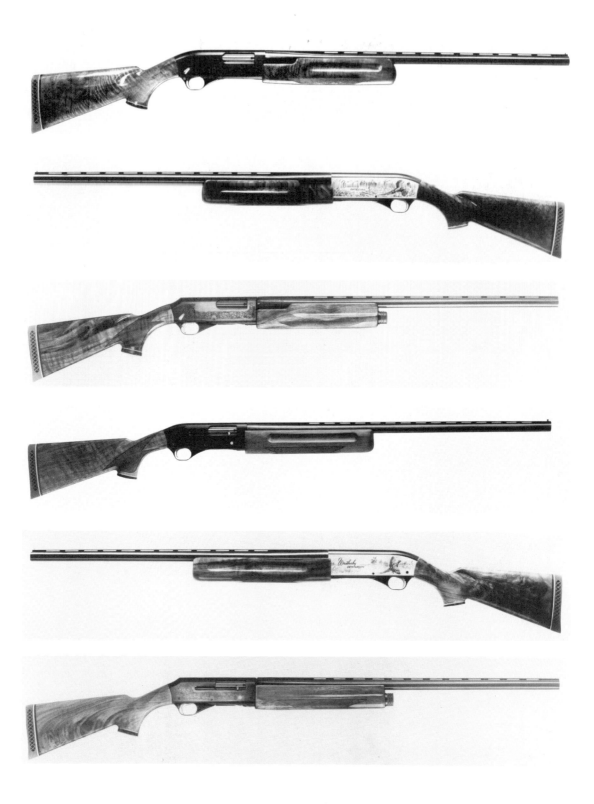

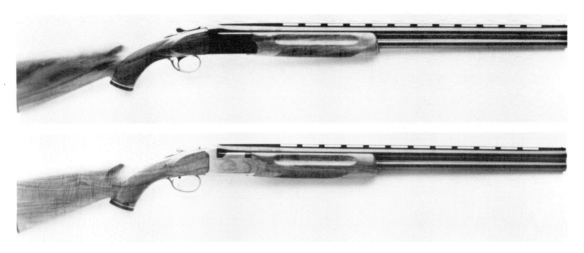

(Opposite page) Weatherby's first repeating shotguns were the Patrician pump and the Centurion autoloader in 1972, followed by the Ninety-Two pump and Eighty-Two autoloader in 1982. All repeating shotgun manufacture was ended in 1989. Top to bottom: Patrician pump, Patrician Deluxe, Weatherby Ninety-Two pump, Centurion Automatic, Centurion Deluxe, and Eight-Two automatic.

The moderately priced Weatherby Orion over/unders are made by New SKB in Japan, and were introduced in 1982 with the Athena. In addition to the Grade I at the top and the Grade III below, a Grade II is available.

One thing is for sure—Roy Weatherby knew how to sell rifles. This advertisement featured the 1953 (6th) edition of the "Tomorrow's Rifles Today" book. In later editions, the name was changed to The Weatherby Guide.

History of Weatherby Firearms - Models and Serial Numbers

Weatherby Centerfire Rifles

"Pre" Mark V Production

Introduced	Discontinued	Mfg. Source	Action	Model	Serial Numbers	Calibers
1945	1961	———	Various	(Made from customers' rifles)		
1949	1963	Wby - So. Gate	F.N. Mauser	Deluxe RH only	1400 - 10962	.257, .270, 7mm, .300 & .375 Wby Mag, plus .270 WCF & .30/06
1955	1959	Wby - So. Gate	Mathieu	Deluxe LH only	L101 - L286	Same as above
1955	1962	Schultz&Larson - Denmark	S & L	Deluxe RH only	1721 - 3690 & S152 - S455	.378 Wby Magnum
1956	1962	Wby - So. Gate	Brevex Magnum	Deluxe RH only	200 - 380	.460 Wby Mag.
1957	1961	Sako -Finland	F.N. Mauser	Deluxe RH only	6000A - 6275A	.257, .270, & .300 Wby Mag., .30/05

Mark V Production

Introduced	Discontinued	Mfg. Source	Action	Model	Serial Numbers	Calibers
1958	1959	Wby - So. Gate	Mark V	Deluxe RH & LH	15000 - 16224	.257, .270, 7mm, .300, .375, .378 & .460 Wby Mag., plus a limited quantity of .220 rocket .270 WCF, .243 Win., .244 Rem., .308 Win., 7x57, .257 Roberts, .300 H&H & 375 H&H
1959	1973	J.P. Sauer-West Germany	Mark V	Deluxe RH & LH	20001 - 43730	.257, .270, 7mm, .300, .375, .378 & .460 Wby Mag., plus a limited quantity of .2~3 Win., .244 Rem., .270 WCF, 7x64, 8x68 & 6.5x68
1963	1973	J.P. Sauer	Mark V	Deluxe RH & LH	37565 - 43730	.340 Wby Mag
1964	1973	J.P. Sauer	Mark V Vrmstr	Varmintmaster	S1000 - S8159	.224 Wby Mag & .22/250

Weatherby Models and Serial Numbers

Introduced	Discontinued	Mfg. Source	Action	Model	Serial Numbers	Calibers
1964	1973	J.P. Sauer	Mark V	Deluxe RH & LH	P1000 —	.257, .270, 7mm, .300, .340, .375 .378 & .460 Wby Mag, plus 7X64, 8X68 & 6.5X68
1967	1973	J.P. Sauer	Mark V	Deluxe RH & LH	P21070 —	.30-06
1967	1973	J.P. Sauer	Mark V	Deluxe RH & LH	P23242 - P63970	.240 Wby Mag.
1972	—	Howa - Japan	Mark V Vrmstr	Varmintmaster Deluxe RH only	S01000 —	.224 Wby Mag. & .22-250
1972	—	Howa - Japan	Mark V	Deluxe RH & LH	00003 - 00400 & H15000 —	.240, .257, .270, 7mm, .300, .340, .378, & .460 Wby Mag plus .30-06
1972	—	Howa - Japan	Mark V Vrmstr	Varmintmaster Deluxe RH only	S01000 —	.224 Wby Mag. & .22/250
1974	1984	Howa - Japan	Mark V	Europa RH & LH	H75015 - H156253	.240, .257, .270, 7mm, .300, .340 .378, & .460 Wby Mag. plus .30-06, 6.5x68, 7x64 & 8x68
1981	—	Howa - Japan	Mark V	Lazermark RH & LH	122284 —	.240, .257, .270, 7mm, .300, .340, .378, .460 Wby Mag. plus .30-06
1981	—	Howa - Japan	Mark V Vrmstr	Lazermark Vrmstr - RH only	S03752 —	224 Wby Mag. & .22-250
1983	—	Howa - Japan	Mark V	Fibermark RH only	H125625 —	.240, .257, .270, 7mm, .300, & .340 Wby Mag., plus .30-06
1986	—	Howa - Japan	Mark V	Euromark RH & LH	H193207 —	.240, .257, .270, 7mm, .300, & .340 .378 & .460 Wby Mag. plus .30-06
1987	—	Howa - Japan	Mark V	Fibermark LH	H198377 —	.240, .257, .270, 7mm, .300, & .340 Wby Mag., plus .30-06
1989	1991	Howa - Japan	Mark V	Ultramark RH & LH	H210828 - H215743	.240, .257, .270, 7mm, .300, .340, .378, .416 & .460 Wby Mag., plus .30-06

Weatherby Models and Serial Numbers

Intro-duced	Discon-tinued	Mfg. Source	Action	Model	Serial Numbers	Calibers
1989	—	Howa - Japan	Mark V	Deluxe RH & LH	H209447 to —	.416 Wby Mag.
1989	—	Howa - Japan	Mark V	Lazermark RH&LH	H211825 —	416 Wby Mag.
1989	—	Howa - Japan	Mark V	Euromark RH&LH	H211845 —	.416 Wby Mag.

Vanguard Production (All models Right Hand only)

Intro-duced	Discon-tinued	Mfg. Source	Action	Model	Serial Numbers	Calibers
1970	1984	Howa - Japan	Vanguard	Vanguard by Weatherby	V0011 -	.243 Win, .264 Win Mag, 7mm Rem Mag, .30-06, .300 Win Mag & .308 Win
1972	1984	Howa - Japan	Vanguard	Vanguard by Weatherby	V8271 -	.270 Win
1972	1984	Howa - Japan	Vanguard	Vanguard by Weatherby	V8471 -	.25-06
1983	1984	Howa - Japan	Vanguard	Vanguard by Weatherby	V78867 - V80966	.22/250
1984	1989	Howa - Japan	Vanguard	V G X	VX0001 - VX25515	.22/250, .243 Win, .25-06, .270 Win, 7mm Rem Mag, .30-06 & .300 Win Mag.
1984	1989	Howa - Japan	Vanguard	V G S	VS0001 - VS17870	Same as above
1984	1989	Howa - Japan	Vanguard	V G L	VL0001 - VL17596	.223 Rem, .243 Win, .270 Win, 7mm Rem Mag, .30-06 & .308 Win
1985	1989	Howa - Japan	Vanguard	Fiberguard	VL06011 - VL17697	Same as above

272

Intro-duced	Discon-tinued	Mfg. Source	Action	Model	Serial Numbers	Calibers
1988	1989	Howa - Japan	Vanguard	V G X	VX24267 - VX25440	.270 & .300 Wby Mag
1988	1989	Howa - Japan	Vanguard	V G S	VS17143 - VS17804	270 & .300 Wby Mag.
1989	—	Howa - Japan	Vanguard	V G X Deluxe	VX25516 —	.22/250, .243 Win, .270 Win, 7mm Rem Mag, .30-06, .300 Win Mag, .338 Win Mag, plus .270 & .300 Wby Mag.
1989	—	Howa - Japan	Vanguard	Classic II	VX17872 —	Same as above
1989	—	Howa - Japan	Vanguard	Classic I	VL18757 —	223 Rem, .243 Win, .270 Win, 7mm-08 Rem, 7mm Rem Mag, .30-06 & .308 Win.
1989	—	Howa - Japan	Vanguard	Weatherguard	VL18207 —	Same as above

Weatherby Rimfire Rifles

Introduced	Discontinued	Mfg. Source	Model	Serial Numbers
Mark XXII Production (.22 LR Caliber)				
1964	1971	Beretta - Italy	Clip	01000 - 43352
1967	1971	KTG - Japan	Clip	J25000 - J42290
1972	1980	Nikko - Japan	Clip	N45000 - N63056
1973	1980	Nikko - Japan	Tubular	T00003 - T22506
1981	1982	Mossberg - USA	Clip	AC01000 - AC01670
1981	1982	Mossberg - USA	Tubular	AT01000 - AT01640
1984	1988	Howa - Japan	Clip	JC10000 - JC13250
1984	1988	Howa - Japan	Tubular	JT50000 - JT54874

Over / Under Shotguns

Introduced	Discontinued	Mfg. Source	Gauge	Model	Bbl Lgtth	Chokes	Serial Numbers
Regency Production							
1967	1967	Angelo Zoli-Italy	12	Field	28	F/M	*13094 – 16219
1968	1972	Angelo Zoli-Italy	12 & 20	Field	28	F/M	17000 – 24112
1972	1982	Angelo Zoli-Italy	12	Field	30 & 28	F/M	R01000 – R08710
1972	1982	Angelo Zoli-Italy	12	Field	28 & 27	M/IC	"
1972	1982	Angelo Zoli-Italy	12	Skeet	26	S/S	"
1972	1982	Angelo Zoli-Italy	20	Field	28 & 26	F/M	"
1972	1982	Angelo Zoli-Italy	20	Field	28 & 26	M/IC	"
1972	1982	Angelo Zoli-Italy	20	Skeet	28 & 26	S/S	"
1972	1982	Angelo Zoli-Italy	12	Trap	32 & 30	F/F, F/IM, F/M	"

* Initial production had game scenes engraved on receiver. All later production had floral engraving on receiver

Introduced	Discontinued	Mfg. Source	Gauge	Model	Bbl Lgtth	Chokes	Serial Numbers
Olympian Production							
1977	1977	Nikko - Japan	12	Field	28	F/M	K801611 – K801912
1977	1977	Nikko - Japan	12	Field	30 & 28	F/M	631663 – 632716
1977	1977	Nikko - Japan	12	Skeet	26	S/S	"
1977	1977	Nikko - Japan	20	Field	28	F/M	255348 - 255352
1978	1981	Nikko - Japan	12	Field	30 &28	F/M	W000001 – W004605
1978	1981	Nikko - Japan	12	Field	28 & 26	M/IC	"
1978	1981	Nikko - Japan	12	Skeet	28 & 26	S/S	"
1978	1981	Nikko - Japan	12	Trap	32 & 30	F/M, F/IM	"
1978	1981	Nikko - Japan	20	Field	28 & 26	F/M, M/IC	R000001 – R001768
1978	1981	Nikko - Japan	20	Skeet	28 & 26	S/S	"
1981	1981	Nikko - Japan	12	Dlx Field*	30 & 28	F/M	W004435 – W004575

Introduced	Discontinued	Mfg. Source	Gauge	Model	Bbl Lgtth	Chokes	Serial Numbers
1981	1981	Nikko - Japan	12	Dlx Trap*	32 & 30	F/M	W004383 – W004441
1981	1981	Nikko - Japan	20	Dlx Field*	28	F/M	R001645 – R001773
1981	1981	Nikko - Japan	20	Dlx Field*	26	M/IC	"
1981	1981	Nikko - Japan	20	Dlx Skeet*	26	S/S	"

* Fully engraved receiver

Athena Production

Introduced	Discontinued	Mfg. Source	Gauge	Model	Bbl Lgtth	Chokes	Serial Numbers
1982	1984	New SKB - Japan	12	Field	30 & 28	F/M	D000001 – D003794
1982	1984	New SKB - Japan	12	Field	28 & 26	M/IC	"
1982	1984	New SKB - Japan	12	Trap	32 & 30	F/IM	"
1982	1984	New SKB - Japan	12	Trap	30	F/M	"
1982	1984	New SKB - Japan	20	Field	28	F/M	F000001 – F001142
1982	1984	New SKB - Japan	20	Field	28 & 26	M/IC	"
1982	–	New SKB - Japan	12	Skeet	26	S/S	D000012 to –
1982	–	New SKB - Japan	20	Skeet	26	S/S	F000002 to –
1984	–	New SKB - Japan	12	Field IMC *	30	F/M/F	D001507 to –
1984	–	New SKB - Japan	12	Field IMC	28	F/M/IC	"
1084	–	New SKB - Japan	12	Field IMC	26	M/IC/S	"
1984	–	New SKB - Japan	12	Trap IMC	32 & 30	F/M/IM	"
1985	–	New SKB - Japan	20	Field IMC	28	F/M/IC	F001102 to –
1985	–	New SKB - Japan	20	Field IMC	26	M/IC/S	"
1988	–	New SKB - Japan	12	Trap Sgl Bbl	34 & 32	F/M/IM	D005636 to –
1988	–	New SKB - Japan	28	Field	28	F/M	DD00001 to –
1988	–	New SKB - Japan	28	Field	26	M/IC	"
1988	–	New SKB - Japan	.410	Field	28	F/M	FF00001 to –

Weatherby Models and Serial Numbers

Introduced	Discontinued	Mfg. Source	Gauge	Model	Bbl Lgtth	Chokes	Serial Numbers
1988	–	New SKB - Japan	.410	Field	26	M/IC	FF00001 to –
1988	–	New SKB - Japan	12	Skeet	28	S/S	D005693 to –
1988	–	New SKB - Japan	12	Trap Combo	32 Sgl/30 OU	F/M/IM	D005999 to –
1988	–	New SKB - Japan	12	Trap Combo	32 Sgl/32 OU	F/M/IM	"
1988	–	New SKB - Japan	12	Trap Combo	34 Sgl/30 OU	F/M/IM	"
1988	–	New SKB - Japan	12	Trap Combo	34 Sgl/32 OU	F/M/IM	"
1988	–	New SKB - Japan	12	Master Skeet Tube Set	28	S/S w/6 Tubes	D005833 to –
1988	–	New SKB - Japan	28	Skeet	26	S/S	DD00245 to –
1988	–	New SKB - Japan	.410	Skeet	26	S/S	FF00194 to –
1990	–	New SKB - Japan	12	Grade V IMC**	30	F/M/F	DA00152 to –
1990	–	New SKB - Japan	12	Grade V IMC	28	F/M/IC	"
1990	–	New SKB - Japan	12	Grade V IMC	26	M/IC/S	"
1990	–	New SKB-Japan	20	Grade V IMC	28	F/M/IC	FA00063 to –
1990	–	New SKB - Japan	20	Grade V IMC	26	M/IC/S	"

* IMC = Integral Multi Choke

** With the introduction of the Grade V model, the original Athena Field IMC models became known as the Grade IV, although there were no cosmetic changes from the original.

Orion Shotgun Production

Introduced	Discontinued	Mfg. Source	Gauge	Model	Bbl Lgtth	Chokes	Serial Numbers
1982	1984	New SKB - Japan	12	Field	30 & 28	F/M	E000001 – E005945
1982	1984	New SKB - Japan	12	Field	28 & 26	M/IC	"
1982	1984	New SKB - Japan	12	Trap	32 & 30	F/IM	"
1982	1984	New SKB - Japan	12	Trap	30	F/M	"
1982	1984	New SKB - Japan	20	Field	28	F/M	G000001 – G001796

Weatherby Models and Serial Numbers

Introduced	Discontinued	Mfg. Source	Model	Gauge	Bbl Lgth	Chokes	Serial Numbers
1982	1984	New SKB - Japan	Field	20	28 & 26	M/IC	G000001 – G001796
1982	–	New SKB - Japan	Skeet	12	26	S/S	E000002 to –
1982	–	New SKB - Japan	Skeet	20	26	S/S	G000003 to –
1984	–	New SKB - Japan	Field IMC *	12	30	F/M/F	E002654 to –
1984	–	New SKB - Japan	Field IMC	12	28	F/M/IC	"
1984	–	New SKB - Japan	Field IMC	12	26	M/IC/S	"
1984	–	New SKB - Japan	Trap IMC	12	32 & 30	F/M/IM	
1985	–	New SKB - Japan	Field IMC	20	28	F/M/IC	G001671 to –
1985	–	New SKB - Japan	Field IMC	20	26	M/IC/S	
1988	–	New SKB - Japan	Field fixed chk	28	28	F/M	EE00001 to –
1988	–	New SKB - Japan	Field fixed chk	28	26	M/IC	
1988	–	New SKB - Japan	Field fixed chk	.410	28	F/M	GG00001 to –
1988	–	New SKB - Japan	Field fixed chk	.410	26	M/IC	
1988	–	New SKB - Japan	Skeet fixed chk	28	26	S/S	EE00283 to –
1988	–	New SKB - Japan	Skeet fixed chk	.410	26	S/S	GG00230 to –
1990	–	New SKB - Japan	Grade III IMC**	12	30	F/M/F	ER00373 to –
1990	–	New SKB - Japan	Grade III IMC	12	28	F/M/IC	"
1990	–	New SKB - Japan	Grade III IMC	12	26	M/IC/S	"
1990	–	New SKB - Japan	Grade I IMC	12	30	F/M/F	EN01360 to –
1990	–	New SKB - Japan	Grade I IMC	12	28	F/M/IC	"
1990	–	New SKB - Japan	Grade I IMC	12	26	M/IC/S	"
1990	–	New SKB - Japan	Grade III IMC	20	28	F/M/IC	GR00175 to –
1990	–	New SKB - Japan	Grade III IMC	20	26	M/IC/S	"
1990	–	New SKB - Japan	Grade I IMC	20	28	F/M/IC	GN00682 to –
1990	–	New SKB - Japan	Grade I IMC	20	26	M/IC/S	"

Weatherby Models and Serial Numbers

Introduced	Discontinued	Mfg. Source	Gauge	Model	Bbl Lgtth	Chokes	Serial Numbers
1991	–	New SKB - Japan	12	Sporting Clay	28	M/IC/S	E010877 to –

* IMC = Integral Multi Choke

** With the introduction of the Grade III and Grade I models, the original Orion Field IMC models became known as the Orion Grade II, although there were no cosmetic changes from the original.

Pump Shotguns

Patrician Production

1972	1974	KTG - Japan	12	Field	30 & 28	Full	50001 – 50643 &
1972	1974	KTG - Japan	12	Field	28 & 26	Mod	S00001 – S05069
1972	1974	KTG - Japan	12	Field	26	Imp Cyl	"
1972	1974	KTG - Japan	12	Skeet	26	Skeet	"
1973	1974	KTG - Japan	12	Trap	30	Full	S03038 – S05069
1975	1976	KTG - Japan	12	Dlx Field*	30 & 28	Full	S00001W – S00113W
1975	1976	KTG - Japan	12	Dlx Field	28 & 26	Mod	"
1975	1976	KTG - Japan	12	Dlx Field	26	Imp Cyl	"
1975	1976	KTG - Japan	12	Dlx Skeet	26	Skeet	"
1973	1975	Nikko - Japan	12	Field	30 & 28	Full	N00001 – N00C11 &
1973	1975	Nikko - Japan	12	Field	28 & 26	Mod	NS00500 – NS12863
1973	1975	Nikko - Japan	12	Field	26	Imp Cyl	"
1973	1975	Nikko - Japan	12	Skeet	26	Skeet	"
1973	1975	Nikko - Japan	12	Trap	30	Full	"

* Deluxe model had etched receiver and fancy grade stock

Patrician II Production

1976	1981	Nikko - Japan	12	Field	30 & 28	Full	NS12922 – NS17115

Weatherby Models and Serial Numbers

Introduced	Discontinued	Mfg. Source	Gauge	Model	Bbl Lgtth	Chokes	Serial Numbers
1976	1981	Nikko - Japan	12	Field	28 & 26	Mod	NS12922 – NS17115
1976	1981	Nikko - Japan	12	Field	26	Imp Cyl	"
1976	1981	Nikko - Japan	12	Skeet	26	Skeet	"
1976	1981	Nikko - Japan	12	Trap	30	Full	"
1976	1981	Nikko - Japan	12	Buckmaster	26	Slug	"
1978	1981	Nikko - Japan	12	Dlx Field*	30 & 28	Full	NS11945 – NS18148
1978	1981	Nikko - Japan	12	Dlx Field	28 & 26	Mod	"
1978	1981	Nikko - Japan	12	Dlx Field	26	Imp Cyl	"

* Deluxe model had etched receiver and fancy grade stock

Ninety-Two Production

Introduced	Discontinued	Mfg. Source	Gauge	Model	Bbl Lgtth	Chokes	Serial Numbers
1982	1983	KTG - Japan	12	Field	30 & 28	Full	92-00001 – 92-11990
1982	1983	KTG - Japan	12	Field	28 & 26	Mod	"
1982	1983	KTG - Japan	12	Field	26	Imp Cyl	"
1982	1983	KTG - Japan	12	Skeet	26	Skeet	"
1982	1983	KTG - Japan	12	Trap	30	Full	"
1982	1989	KTG - Japan	12	Field IMC**	30 & 28	F/M/IC	"
1982	1989	KTG - Japan	12	Field IMC	26	M/IC/S	"
1982	1989	KTG-Japan	12	Buckmaster	26	Slug	"

* Deluxe model had etched receiver and fancy grade stock

** IMC = Integral Multi Choke

Autoloading Shotguns

Centurion Production

Introduced	Discontinued	Mfg. Source	Gauge	Model	Bbl Lgtth	Chokes	Serial Numbers
1972	1974	KTG - Japan	12	Field	30 & 28	Full	A00001 – A07405

Weatherby Models and Serial Numbers

Introduced	Discontinued	Mfg. Source	Gauge	Model	Bbl Lgtth	Chokes	Serial Numbers
1972	1974	KTG - Japan	12	Field	28 & 26	Mod	A00001 – A07435
1972	1974	KTG - Japan	12	Field	26	Imp Cyl	"
1972	1974	KTG - Japan	12	Skeet	26	Skeet	"
1973	1974	KTG - Japan	12	Trap	30	Full	A03411 – A07405
1974	1976	KTG - Japan	12	Dlx Field *	30 & 28	Full	A00001W – A00209W
1974	1976	KTG - Japan	12	Dlx Field	28 & 26	Mod	"
1974	1976	KTG - Japan	12	Dlx Field	26	Imp Cyl	"
1974	1976	KTG - Japan	12	Dlx Skeet	26	Skeet	"
1973	1975	Nikko - Japan	12	Field	30 & 28	Full	NA00400 – NA10091
1973	1975	Nikko - Japan	12	Field	28 & 26	Mod	"
1973	1975	Nikko - Japan	12	Field	26	Imp Cyl	"
1973	1975	Nikko - Japan	12	Skeet	26	Skeet	"
1973	1975	Nikko - Japan	12	Trap	30	Full	"

Centurion II Production

Introduced	Discontinued	Mfg. Source	Gauge	Model	Bbl Lgtth	Chokes	Serial Numbers
1976	1979	Nikko - Japan	12	Field	30 & 28	Full	NA10884 – NA17754
1976	1979	Nikko - Japan	12	Field	28 & 26	Mod	"
1976	1979	Nikko - Japan	12	Field	26	Imp Cyl	"
1976	1979	Nikko - Japan	12	Skeet	26	Skeet	"
1976	1979	Nikko - Japan	12	Trap	30	Full	"
1976	1979	Nikko - Japan	12	Buckmaster	26	Slug	"
1978	1979	Nikko - Japan	12	Dlx Field *	30 & 28	Full	NA11793 – NA16600
1978	1979	Nikko - Japan	12	Dlx Field	28 & 26	Mod	"
1978	1979	Nikko - Japan	12	Dlx Field	26	Imp Cyl	"
1979	1981	KTG - Japan	12	Field	30 & 28	Full	A17755 – A18878

Introduced	Discontinued	Mfg. Source	Gauge	Model	Bbl Lgtth	Chokes	Serial Numbers
1979	1981	KTG - Japan	12	Field	28 & 26	Mod	"
1979	1981	KTG - Japan	12	Field	26	Imp Cyl	A17755 – A18878
1979	1981	KTG - Japan	12	Skeet	26	Skeet	"
1979	1981	KTG - Japan	12	Trap	30	Full	"
1979	1981	KTG - Japan	12	Buckmaster	26	Slug	"
1980	1981	KTG - Japan	12	Dlx Field *	30 & 28	Full	A18501 – A18968
1980	1981	KTG - Japan	12	Dlx Field	28 & 26	Mod	"
1980	1981	KTG - Japan	12	Dlx Field	26	Imp Cyl	"
1980	1981	KTG - Japan	12	Dlx Skeet	26	Skeet	"

* Deluxe model had etched receiver and fancy grade stock

Eighty-two Production

Introduced	Discontinued	Mfg. Source	Gauge	Model	Bbl Lgtth	Chokes	Serial Numbers
1982	1983	KTG - Japan	12	Field	30 & 28 *	Full	82-00001 – 82-11527
1982	1983	KTG - Japan	12	Field	28 & 26	Mod	"
1982	1983	KTG - Japan	12	Field	26	Imp Cyl	"
1982	1983	KTG - Japan	12	Skeet	26	Skeet	"
1982	1983	KTG - Japan	12	Trap	30	Full	"
1982	1989	KTG - Japan	12	Field IMC **	30 & 28 *	F/M/IC	"
1982	1989	KTG - Japan	12	Field IMC	28 & 26	F/M/IC	"
1982	1989	KTG - Japan	12	Field IMC	26	M/IC/SK	"
1982	1989	KTG - Japan	12	Buckmaster	26	Slug	"

* 30" and 28" barrels were available with 2-3/4" and 3" chambers

** IMC = Integral Multi Choke

Weatherby Commemorative and Limited Edition Models

1976 - BICENTENNIAL MODEL MARK V RIFLE

    1000 - 400 in .300 Wby Mag.

    200 each in .257, .270 & 7mm Wby Mag. - S/N B0001 thru B1000 - Mfg by Howa in Japan

1979 - Produced for WORLD WILDLIFE MUSEUM in Tucson, AZ

    5 - Patrician II Pump Shotguns - 28" Mod - S/N WWM0001 - WWM0005 - Mfg by Nikko in Japan

    4 - Mark V Deluxe Rifles - 7mm Wby Mag. - S/N WWM0000 - WWM0003 - Mfg by Howa in Japan

    3 - Mark V Deluxe Rifles - .300 Wby Mag. - S/N WWM0004 - WWM0006 - Mfg by Howa in Japan

1979 - DUCKS UNLIMITED COMMEMORATIVE MODEL PUMP SHOTGUN

    1601 - Patrician II Pump Shotguns - 30" Full - S/N 79DU0001 thru 79DU1601 - Mfg by Nikko in Japan

1979 - DUCKS UNLIMITED TRADE MODEL PUMP SHOTGUN

    1603 - Patrician II Pump Shotguns - 30" Full - S/N 79DU2001 thru 79DU3603 - Mfg by Nikko in Japan

1980 - DUCKS UNLIMITED COMMEMORATIVE MODEL AUTOMATIC SHOTGUN

    2001 - Centurion II Auto Shotguns - 30" Full - S/N 80DU0000 thru 80DU2000 - Mfg by KTG in Japan

1980 - DUCKS UNLIMITED TRADE MODEL AUTOMATIC SHOTGUN

    1003 - Centurion II Auto Shotguns - 30" Full - S/N 80TM3000 thru 80TM4002 - Mfg by KTG in Japan

1980 - 35th ANNIVERSARY MODEL MARK V RIFLE

    1000 - 400 in .300 Wby Mag.

    200 each in .257, .270 & 7mm Wby Mag. - S/N C0001 thru C1000 - Mfg by Howa in Japan

1981 - "LIMITED STATE SERIES" MARK V RIFLE

    100 - All .300 Wby Mag. - 2 for each State, with serial numbers depicting the year, postal abbreviation for the State, plus 01-02 for the two rifles. Ex: 81AL01 & 81AL02 thru 81WY01 & 81WY02

1981 - WEATHERBY LIMITED EDITION SILHOUETTE GUN

    200 - 150 in .308 caliber   - S/N M00001 - M00075   Mfg by Howa in Japan (Barreled action)

                                  M00101 - M00175   Mfg by WBY in So Gate (Stock & trigger assembly)

    50 in 22/250 caliber -   S/N M00076 - M00100 & M00176 - M00200

1984 - OLYMPIC COMMEMORATIVE MODEL MARK V RIFLE

    1000 - 400 in .300 Wby Mag. - S/N OL0001 thru OL1000 - Mfg by Howa in Japan

    200 each in .257, .270 & 7mm Wby Mag.

1985 - 40th ANNIVERSARY MARK V RIFLE

    200 - 95 in .300 Wby Mag. - S/N 40-001 thru 40-200 - Mfg by Howa in Japan

    35 each in .257, .270 & 7mm Wby Mag.

1986 - DUCKS UNLIMITED SPONSOR O/U SHOTGUN

    850 - Orion Over/Under Field Grade - 28" IMC - S/N DU0001 thru DU0850 - Mfg by New SKB in Japan

Index

.22/250 Remington, 251
.220 Rocket, 10, 14, 26
.220 Swift, 10, 181, 183
.220 Weatherby Rocket
    See .220 Rocket
.224 Weatherby magnum
    See Weatherby magnum cartridges
.240 Weatherby magnum
    See Weatherby magnum cartridges
.257 Weatherby magnum
    See Weatherby magnum cartridges
.270 Weatherby magnum
    See Weatherby magnum cartridges
.270 Winchester, 181, 184
.30-06 Springfield, 32, 148, 152, 160, 186
.300 H&H Magnum, 11, 181
.300 Weatherby magnum
    See Weatherby magnum cartridges
.308 Winchester, 251
.338 Winchester Magnum, 184
.340 Weatherby magnum
    See Weatherby magnum cartridges
.375 H&H Magnum, 14
.375 Weatherby magnum
    See Weatherby magnum cartridges
.378 Weatherby magnum
    See Weatherby magnum cartridges
.416 Weatherby magnum
    See Weatherby magnum cartridges
.458 Winchester Magnum, 185
.460 Weatherby magnum
    See Weatherby magnum cartridges
.470, 164, 176
.600 Nitro Express, 176
40th Anniversary commemorative, 254
7mm Mauser, 184
7mm Remington Magnum, 184
7mm Weatherby magnum
    See Weatherby magnum cartridges
82 Auto, 225
92 Pump, 225

A

Aberdeen Proving Grounds, 97
Ackley, P.O., 29
Africa, 23, 65, 76, 84, 117, 125, 229
Alaska, 86, 121, 123
Aleman, Miguel, 61
Allyn, John, 51, 53
    See also Partners
American Rifleman (magazine), 12, 196
Ammunition, 203, 207
    Norma, 193
    powder, 208
    primer, 209
    RWS, 44
    Speer, 205
Anderson, Judge, 241
Angelo Zoli & Sons, 222
Antonio Samaranch, Juan, 254
Argosy magazine, 186
Asia Optical Company, 214
Askins, Major Charles, 1
Astronauts, 60
Athena, 224
Atkinson, Lt. Gen. Hamp, 60
Automobiles, 68
Autrey, Gene, 59

B

Baker, Art, 72
Bates, J.D., 33
Beall, Walt, 211
Bear
    Kodiak, 121
    polar, 123
Beretta, 51, 215
Bicentennial Mark V, 249
Birmingham Small Arms
    See BSA
Blankenbaker, Jim, 54
Borgnine, Earnest, 59
Branham, Bud, 84

Brevex, 194
British Columbia, 115
Bronze Point bullet, 151, 155, 159
Brooks, Berry, 109
Brooks, Oscar, 88
Brown, Pete, 86
Brownell, Bob, 75
BSA, 188, 192
Bucklin, Ken, 31
Buehler Scope Mount Company, 188
Buehler, Maynard, 188
Bush, President George, 233

C

Canada, 23
Cape buffalo, 143, 149, 158
Celebrities, 57
Centurion, 222, 224, 250
Chrysler Corporation, 59, 70
Coapman, John, 36
Coleman, Sheldon, 10, 11
Colt Firearms, 50
Commemorative guns, 249, 252
Connor, Chuck, 59
Connors, Mike, 59
Cooper, Gary, 10, 57
Corelokt bullet, 133, 135, 146, 148, 152

D

Dale, Lyle, 35, 41, 43
Dawson, George, 18
Dealers, 24
Defense contracts, 27
Devine, Andy, 59, 62
Doolittle, Gen. Jimmy, 61
du Pont, 204
Ducks Unlimited, 249, 255
Dynamit-Nobel, 42, 46

E

Eisenhower, Dwight D., 61
Eland, 134
Elephant, 101, 176
Enfield, 22
Engle, Gen. Joe, 60
Engraving, 191
Estrada, Julio, 110
Europe (travels), 40, 74
Excise tax, 28

F

F.N., 187
Fadala, Sam, 90
Federal Cartridge Company, 18, 209
Fiberguard, 245
Fibermark, 242
FIC
    See Firearms International Corp.
Field & Stream magazine, 19, 107
Firearms International Corp., 16, 190
Firestone, 74
Flying Tigers, 60
FN, 193, 207
Foss, Joe, 61, 79, 107
Frankford Arsenal, 18
Freeland, Al, 75
Fuller, Bob, 83
Fuller, George, 2, 80

G

Garand, John, 196
Gates, Elgin, 36, 62, 113, 123, 197, 198, 225, 251
Gazelle, 132, 136
Giraffe, 169
Glaser, 191
Glaze, Wayne, 33
Godfrey, Arthur, 58

Gradle, Roy, 29
Green, Lorne, 59, 73
Gresham, Grits, 1, 97
Gresham, Tom, 1
Griffin & Howe, 19
Grissom, Gus, 60
Gulf Oil Company, 60
Gun World magazine, 82

H

H.P. White Laboratories, 91, 196
Hammerli, 216
Hanson, Bill, 33
Harrington & Richardson, 50
Hatcher, Gen. Julian, 18
Hayes, Gabby, 62
Henrijean, James, 112
Hertel & Reuss, 40, 191, 213
Heym, 190
High Standard, 50
Holmes, Pitcairn, 102
Holzach, Manfred, 42, 218
Horn, Charles, 18, 209
Howa, 51, 93, 221
Howe, Walter, 196
Hunting trips, 115
Huntington, Fred, 80
Husqvarna, 190

I

I.R.S., 28
Impala, 133, 136
Imperial Scope, 63, 213, 242
Ithaca, 50

J

Jackal, 128
jaguar, 87
Japanese manufacturers, 51

Jeager, Paul, 18
Jennie, Fred, 32, 41, 202, 215, 220
Johnson, Mel, 20
Jonas, Coleman, 66, 107
Jordan, Earl, 54

K

Kansas, 13
    Roy's early years, 4
Keel, Howard, 58
Kenya, 118, 125
Kerr and Downey, 117
Kerr, Alex, 29
Walter Kidde Company, 50
The King of Nepal, 61, 62
Klein, Herbert W., 14, 16, 22, 23, 30, 33, 63, 78, 107
Klein, Lloyd, 40
Kleinguenther, Robert A., 49
Klineburger, Bert, 85
Kodiak Island, 122
KTG, 51, 219, 222, 225
Kuhlhoff, Pete, 186

L

Laird & Company, 50
Lancaster, Burt, 57
Law suits, 207
Le May, Gen. Curtis, 59
Leisure Group, 50
Leopard, 146
Lewis, Jack, 82
Life magazine, 108
Limited State Series rifle, 252
Lion, 134, 137, 143, 157, 161
Lister, C.B., 29
Loans, 50, 51
Lovell, Jim, 60
Lucky Bwana, 78
Lutes, John, 26

M

Maddox, Ralph, 33
Manufacturer's reps, 25
Mark V, 26, 30, 83, 191, 221, 228, 249
    design, 193, 195, 197
    naming, 196
    production, 200
    testing, 91, 198
Mark XXII, 41, 51, 215, 221
Mark XXII scope, 52
Martin, Wilbur, 9
Masai, 165
Mathewson, Dave, 196
Mauser, 22
May, Wilbur, 60
McClay, Booker, 16
McClung, Sherie
    See Weatherby, Sherie
McDivitt, Jim, 60
McMillan, Gale, 244
Merrill, Howard, 2
Mews, Leonard, 33, 210
Miller, Col. George, 18
Model railroads, 67
Morrissey, Bob, 35
O.F. Mossberg, 219
Mossberg, Alan, 221

N

Nairobi, 117, 163
NASCO Industries, 48, 52, 53
National Rifle Association, 18, 24, 29,
61, 75, 94, 195, 238
Naude Cordova, Juan, 87
Nickelsen, Ed, 117
Nikko, 219, 221
Niles, Ken, 65, 66, 74, 115
Noonan, Betty, 1, 237
Noonan, Marty, 25, 26, 33, 81, 237
Norma, 40, 91, 104, 193, 208
    See also Ammunition

NRA
    See National Rifle Association
NSGA, 24, 25, 40, 201

O

O'Connor, Jack, 26, 63, 109, 116, 117,
205
O'Malley, Walter, 59
Olympian, 223
Olympic commemorative rifle, 254
Olympic games, 253
One-shot antelope hunt, 85
Optics, 52, 75, 212
    See also Imperial Scope
    scopes, 63, 213
    See also Sightmaster
Orion, 224, 251
Outdoor Life magazine, 26, 79, 107,
116, 117

P

Page, Warren, 19, 109
Pahlavi, Prince Abdorreza, 61
Parker-Whelen, 18
Partners, 32, 33, 47, 52, 54
    problems with, 43
Patrician, 224, 250
Peters belted bullet, 152
Petersen, Robert, 73
Peterson, Ron, 220
Photography, 66
Point Barrow, 124
Powell, Jane, 58, 62
Pratt & Whitney, 19
Premier Scope, 214
Promotions, 71, 75, 78, 241
Public relations
    See Promotions

Q

Quinn, Ed, 59, 70

R

Railway Express, 74
Reagan, President Ronald, 254
Reedbuck, 130
Regency, 51, 52, 222
Remington Arms, 18, 19, 94
    7mm magnum, 26
    Model 700, 187
    Model 721, 21
Retail store, 23, 241
Rey, Bunny, 102
Rhino, 104, 118
Roethe, Leo, 48, 53, 93, 229
Rogers, Roy, 62, 121
Roy E. Weatherby Foundation, 111, 237, 247
Russell, John, 59
RWS, 42, 46
    See also Ammunition

S

Sako, 189, 192, 193
Salesmen, 25, 27, 40
Sauer, 30, 40, 42, 74, 92, 201, 216, 218
Schirra, Wally, 60
Schultz & Larsen, 189, 192
Scott, Brig. Gen. Robert L., Jr., 60
Scott, Gen. Robert, 107
Seidel, Ed, 3
Shah of Iran, 61, 62
Shakespeare Company, 50
Sharpe, Philip B., 13, 14, 75
Sheep (hunting), 36, 78
Shepherd, Sam, 101
Shikar Safari Club, 48

Shotguns, 51, 222, 225
    See also Athena
    See also individual model names
    See also Regency
Sightmaster spotting scope, 52, 213
Silhouette pistol, 251
Silvertip bullet, 146, 148, 155, 159, 168
New SKB, 224
Smith, Robert T., 24
Speer Cartridge Company, 64, 205
Speer, Richard, 205
Speer, Vernon, 205
Sporting clays, 235
Sports Afield magazine, 1, 18, 95, 97, 101, 107
Springer Company, 191
Springfield, 22
Stack, Robert, 59
Steyr-Daimler-Puch, 191
Stock (Weatherby company), 52, 54
Stock design, 83, 210, 242
Storm, Walter V., 117
Strauss, Ralph, 26
Swan, Roy, 18, 19

T

Taxidermy, 66
Taylor, Robert, 58
Television, 72, 121
Thompson, Larry, 82
Thompson, Tommy, 123
Timken, Henry, 60, 193
Torme, Mel, 58
Tradewinds, Inc., 190
TWA, 74, 76, 119
Twining, Gen. Nathan, 59, 107

U

Ueberroth, Peter V., 254

V

van Meeteren, Udo, 42
Vanguard, 52, 221, 242
Varmintmaster, 27, 45, 251
Velocity, 91, 97, 101, 148, 155, 159, 181
    testing, 186
Volkswagen Company, 59
Von Edel, Curt, 117

W

Walther, 216
Warthog, 132, 155
Waterbuck, 130, 135
Waterbury Farrel Company, 19
Waterfield, Bob, 60
Wayne, John, 59
The Weatherby Guide, 76
Weatherby Big Game Trophy Award,
64, 84, 107, 240
    beginning, 107
    recipients, 61, 62, 63, 114
Weatherby Collectors Association, 227
Weatherby Foundation
    See Roy E. Weatherby Foundation
Weatherby magnum cartridges, 75, 81,
181
    .220 Rocket, 183
    .224, 45, 183
    .228, 14
    .240, 183
    .257, 10, 14, 90, 131, 134, 138, 148,
    183, 254
    .270, 10, 14, 63, 82, 90, 128, 131,
    184, 234, 254
    .300, 10, 14, 58, 91, 96, 104, 116,
    122, 184, 254
    .340, 45, 184
    .375, 14, 32, 149, 185
    .378, 32, 185
    .416, 185

.460, 185, 194
7mm, 14, 84, 184, 254
    bullet weights, 91
    development of, 181
Weatherby silhouette pistol
    See Silhouette pistol
Weatherby, Adam, 98, 232, 246
Weatherby, Camilla, 13, 48, 239
    Camilla Jackman, 6
Weatherby, Daniel, 98, 232, 246
Weatherby, Diane, 67
Weatherby, Ed, 1, 53, 185, 222, 229,
242
Weatherby, Jessica, 232
Weatherby, Melissa, 232
Weatherby, Sherie, 230, 233
Western
    See Winchester
Whelen, Col. Townsend, 18
Wilde, Cornell, 59
Wildebeest, 156
Winchester, 18, 19, 94
    .264 magnum, 26
    .270, 32
    .338 magnum, 26
    .458 magnum, 26
    Model 70, 21, 22, 187
Winter, Jan, 16
Wittman, Bill, 9, 12, 13, 14, 16, 33, 43,
53, 238
Wright, Earl, 27

Z

Zebra, 131, 154
Zieg, Steve, 244
Angelo Zoli & Sons, 51
Zuno Arce, Alvaro, 89